BENEATH MULHOLLAND

ALSO BY DAVID THOMSON

Rosebud: The Story of Orson Welles
4–2
Showman: The Life of David O. Selznick
Silver Light
Warren Beatty and Desert Eyes
Suspects
Overexposures
Scott's Men
America in the Dark
A Biographical Dictionary of Film (three editions)
Wild Excursions: The Life and Fiction of Laurence Sterne
Hungry as Hunters
A Bowl of Eggs
Movie Man

BENEATH MULHOLLAND

Thoughts on Hollywood and Its Ghosts

David Thomson

LITTLE, BROWN AND COMPANY

A *Little, Brown* Book

First published in Great Britain in 1998
by Little, Brown and Company
by arrangement with Alfred A. Knopf, Inc.

All photographs by Lucy Gray except:
p. 1, bottom (Paramount); p. 3, bottom (National Film Archive);
p. 5 (Universal); p. 7, middle (Paramount/Long Road Productions);
and p. 8, top (Harry Ransom Humanities Research Center,
University of Texas)

Excerpt from "Aubade" from *Collected Poems* by Philip Larkin
© 1988, 1989 by The Estate of Philip Larkin. Reprinted by
kind permission of Faber & Faber Ltd.

A CIP catalogue record for this book is
available from the British Library.

ISBN: 0 316 64399 8

Typeset in Berkeley by M Rules
Printed and bound in Great Britain by
Clays Ltd, St Ives plc

Little, Brown and Company (UK)
Brettenham House
Lancaster Place
London WC2E 7EN

for
Virginia Campbell
and
Andy Olstein

Contents

Acknowledgments

Some of these essays were originally published, sometimes in rather different form, with illustrations, and even different titles, in various magazines. "20 Things People Like to Forget About Hollywood," "Beneath Mulholland," "Perkins Cobb," "Suspects," "Ask the Anaconda" and "Beyond Hara-Kiri" appeared in *Movieline*. (The author takes this opportunity to thank not just his editor there, Virginia Campbell, but *Movieline*'s exemplary publisher, Anne Volokh.) "Educated Archie," "Gone Away," "How People Die in Movies," "Follow the Money" and "Happiness" appeared in *Film Comment* (thanks here to the editors Richard Corliss and Richard Jameson, and to the publisher, Joanne Koch). "Garbo at 75" appeared in *American Film*. "The Towne" appeared in *Vanity Fair*. "The Technical Sense of Money" appeared in *Los Angeles*. A version of "Driving in a Back Projection" appeared in the book *West of the West: Imagining California*, edited by Leonard Michaels, David Reid and Raquel Scherr, and published by North Point Press. The other essays appear here for the first time.

Introduction

How does the poem go . . . . ?

> *Beneath Mulholland there are bodies buried:*
> *Ghosts, spooks, those flaming images so pale and filmy,*
> *The intimates we never met. O how they stir,*
> *Fretful, sleepless, and how steadily fond parents*
> *School their young—it's only an earthquake, dearest,*
> *5.0 or 5.1.*

I quote from unreliable memory—Nabokov's unfinished Los Angeles rhapsody (going back to his brief Stanley Kubrick period) was, as far as I know, never committed to paper or index cards. Truly, a phantom verse. I wish I could remember more.

   Not that the rich slopes beneath Mulholland Drive would ever be given up to anything as fixed or unprofitable as a cemetery. That ground is meant to flower as wildly as hope or dread. Still, Bel Air is a place that can provide private funerary arrangements, like the small ceremony for the monkey early in *Sunset Boulevard* (that special pleading for a starry life after death). There *are* bodies buried, hopes smothered, stories not quite played out yet. It reminds me of Susan Alexander Kane, watching the dawn come up in the El Rancho, Atlantic City, telling Thompson the reporter that when he goes to Xanadu he really needs to talk to Raymond, the butler. "He knows where all the bodies are buried," she says wistfully.

That's a lovely throwaway line, late in the game of *Citizen Kane,* as if to say, whether or not "Rosebud" is pinned down, there are stories left from Xanadu days, other outrages quietly covered up, or handled, and other lives—not really explored in the movie— that might have made another picture. Was there something between Susan and Raymond? Was Raymond just the deft butler, director of the household or the agent of other enterprises put there as a spy? Is he FBI, patient representative of Cosa Nostra, or a scout from some famous museum who has hopes of getting away with a Florentine ceiling? One thing that prompted me to write my book *Suspects* was the feeling in some of our best movies of the rest of a story itching to be uncovered (like a photograph taken but not developed).

This book is a gathering of essays and stories written over a period of nearly twenty years. Some have been published previously, others have not; some were my idea, others came at the suggestion of editors. But they are collected here because the years and the varied circumstances cannot conceal a dogged, even morbid preoccupation with a kind of life on-screen and off that's not quite alive, or verifiable. I was returning to the subject more than I ever realized at the time. Indeed, I can easily imagine a posthumous publication of this book with a sad, but not unrelieved introduction from some friend bound to say, Thomson's chronic pursuit of half-lives, or less, of ghosts and fabrications, was his own habit. It makes for challenging reading, for we must pick our way between criticism and fiction, an objective style and its haunted undertone, as if a movie was not something for us to weigh and inspect but a version of weather that has warmed us over the years or let a damp achiness into our bones.

It was my fate to slip into the dark at a very early age, and at a moment, around 1947, when the movies were near their best. They amounted not just to weather but to a malaise, such as others seldom noticed or remarked on. Not that I was a lone victim—millions walk on in the same fog of daydream or *noir* anxiety. There is no limp, no hacking cough, no blood on our pillow. But I and other sufferers have this difficulty in separating the real from illusion, or believing in the first while knowing the latter is a trick. And so Howard Hawks's and Montgomery Clift's Mathew Garth (in *Red River*) has been a figure in my life, a presence, and even a companion, as encouraging and as much of an example (if not quite as much his own man) as Kieran Hickey, Mark Feeney, Richard Corliss, James Toback, Steven Bach, Laura Morris or Irene Selznick. Real friends.

Of course, Garth never existed in history or Texas (though I added to the notion of his biography in my book *Silver Light*); as such he has never had to die. *Red River* is still seen, and Clift's lean cowboy is something of an icon, without the unease the real Clift felt in cowboy costume, and despite the jitters that killed the actor's confidence and then the man himself. Kieran Hickey and Irene Selznick, however, and alas, are dead, though I can imagine their amused, snarly dialogue in some waiting room out there. For theirs are two voices that unwind in my head more purposefully than those of some living people I talk to now. They are chatty ghosts, vital presences still. I remind myself to call them with this or that piece of news; I invent their laughing response, and feel better because of it.

This book is inhabited by ghosts like that, people I want to know or talk to (Perkins Cobb and Robert Towne, Joan Didion and Dale Harkness, all of them a little uneasy about being here, or there), personages, characters—"characters" even—yet dummies on my knee, or books in my lap. Of course, movies generate such stateless souls at an alarming rate: images on the screen bigger than life; absurdities with social security numbers lunching at the Ivy, so implausible it is a marvel they need to eat.

More thorough autopsy can wait for the essays themselves. Yet I don't propose to offer a reliable test for telling the living from the dead, or the fictional from the bogus. The question is too penetrating for an answer. The consequent uncertainty intrigues me most, for uncertainty is close to the base condition of life and being on a screen. One quick cut and we're gone. This book is meant for anyone who has felt the precarious charm of Hollywood and the beautiful hesitations in film, and elected to soldier on in good humor. That covers filmgoers who will never get to America as much as Angelenos reluctant to escape the fertile ground to the south of Mulholland Drive. Near and far, such people are somewhere between sleepwalkers and the sick. I daresay the condition is all the graver for being beyond medicine. Just because we don't die of it doesn't mean that we and our culture are not deformed or misled. (TV is more dangerous than the Bomb.) Yet it is a malady to be borne with amusement. For we have got ourselves into a strange fix where claims for sincerity and authenticity sound especially specious and incriminating.

This book is for my editors over the last twenty years—Laura Morris, Sonny Mehta, Bob Gottlieb, Jonathan Segal, Richard Corliss, Richard Jameson, Patrick McGilligan, Andy Olstein and especially Virginia Campbell. I can hear all their voices over the phone, wondering about this or that story idea, this or that sentence. They have been great company, and I owe them plenty.

BENEATH MULHOLLAND

20 Things People Like to Forget About Hollywood

1. All People in Hollywood Are Dysfunctional.

More than any other society on earth, picture people are into health. And that is only proper, because they are a lot of very sick bunnies. Don't be misled. Hollywood obits are regularly in the high eighties—these are people who live a long time, which is what happens if you don't smoke, you work out every day, you get your body fat awesomely low and you do only the best cocaine. But illness is rife. It comes in the form of maladies of the ego and afflictions associated with conflicted interests. Despite the healthiest regime money can buy, most people in Hollywood feel at least several degrees under. People in clinically good health feel headachy, sad, precancerous. Why? To hold attention, to excuse bad or no work, to support the burden of being paid too many millions a picture. Take basic narcissism, add a vulnerable point of view, and you get neurotic un-health. Health practitioners in Hollywood have it made as long as they never threaten their patients with a cure. An AIDS cure might make for so much depression the town would need a new generation of Austrians to deal with it. For above all, the invalid is the center of his or her own universe. And when ego rules, everyone's in pain.

2. The Apocalypse Has Already Happened—in Hollywood.

The "there" isn't here anymore. No pictures get shot in the district that is officially Hollywood. The place is really just another drab, tacky stretch of mid-America, except that so many of the stores and local forms of prostitution are more lurid and inventive. But just because the mine seems to have been abandoned, and a ghost been left behind, you should not be deceived. Think of what happened as an explosion—a very dirty bomb. The explosion occurred years ago, and the toxic stickiness on the surfaces in Hollywood is the residue of that blast. But the fallout went into the air and has drifted all over the world, surmounting foreign political creeds and varieties of language to put everyone into its dream of L.A. (Lies Allowed). They're all dreaming now, their heads filled with the haze, their outer eyes turned off. Sleep-walkers, ghosts, dead men walking—call them what you will, the members of a sad, collective delusion in which we all believe we are alone with our hopes and dreads, alone with the camera. The jazziest ghosts still haunt Hollywood. They know the art and business are dead, as dead as Norman's mother. But that's not the same as defunct. The dead have their magic.

3. You Are Their Playthings, Not the Other Way Around.

If someone told you tomorrow a technology had been invented, out of nowhere, that let the people who had it stare at you with impunity, without mercy or pity, smothering their giggles at seeing you so naked, so unaware, you would say, That's indecent, it would never be allowed. But it is. Hollywood's like a huge, secret smoked glass with invisible people behind it watching you walk up close to see if you have a zit on your cheek. There are buildings and limos with people inside studying those out-side as a rather pathetic species of wildlife—aberrant, untidy, uncool. In the movies, it's us in the dark, them in the light—voyeurism, a way of being substanceless while watching. But they are the ultimate voyeurs; they're seen only on their own terms, in a flattering light, yet stare freely at you without a trace of shyness, like monsters eating you up, inhaling you.

4. Everyone in Hollywood Is in a Movie.

This happens all the time in Hollywood: you are walking in the breezy afternoon sunshine when a van packed with alarmed faces suddenly cuts across the street. Two or three people only steps away from you are nearly knocked down. Brakes howling, the van lifts half off the street, veers, steadies and roars up a side street. As you marvel at the reckless driving, two cop cars, sirens blaring, come racing toward you, and go right by the side street. Someone on the sidewalk steps out and waves them back, and the cops reverse with a fury and take the side street. You notice: one of the cops was smoking a cigar. For color? A strange air hangs over the scene. Was this real or were you all being filmed? You can't see a camera. But the cop with the cigar looked just like Brian Dennehy. And you've heard the soundtrack before—the brakes and the sirens. Will you have to sign a release? It's an old joke that if you ever need to murder anyone in L.A. (and most people do) you only have to take along a camera crew, shoot a murder scene and then do the deed on the second take. Everyone will understand that filming is going on and agree not to look at the camera. It's like that moment in *Heat* when Pacino and his cops follow De Niro and his gang to a dead-end industrial site and wonder what the hell is going on, until Pacino gets it—they're being watched by the guys they thought they were tracking. Everyone in the town is on candid camera, and knows it, and has his motivation down.

5. Information Matters, Knowledge Doesn't.

As in that seminal game of the eighties, Trivial Pursuit, what matters in Hollywood is not knowledge but irrelevant, obscure, cute "facts," like the numbers on *Independence Day* (momentous, unprecedented but subject to instant oblivion, like a tape in *Mission colon Impossible*), or who is sleeping with whom. At Hollywood occasions, one must be thoroughly prepared with information so recondite as to be absurd. The talk should be vivid, grabby, tasteless and superior, pertaining to no known level of reality, consequence or philosophy. Like lines an actor says, every remark should be designed to be immediately disowned, trashed and dismembered. People in Hollywood never speak from the heart; they speak from the script, with the slightly apologetic wryness that comes from having expected a late polish which did not arrive in time. Taken to its highest level of nullity, this pursuit of the inane can turn into a decision to vote for Bill Clinton (or not) entirely on the question of whether he ever actually fucked Sharon Stone. And whether she was there at the time.

6. The Most Important Talent Is Lying.

The only time that exists in Hollywood is the Present. The Civil War was Vivien Leigh and Clark Gable; Pearl Harbor was Montgomery Clift and Donna Reed. All of those scenes are what pass for History. There is no reason to regard Time as a process of cause and effect, or of progress, or of anything that would require anyone to be responsible for it. There is only the Present, in which stories are getting told all at once, and everything is happening simultaneously. The actor working out on the stair machine is also learning his lines on his earphones. The young development executive at a party is drinking and attending to the asshole producer in front of him, and also listening to what the suit from CAA is saying to the VP at Warner Bros., and at least getting the gist of what the late, great Michael Ovitz is saying to Warren Beatty. You'd think all this data processing would drive people crazy, but the actual, unfailing effect is that it just makes people eerie—which is a major thing to be. Now, the obvious result of this simultaneity is duplicity (a technical term). That young development executive is negotiating concurrent, conflicting contracts with different entities (think of them as entities) in serene good faith, straight-faced, without one smear of guilt. Soon he'll be into the big time: direct lies, multiple love affairs, secret lives. Actors come by this naturally—lying is the magic in great acting. There are people who won't hire or even read an actor until he's a proven, expert, drop-dead, unaging liar. This talent for lying is the key to the true fragmented soul. There are twelve-week courses on it all over town, though they have cover names, like "Building a Role" or "Getting Back to the Self."

7. Hollywood Is *Chinatown*.

The Holly and the wood, the new girls and the scripts in development, have to flower and flourish, no matter that Los Angeles is a parched shore and desert scrub valley without moisture of its own. The freshness has to be brought in so that the gardens on the steep slopes of Bel Air can have the springy carpets of grass, the suffocating sweetness of jasmine and the clenching of crimson plants that hold daring architectural achievements to the dry-cake crumble of the earth. Every last drop of water must be traded and piped down from Owens Valley, the Sierras, the Rockies, to make the showers in which those shat upon by the System can erase humiliation and feel precious loss of memory. And Hollywood people must be able to contemplate the flawless water in glasses at Morton's and in their own lap pools, without imbibing or entering, as "a symbol not of affluence but of order, of control over the uncontrollable" (that's Joan Didion).

8. Drugs Are Necessary.

I like to think of drugs as part of the defiant, ongoing and really rather miraculous spiritual life of Hollywood. After all, we know that drugs are bad—they destroy brain cells, warp the individual's sense of order, reason and responsibility, undermine the family and unravel the social fabric, not to mention what happened to River Phoenix. Plus, drugs put you in the company of lowlifes in deals where you have no protection, and they're humiliating and they never last long enough. In the end, they are not even photogenic, so if they boost a career for a while, they end up cutting it short. On the other hand, just between *vous et nous,* drugs are to-die-for sublime, which the drug czars never mention. Why in the world do we have to lose our sense of humor and ignore that, bottom line, drugs make you feel good *now*? And *now* is nice, as well as near, and *now* can keep happening. Drugs are easily the best way to handle the paranoia God invented, and sooner or later in Hollywood everyone ends up doing paranoia in a serious way. I mean, suppose the Bomb is sixteen minutes away—are you going to read the new Joan Didion novel, or do the smack you've been hoarding? What is Joan going to do? I don't ask.

9. Friendship in Hollywood Isn't Friendly.

Old chestnut: it is not enough for me to succeed, my friends must fail too. Anecdotally, there was the Hollywood wife who, after years of silent suffering, decided to divorce her husband because he kept having affairs. "Darling," he'd told her, "they don't mean a thing—they're only with friends." The day after she began proceedings, she received lavish flower arrangements from several of her lunch and bridge and tennis chums. That's how she found out exactly with whom her husband had had his affairs. Which, incidentally, is one of the reasons floristry is such a blue-chip business in Hollywood.

10. Movies Aren't the Point Anymore.

"Synergy." They're all saying synergy is the thing the business is all about now. The dictionary says "synergy" is "combined action or operation," which in Hollywood supposedly means that you do a picture that also feeds into the theme parks and merchandising outlets owned by the conglomerate that owns the studios. Rides, T-shirts, toys, video games, CDs, board games. The business is working on multiple fronts, screwing the public in every orifice it can find. There's talk about synergy everywhere now, so you know it must be covering a multitude of sins. Put that in your dictionary. Call me conservative, but I look at the people who are talking synergy and I see what I have always seen: thin-faced guys who are into pulling down $500,000 a year and fucking bimbos like shooting antelope in Africa.

11. Hollywood Is Fundamentally Un-American.

It's a mistake to believe that the first generation of moguls, who escaped the cruelty and poverty and tyranny of life under the czar or king or emperor, left that world behind. Rather, they brought that system to the new world and cast themselves—at last, the dream realized—as the monarch, Mr. Big. In the land of the free, they fashioned a city-state where medieval powers existed, and to go with it they invented a cult that was close to the idolatrous nature of religions before the age of reason and science. So their Hollywood was intensely un-American if you're thinking Jefferson, the Bill of Rights and the code of independent intellect. Hollywood was a harkening back to despotism, slavery and a belief in the divinity of supernatural monsters. Every fourth year a Dole and a Clinton feel the need to woo, warm and co-opt Hollywood, while any halfway intelligent politician must realize that the movies are—in their appeal to unreason and unreality, in their excitation of desire and instability, in their worship of power and glamour— the most abiding, virulent virus in the American organism.

12. Everybody Is Always Acting.

It was always said in the grand old days of Metro-Goldwyn-Mayer that Louis B. Mayer was the most chronic actor on the lot. This was often said with fondness, and with respect for Mr. Mayer's profound—indeed, helpless—love of movies. But in truth Mayer was a power monger who yearned to be regarded as everyone's father so that he could better abuse, degrade and exploit. He acted to outdo the professional actors, those loathed beauties he hired, half-owned, envied and despised. He had his private deals with all of them. The ones whipped from birth, like Judy Garland, feared him; tough spirits like Katharine Hepburn chuckled and jousted with him, man to man. Mayer dramatized all exchanges, day and night, stealing from scripts with an unconscious ease matched later by Ronald Reagan. No professional actor could top him; it was his way of always being right. Professional actors went deeper and deeper in search of Sincerity and Truth, but Mayer exulted in the thing that only amateurs and hysterics know: that acting is the guardian of an absolute, complete falsehood that has crept off the screen and polluted real life, creating an America as delirious as Mayer's childish dreams. We act up to show we are here. And we think that fake orgasms are the truest.

13. Only Stupid Stars Complain About Bad Publicity.

There are tales of the young and tender in Hollywood who have been wounded by something written or said on TV about them. They howl and their personal PR reps and the studio's PR reps agree that what's been said is out of line. The PR people then speak to the offending entity, and sometimes even suspend relations to register their outrage over some quite ghastly revelation that is a fraction of the horrendous truth. There is seldom any deeper disturbance, for the studios and the press and the publicists all need one another. And anyway, bad publicity is an esoteric concept nowadays. After all, every kind of wickedness, frivolity or arrogance that discretion might rather hush up can be read as simply a young, headstrong independence. Revelation is always wondrous and casts a magic light on those revealed. The only real danger is flinching, seeming to notice your own nakedness. If you don't flinch, you're merely nude, which is a classically recognized form of beauty. Smart stars know the trick of being photographed: act as if there is no camera there, no camera yet invented. When they get abused by the press, they play with their hair, think great thoughts. They don't explain, don't complain and never, ever ask to be liked. O.J.'s problem is that he still wants to be popular. If he were stronger, he'd just keep utterly calm. The point with O.J. and with all stars who've been caught in a misdeed is that they must convince us how easily they could do it again.

14. Everyone Does It for the Money.

There are three colors of money in the business: *up-front, gross points* and *net points. Up-front* is when maybe 25 percent is actually up-front and the rest comes in installments as the job gets done. Most people get their take up-front in studio checks (which is how un-dead the studio system really is) minus deductions, which run somewhere over 30 percent of the 25 percent, and the 10 percent their agent is taking. So up-front is, tops, 15 percent of what they thought they were going to get. *Gross points* means a percentage of the money returned to the distributor of a film from the first dollars earned. As a gross participant (no need to feel bad about that term) you get, say, fifty cents of every five dollars of ticket money if your points are 10 percent. This is the only real way to make money; *net points*—points on the profits after everyone with gross points has had his share—never "happen." Now, here are the minimum estimated average annual expenditures for your normal, upwardly mobile VP in the business, with wife, two children and one former marriage:

Mortgage	$35,000.00
Insurance/property tax	8,000.00
Child support	30,000.00
Children's education	20,000.00
Agent/lawyer/accountant	15,000.00
Analysts (4 or 5 patients)	25,000.00
Telephone/fax	15,000.00
Automobile	15,000.00
Entertaining	10,000.00
Clothes	10,000.00
Travel	15,000.00
Trade papers	500.00
Books	39.99
Medical	12,500.00
Living costs	50,000.00
Maid/cook	25,000.00
Gardener	10,000.00
Trainers, etc.	10,000.00
Child care	25,000.00
Charities	10,000.00
	$341,039.99*

*The only way to write off most of the above is to have an independent deal instead of working directly for the studio. Better to be a president in your own hell than a vice-president at one of the majors.

All of which is to say: everybody does it for the money.

15. Scripts Are Bad Because Nobody Really Reads Them.

The script is the literary form for a society giving up literacy. People in Hollywood don't read them. Not even the writers read them. They write the scenes out of order and seldom need to scan the whole thing through except to check for page numbers. One writer told me, "Reading is an alien rhythm to what happens on the screen. So reading is no help. It has to happen." At studios and agencies, no one with real power has the time or patience to read anything but contracts and deal memos. They buy coverage. Once a movie is in preproduction, a producer gets so many versions of the script there's no sense reading any of them because there will be a new draft by the time they're finished. They stay loose and pick up the "story" of the picture, its mood. They don't worry if there's no ending yet—if there were one, it would just change. Actors read only their own lines; they want to retain their creative space. And they will want to talk to the writer themselves, slip in some lines they like—it's amazing how often those lines come back on paper. In the end, everyone just lets the script breathe, so it can be amorphous and organic. The only people who actually read scripts are Writers Guild arbitration committee members, and those are some pretty sad people.

16. Budgets Are for Simps.

Like the script, the budget is there, but no one ever quite looks at it. Most of the time, there's no such thing as "budgetary control." It's possible that, once upon a time, several grim-faced accountants went around the studios keeping score. Now, when $40 million is going out of style as an average cost, who counts? And you, the fannies in the dark, are right when you suspect that as budgets get bigger, movies get stupider. Because, of course, there are scumbags skimming the system if they can find spoons big enough. The bigger the budget, the more leaks out in the way of technical adjustments, per diems, overtime, expenses, petty cash and *what is this $555 doing in my pocket?* And so, the budget is going to be what it's going to be. The budget is simply what everything adds up to at the end, plus or minus.

17. Gangster Movies Get Made Because Moguls Want to Be Gangsters.

Remember the way Warren Beatty in *Bugsy* is always practicing his elocution so he might have a shot at being in pictures? A nice touch, but it would have been sweeter still if we'd seen some movie executives studying the Bug to get their own gangster acts down. The opportunity to wear slick clothes while talking filthy, to exude the sangfroid of men of the world while having your enemies killed, to be the epitome of cool with dames on your arm while being a Hitler—ever since pictures began, the guys in charge of the business have aspired to the manner of *GQ* mobsters. It was *The Godfather* that locked the image down. Michael Corleone has been the guiding light of style and stealth in Hollywood for the last twenty-five years—withdrawn, austere, shy, a dandy, indifferent to the flesh, a beetle on the dung of money, whispering orders for destruction or elimination, all for the sake of the business. There is a rowdier model, too—Joe Pesci in any number of roles, always about to attack, always saying "fuck," always degrading women, always dangerous and unschooled. The only reason to see *Casino* is to watch the struggle in Scorsese's soul as to whether he most wants to be Pesci or De Niro, the unbridled Kong mobster or Mr. Cool, who fusses over every detail of his business and likes to sit in his plush office with his pants hanging folded in the closet so as not to lose their hard crease.

18. Appearances *Are* Everything.

Los Angeles is best thought of as a set. Plenty of long, scholarly books go on about the "illusory" nature of the city, about the "dystopia" that is always shifting, about buildings that go up and down like sexual arousal—and those books are part of the set decoration, like throw cushions that complement the steel-and-glass coffee table. Of course, the movies are behind this, because in picture-making everywhere you go is a location or a set, something you can paint as you like, knock down, move around, work until you get it right. In the end, the decor is whatever is "right" for the character. So, on the big set of Hollywood, if you look "right," you have found yourself. It is at this nexus that diction meshes with therapy and shopping. "I thank God for the Northridge earthquake," you hear people mutter, "it was the impulse I needed to re-see the living room." They want the wall color "right" for them, for their mood and their designer drop-deads and their important guests. The breakthrough will come when walls are invented that are actually screens with control panels you can play around with to find the "right" balance, the "right" hues, the "right" themes. Then the ultimate movie experience will be just staying at home and running different dialogue and decor with the "right" people.

19. Fantasy Is Religion.

Whenever Hollywood does Christ, whether it's Jeffrey Hunter or Max von Sydow or Willem Dafoe, the result is not just ridiculous and embarrassing and tedious and about as atmospheric as a paper cup. It is also the complete expurgation, elimination and eradication of any hint of the spirit. Those kinds of movies are the guaranteed death of religion, the way NBC's coverage of the Olympics would have destroyed sports and patriotism if it had gone on long enough. Such things are sins against photography and deterrents to inner life, eternal prospects and moral being. Now, one shot of Ingrid Bergman in *Casablanca* wondering what to do, and the whole Ouija board shakes—that's the movies. Movies have been a hundred-year séance called fantasy. But what about God? The terrific thing about fantasy is that you, *you* are God.

20. Movies Are No Longer About Anything.

There was a time when movie audiences sighed in rapture because they were seeing, as if for the first time, a sunset in

Monument Valley, a pretty girl taking off her clothes, a car crash. By now, we've learned how fake what's on the screen is, and we've gone blind. We don't care to be naive enough to believe anymore. And the movies have given up photographing the real thing. Just think how many pictures of the last ten years have involved impossible places and people or creatures who could never exist. Special effects, they call it, and everybody's happy with it, but what *special effects* implies is that the basic effect—the magic of movies—doesn't work anymore. What we have seen in our lifetime is the final abandonment of reality and life as points of reference. The ghost town can only tell ghost stories. Which is why an air of campiness has taken over. Camp doesn't play just because Hollywood is so gay but because it carries with it a faint, superior sneer for all movies, and that is the underlying attitude of so many who make pictures now. You see, no one—except maybe Steven Spielberg and Ron Howard—believes anymore in a picture for the story it tells. Everyone else has seen so many movies, absorbed so many tropes and rhythms of movie-ness that nothing is ever fresh or authentic. People once loved Hollywood because they hoped that the light on the screen could tell great stories to everyone. We know now that the flicks are only lies told for exploitation. Which is very likely what they always were, only now we are less gullible. We have become the cynics. Hollywood and L.A. are the shambles of destroyed hope. That was the explosion that left a congealed scum of shame and disappointment on every stretch of concrete. And hope really is all America ever had to offer.

(1996)

Beneath Mulholland

It is a drive and a highway, running east–west, the supreme vantage point for the entirety of Los Angeles and the San Fernando Valley. You can stand up there and feel like Christ—or the Devil. Mulholland Drive allows both roles.

Like any road, it has an A and a B that it connects. But Mulholland is more concerned with being up there than with destination. Few travel its length, except as explorers; and as it makes that winding automobile journey it is several different roads and moods, going from *Shampoo* to *Shane*. Mulholland is a phenomenon of Los Angeles, both an idealized spectacle and a place from which to survey the classic city of visibility. Even as you drive, the panorama turns into a model for grace and dread.

Imagine Marilyn Monroe, fifty miles long, lying on her side, half-buried on a ridge of crumbling rock, the crest of the Santa Monica Mountains, with chaparral, flowers and snakes writhing over her body, and mists, smog or dreams gathering in every curve. You'd need a certain height to recognize that intricate course as a body. But that's Mulholland, and you can drive it whenever you've got an hour and a half to spare, pursuing the ridge between Cahuenga and the Pacific. It's about as long as an old movie, and as full of scents and half-grasped fears and splendors as Marilyn's drowsy state.

Play with that fancy. Her toes twitch at the Hollywood
Freeway, vaguely disturbed by the furious traffic of gnats. From
the knob of her ankle you can look down on the Hollywood
Bowl, turn east to the HOLLYWOOD sign or see downtown sky-
scrapers looming in the steam like guns in a Turkish bath. As the
legs become thighs, Mulholland enters its richest stretch, full of
designer security systems for houses hiding from the road, of
sprinklers hissing at the bougainvillea and the blinding roses, of
glamorous real estate, the Mulholland where young giants of the
city live, some of them with views north and south, of San
Fernando's pimento suburbia and the gray daytime swell of L.A.,
which at night goes MTV in black fur and diamond lights. At that
most precious, privileged part of the body, where the thighs
widen and foliage starts, you can find the secret mansion of
Warren Beatty, high on its own escarpment, guarded by trees
and Bauhaus bars.

There are those who think of only this Mulholland, who would
not go beyond the low belt that is the San Diego Freeway. But
there's much more to find. A little west of the freeway, Mulholland
becomes a dirt road for nearly eight miles, as far as Topanga
Canyon Boulevard. In a minute of driving, you give up the serene
sway from one curve to another for a violent, jolting surface and
roadside weeds so dusty their short season of green looks like the
color of dollars.

This must be the belly of the beast, grumbling at what it has
eaten. There are no houses or telephones, none of the firehouses
from the wealthy, worried section. If you broke down, you would
be stranded. To the north you can see the sharkskin surface of the
Encino Reservoir, but to the south there are only empty con-
certina folds of hillside where hawks spin in the mauve and gold
dust of sunset. You could lose a Live Aid concert down in
Topanga State Park. How much easier for a few desperate people
to lurk there. The dirt road section of Mulholland is a place for
paranoia—eerily empty on weekdays at noon, a bikers' track on
weekends and a place for furtive love and dealing. You sometimes
come upon a parked car with talk too delicate to approach. And

there are mattresses dying in the brush where who knows what trysts were enjoyed, or how long ago.

Just as you think you are lost, the hard-top resumes and you slide into a little patch of community before the last long section—the ribs, the breasts, the shoulders and throat. This rolling countryside contains a distant dewdrop green golf course, a ranch where stunts are filmed, riding trails, the homes of solitaries, artists and eccentrics, a mock Alpine section, a trashy trailer park, the three satellite dishes of a Jewish recreation center, hillsides burnt black by the latest fires and, at last, the highest number on Mulholland, 35375, a camp for blind children set among eucalyptus trees. Then there's the sea, a beach named after actor Leo Carrillo, sidekick to the Cisco Kid, and platinum surf like Marilyn's hair in her last pictures.

Some say the road was built for that journey, so that the sweaty poor of Bunker Hill and Fairfax secretaries could get to the sea for relief. There are faster ways now, of course, on the freeways or Santa Monica Boulevard. And even in 1923–24, when Mulholland was built, the road was more a gesture of triumph and philosophy than a means of transport.

That's why it was named after William Mulholland (1855–1935), the superintendent of the L.A. Water Department, who designed and presided over the scheme that sucked water from the Owens Valley, 250 miles away, to make Los Angeles fertile, flush-friendly and be-pooled. No water tanks need more pumping than those on Mulholland, and the well-watered thighs still bloom in William's honor. Mulholland is regarded now as a robber baron and an ecological rapist: this is the "Bless me for I have sinned" the Angeleno murmurs whenever he enters the shower or drops into the copper sulphate pools that fill every navel and armpit along Mulholland. In other words, no one is sending the water back to the parched and desolate Owens Valley. They're keeping it, along with the casual guilt.

"There it is—take it" is what Mulholland is supposed to have said, of the water and the brutal advantage of clout. Mulholland Drive still lives on that advice, just as Hollywood taught us to cherish scoundrels. The road is like a location in a film, chosen and dressed for its magnificent vantage and for the juxtaposition of inane civilization and a dangerous wilderness. This is where the desert touches Gucci and Mercedes, where pet chihuahuas can be eaten by coyotes. Mulholland has buildings that could topple into the canyons: the John Lautner Chemosphere stands on one concrete stem, and there is a tennis court on stilts. It has rich homes that might be descended on at night by anarchists, murderers or nightmare Apaches. There is even a Manson Avenue that runs off Mulholland: you have to wonder whether it was scripted tribute or magical impromptu.

Mulholland is a pinup and an idea: it has Brancusis in some groomed gardens, and beer bottles shattered from target practice a few miles farther on. Its function is to embody that contrast: it is a highway made for narcissism and envy, an example of privilege, luxury and airy superiority that whispers, "Look at me—take me, if you can." The road, the drive, the highway all thrill to the way man has commanded natural power and beauty here and turned them into a property or a story. That HOLLYWOOD at the eastern end, letters fifty feet high, is a title, a caption: it's there to tell us the landscape is a kept woman as well as collapsing topography. And the road is called Mulholland Drive so that you know you should be wary of anyone on foot.

(1985–96)

Educated Archie

You may remember that during the first part [of North by Northwest] all sorts of things happen to the hero with such bewildering rapidity that he doesn't know what it's all about. Anyway, Cary Grant came up to me and said, "It's a terrible script. We've already done a third of the picture and I still can't make head or tail of it." . . . Without realizing it he was using a line of his own dialogue.

— Alfred Hitchcock in *Hitchcock*,
by François Truffaut

It doesn't get us far wrestling with the solemn question, How good an actor was Cary Grant? To appreciate this auteur, it is better to practice standing still, listening and watching. He was as poised and attentive as the medium. Whenever he tried hard—in *None But the Lonely Heart, Arsenic and Old Lace, The Howards of Virginia*—he seemed noisy and embarrassed, like someone explaining a joke to a deaf aunt. Perhaps he was an unconvinced liar as well as a guarded soul. He does handle lies gingerly, and he lets us feel that the soul is private, inestimable and vulnerable. There is no sanctimony in this, just respect for the free, lonely course of intelligence. Other people talk and posture, Grant simply listens until their foolishness sinks in on them. His reticence fosters cool wisdom in a picture and underplaying among alert actors.

None But the Lonely Heart was a novel he liked enough to buy. It had a role from roots similar to his own; it reminded Archie Leach of losing his mother to an institution when he was a boy and meeting her again twenty years later. (Is it coincidence that this actor whose boyishness is so hopeful and sometimes so chronic seems never to have been a child?) If sense-memory and shared experience of character are relevant to acting, then *Lonely Heart* was his most personal picture. But he was such a skeptic about emotional disclosure. He was shy, but it is his taste that feels the indecency of showing off when the medium is already a huge display. Whoever it is in there, he has preferred to tease the idea of "Cary Grant" (costarring with Tony Curtis soon after *Some Like It Hot*) instead of becoming other characters. He is something more and less than an actor, like E.T., a presence in whom sincerity and intelligence are parallel modes, not a braid of life.

Few people now remember Grant from the stage; when he was a Broadway actor, in the late twenties and early thirties, he kept to musical comedy and light romance. Invariably, he has been too serious to invite momentous or classical roles; he is uncomfortable out of a lounge suit. In *Only Angels Have Wings* one can suppose him wondering if the banana republic setting explains the swag of his trousers. We can imagine the whatever next? grin, the fastidious discretion in turning away to smile, the cock of the head between perplexity and disdain—if anyone ever suggested that he might try Hamlet, Malvolio, Astrov, Solness, James Tyrone, Shylock, the real Cole Porter (as opposed to Warners') or Archie Rice—no matter that Grant had grown up in Archie's world of empires, while Olivier had to be taken to the last active music halls to get a look at stand-up comedy.

You can hear his self-effacement: *Oh golly, Susan* (Grant could feast on a woman's name, in a way lechers need a CinemaScope of thighs), *he's an actor, and I'm just a* . . . His awe for the real

thing was plain to see, in 1979, when Grant came forward to present the Academy's life achievement Oscar to Olivier. Grant was
spiffed up with pleasure: no one else on-screen has ever made
that spirit more touching or philosophical. Never a Flynn or a
Power (he was humiliated and grim in *The Pride and the Passion*),
he conveys a disposition for scrutiny that is the most intriguing
moral stance in American film, distinct but elusive—we have to
work to comprehend it. He gives fun its proper, high status; and
in its pure form, fun is so rare. Which other movie actor makes
well-being so subtle or attractive, or so rarely succumbs to self-
pity?

With Olivier's Oscar in his happy grasp, Grant seemed diffi-
dent about his own vigor standing beside Olivier's guttering
organism. He was too trusting or too amiable to wonder whether
malady has been Olivier's richest role for the last decade. Yet the
screen's Grant is the quickest detector of indulgence in others,
and so suspicious of it in himself that he seems instinctively
averse to the close-up and its luster of selfhood. Grant wills the
group shot in his films just as C. K. Dexter Haven wants us all to
behave: naturally. Honoring the frail lord of living theater, Grant
fell into the wide-eyed wonder that often spells trap in his
pictures. He was like an Englishman's version of a delighted
American tourist, let in at the stage door of the National Theatre.
Gee, Sir Laurence, I just wanted to say . . . I know, dear boy, I know.

But Olivier didn't notice, and perhaps it has been a mystery
that old Cary Grant chose not to get into. Still, on that Oscar
night, we were being asked to assent to a myth: that it is noble to
pretend to be others but silly to pretend to be yourself. As if
Grant's screen work was not ridiculously superior to Olivier's.
Olivier's vibrant ghost brought a shiver to every spine; when he
felt the tingle in his body perhaps he believed he could expire
from the exaltation of being admired. Grant is suspicious of affection or praise; his ego is too dark, his doubts too great.

He has the grin of someone who learned to trust no one, but
who managed it politely and without ever giving up on people.
He is as narrow and deep as any lonely person. In trying to say

why he is the most fascinating male personality in pictures, we have to recognize him thinking ahead of his films, never turning a blind eye to where he is, making an unspoken aside to the audience: *But this is a movie, didn't you know? No, don't drift off. You can't sleep here; Jerry the Nipper'll get you if you do.*

In movies, acting yields to fascination. The medium winces at bold, dramatic declaration; it wants to creep up on beautiful people. Whereas Olivier elected to make himself a Moor, with a new voice and a fresh face, Grant preferred as little alteration as possible. He guesses that the movie audience will imagine more adventurously if his face is enigmatic, better half-closed than overfull. That leaves room for the spectator. Always thinking, he seldom sends up thought balloons. We know him for a mind, and so we don't need signals. We should ask not, Can he act, but Can he be watched? How was he watched for thirty-five years and seventy-odd films without him or us becoming bored?

Cary Grant has never settled for being a glossy, romantic star, a ghost in our dreams. He has instead lent himself to the kind of dismantling that culminates in *North by Northwest,* where he plays the epitome of "Cary Grant," a dry-gin figment of Madison Avenue put through an insane obstacle course to regain his humanity. But that aim had always been part of Grant's approach; his faith in fun is based in moral propriety; it is never facetious and never content with surface allure. Grant takes a film deeper into itself, adroitly slipping away from all the easy lies of screen authority—that the camera is not there, that the situation on the screen is real and the feelings heartfelt.

Pauline Kael once joined with Mae West in saying that Grant "could be had." I think not. He never gives himself up, he stands for the principle that group shots are composed of separate people joined in lines of observation and judgment. That web appeals to his curiosity; he is cut off from life in close-ups. He is always fretting at, muttering against or edging away from the solitude that stars generally inhaled with the light. He does not quite talk to the audience or look at the camera, but he communes with the film. Grant constitutes an edge of heckling scrutiny around his best films, like the real space that makes a stage audience into jurors, not voyeurs. It encourages distance, argument and respect to think we are watching not life but a game. His best films are by good or better directors. But his achievement is so discerning of the medium, and of the change from acting to being there (but hidden) on the screen, that it transcends and educates his directors. Perhaps he responded most to comrades, or people he enjoyed. There is a remarkable feeling for friendship when he looks at others on the screen. In *Holiday,* it is his love for Edward Everett Horton and Jean Dixon that helps us see the importance of his friendship with Katharine Hepburn, the woman he loves. This affinity is more critical than his quizzical view of love or sex. He is so much more in harmony with values that can work against each other—discrimination and loyalty.

Nothing is as heady for him as fun, or as much fun as the head. Because he is often a surrogate director, he teaches us how the people in a picture indicate a director's attitude. Some stars slow or lull their pictures, dragging them toward narcissism. But Grant stimulates his colleagues. In saying keep your wits about you, he raises the possibility of wit. As he glances and notices, we pick up the pace and shift of his attention—and give credit to lucky directors.

His persistent note of questioning leads us into the issues of his films, as when early in *Penny Serenade* he and Irene Dunne have this brief exchange:

"When you're with me you're safe," he tells her.

"I don't know if it's safe."

"I'm darned if I do, either."

The best Grant films have to acknowledge that having him around has diverted their subject matter. His mild but subversive presence has urged a new reflexiveness on filmmaking. He is too sensible to suppose that good audiences (and he does require the best in us) could believe in the illusion. He thinks we're worthy of seeing the story and its intricate process of being told. Just as in a good joke, we observe the pleasure of the person telling the story. It would take a frame analysis to show how dexterously Grant nurses teeming full shots with his casualness; he can knit up disorder and deliver a joke with one double take that flicks across the nerves of a scene. He is looking and reacting within a scene the way some directors hope to impose meaning with a variety of points of view and cutting. It appears that he must always play the cleverest person in a film. The wonder is that sometimes he was a very learned idiot (*Bringing Up Baby*), still guiding our eyes with the frowns and frosts of injured innocence.

It's as if an astute referee was teaching pugs how to box, or a ghost (*Topper*) advising mortals where to step and how to speak, and watch out for the joke. He was so well balanced—and his physical aplomb so gentlemanly—that he could look like a layman who'd wandered in unawares on some tumblers and yet somehow, without plan or knowledge and looking off in the wrong direction, caught the girl flying through the air: *Oh, hallo,* her pretty bundle landing in his available arms: *Well, hallo!* He contrives to let us feel we have seen a rehearsal that turned out so well that there is no need to do a real take. Cary Grant's taunting charm springs from his passionate reluctance to quite do it, properly.

There is little in print on how Grant behaved and worked on-set, but in a 1975 *New Yorker* article Pauline Kael said, "Although Grant is a perfectionist on the set, some of his directors say that he wrecks certain scenes because he won't do fully articulated passages of dialogue. He wants always to be searching for how he feels; he wants to waffle charmingly." How else do we gain the piercing sense that Grant is thinking before he speaks, and discarding some thoughts as unworthy or unnecessary?

It is his policy in films, and the thrust of his casting, to skirt our foolish, fond expectations for him by the simple ploy of having us reflect on them. There is immediate humor in the possibility that Grant might have spent a part of his life clambering over roofs, crawling into windows. Thus the appeal of the preposterous casting of *To Catch a Thief*. And when John Robie actually takes to the Riviera rooftops, we think of a witty set of sharp angles with an Astaire dandy anxious not to step on the lines. On the few occasions when Grant is required to hurry in a film, even as the skeleton collapses around him, we are reminded that he was once a damned acrobat.

John Robie's head for heights is better employed deciding just how a casino chip can slip down between the breasts of a lady sitting beneath and in front of him. And that, of course, is a "bet" designed to be seen—by Jessie Royce Landis (one of his most appreciative screen friends) as well as by the camera. It is a superb unobtrusiveness in Grant that flashes through his eyes: *Oh, did you see that from there?* This is rococo shyness. No other actor admits the gratification in having himself be seen, or so kids the pretense that no one is watching. The most famous line in *To Catch a Thief*—reason enough for making it—has Grant and Grace Kelly stopping for a picnic. He is between her and the camera, nicely played in the kind of triangular discourse common in Grant films (action-Grant-audience), when she opens the hamper of cold chicken and asks him whether he'll have a leg or a breast.

Grant doesn't eye the camera with a how-d'ya-like-that? (He did that once in movies, at the end of *The Philadelphia Story,* when the ensemble turns to the "wings" and the cheeky appearance of Sidney Kidd, Spy himself, with camera.) With Kelly, Grant never moves or flickers: it is his acme to sit quiet and still, trusting we are there, falling about, knowing the humor is more acute because this is happening to "Cary Grant." He tells Kelly, "You decide," always deferring. Stanley Cavell has noticed, in *Pursuits of Happiness,* how in *The Philadelphia Story* Dexter deflects leading questions with an "Am I?" or "Is it?"—"as if always aware that a liberating interpretation must be arrived at for oneself."

The picnic with Kelly follows a pattern set up a little earlier when Grant's alleged Oregon timberman walks her to her room and, in the open doorway, she pauses and rises to kiss his passive consort figure, like a blue chiffon trout taking a fly, the rod, the angler and Izaak Walton, too. There is a beatific smile on his face when he turns, but he isn't just impressed by the lady or the kiss. His smile is asking, *How would you like to be in a movie? Think how many times we had to take that.*

This is late Grant, escorting the cinema closer to a realization that its nature is camp. But his testy reluctance to be in, or immersed in, his own films, to do them properly or take them seriously, had been there from the beginning. The wonder in his films with Mae West is not that she had found a cute partner, so that the audience went wild imagining those two getting it on, but that someone had stepped up on her stage (so hard to inhabit if you weren't a sofa) and whispered in her silk purse, *Good Lord, you are an old fraud, aren't you? But keep it up . . . nudge me in the loin and I'll blush.* Not once was Grant sexual on-screen. Instead, he knew that watching was erotic, that the glow of imagery was suggestive, but no one was actually going to do it.

The finest romantic implication of any film is that, up there, or after the "cut," or tonight, or sometime, there's going to be an orgy—isn't that the sex of bodies so large?—but as for here and now . . . *Susan, that's out of the question. They're watching. Anyway, I go gay when I'm being watched.* His allure, his seductiveness, rests on his clear preference for some future loving condition of intimacy and invisibility. *Oh, you can't wait, eh? Well, you'll just have to. We're having fun now.*

It's surely no accident that for his two most prolonged kissing sequences, Hitchcock waited for Cary Grant. They occur with Ingrid Bergman in *Notorious* and with Eva Marie Saint in *North by Northwest,* and in both cases the lavish embrace is hiding trap or dishonesty. No Borzage, Hitchcock wants to warn us about mistake, misunderstanding or theft in a kiss. As he admitted, he embarrassed the players with the length and engineering of the kisses. But he is goading the audience, too, making them an offer that can never pay off. This explicit nagging at Grant's restraint is as calculated as having the back of his head be our first look at him in *Notorious,* surveying Alicia Huberman and Ingrid Bergman, spinning a scheme around them. Hitchcock felt the cold, disapproving edge in Grant's urge for withdrawal, just as Hawks and others read into it the warmth that likes to keep love out of camera range.

Still, I doubt if the *Notorious* kiss would have been set up if Hitchcock hadn't first learned from films by Hawks, Cukor and McCarey. In Hitchcock's gradual discovery of the links between universal voyeurism and filmmaking, *Notorious* brings a new confusion of arousal and discomfort in the audience. As he told Truffaut about the kiss, "I felt it was indispensable that they should not separate, and I also felt that the public, represented by the camera, was the third party to this embrace. The public was being given the great privilege of embracing Cary Grant and Ingrid Bergman together. It was a kind of temporary *ménage à trois*."

No Grant admirer should turn away from his brusqueness in *Notorious*. There is a risk of being cutting in all game playing. Hawks had already used it in *Only Angels Have Wings* and *His Girl Friday*, the latter the fiercest proof that if the fun or the game ever stops then we'll die like rats in poisonous boredom. But *Notorious* is just about the only major Grant film without a laugh or a smile, the work in which his relaxed dynamo is most subjugated by a film's oppressiveness. It's as if Grant had fallen quiet and morose, not quite sure that he wouldn't prefer the Claude Rains part. He seems bitter, which suits his blaming security agent: *If you ask me, Rains has got the plum. You know, I like Claude. Look at him do that bit there—effortless.*

Hitchcock had already helped Grant appreciate the ambiguity in a husband's attentiveness. *Suspicion* is unthinkable without Grant's bravura insouciance; surely Hitch was on more fruitful ground in letting Cary go sunny and brisk if he wanted him to be disturbing. It is also the perfect means for Hitchcock of having murder seem resourceful, understandable and playful to make Grant embody the good-humored sportiveness of the classic reader of an old English thriller: *Did he do it or not? I can't tell.* Nor was Hitch sure that he could get away with this blithe killer. To the very end he didn't know if censorship would permit Grant's cheery malice, or whether the Francis Illes original would have to be stood on its head with a happy ending. *Not to worry, I'll play it in the middle—"Hallo, dear, how are you, had your milk yet?"—and you'll be able to use it however the thing ends.*

In the film, Grant turns out not a murderer, or not for the moment; he is just the spirit of irresponsibility, someone who enjoys murder mysteries more than hard work. Hitch wanted an ending in which Grant does poison Joan Fontaine, but not before she has reported everything in a letter that he conscientiously posts in the last shot. RKO settled for the "happy" ending: Joan living on with unreliability. To that end, in the director's absence, they looked at the picture with eyes of righteous woe and planned to take out all the scenes in which Grant looked like a murderer. That brought a ninety-nine-minute movie down to fifty-five minutes. *Well, of course I look like a murderer. You listen to anyone on-screen long enough, and you look as if you want to go to bed with them, or kill them . . . or both.* The movies are always about sex and violence, even if people are standing still and regarding one another.

I hope I'm making a fair attempt at talking in Grant's voice. I'm trying it because so often Grant speaks out of a film as well as within it. He's like an uncle in a children's game, who knows the kids are hiding and listening, and who throws them lines occasionally or—as with the leg and the breast—aware that they are growing up fast, allows them just a beat and then carries on, talking to cover their laughter in the dark. It's a modest trick, maybe, to be a dummy on the knee of the film, but Grant is an Archie who can nudge the ventriloquist, scold him a little and then make fun of his pursed lips. Magic.

Grant's films picked up on this possibility very early, in a way that occurred with no other great star. Everyone played fair by the rules of a Joan Crawford vehicle, or a Gary Cooper picture. The filmmakers knew the routines by heart; they ignored the joke in the special lines, situations and camera angles that displayed the stars. Kidding was very rare: Cagney might pick up the odd grapefruit after *Public Enemy* and smile demurely at the continuity girl; *The Big Sleep* is beguiling because the Burbank house party ignores the rigged-up nonsense of its story.

But that is Hawks again, perfecting a disregard for all but fun that Grant helped crystallize in the screwball comedies. *I've seen you, you're doing my thing, aren't you? Got Bogart to look happy at last.* Mae West gave it license, and Cukor seems to have understood the liberation of *Sylvia Scarlett,* in which Grant could play an English con artist. The slyness there is all the sharper because it confronts the fatuous grandeur of Brian Aherne. And thank God for Ralph Bellamy, the essential stooge in two movies about the special but not quite kind fun a loving couple have in pretending they might to be divorced: *The Awful Truth* and *His Girl Friday.*

Pauline Kael noticed that in both *The Awful Truth* and *Bringing Up Baby* there are references to Grant as Jerry the Nipper. In *Gunga Din*, he makes his character's name, "Archi-bald?" feel like a yawn that impedes full waking. In *Holiday,* in the first sequence, when Grant calls his fellows—Edward Everett Horton and Jean Dixon—to tell them he's in love, he leaves with a cartwheel to the door. This isn't out of place; it fits the pilgrimlike quest for well-being in Johnny Case that he might have studied acrobatics in the evenings. But one feels that the film has gauged the pent up physicality in Grant's borrowed-tie courtliness and whispered to him about a somersault. *What, do it here? In a picture? You're kidding.* How easily the most elegant teases put themselves in the position of being sent up. But it happens; the story and the illusion halt and Grant at last goes end over end. But this is allowed because he has managed to let us hear his thoughts: *Look, suppose we do this. . . . I'll show you. . . . There, you like it? Yes, I like it, too. So, let's do it. . . . What? You mean you shot it? You are a fox. I haven't seen anything as sharp as you since the knife old Archie Leach used to cut his throat.*

Which brings us to the haunting moment in *His Girl Friday,* a tremor in the great satin shroud of Hollywood illusion, when a razor slashes the cloth and a picture breathes, for an instant, with an idea ahead of its time—that nothing is so intriguing about

Hollywood as the pious gravity with which everyone is lying and dry-cleaning the lies. The authorities are threatening Grant's editor with jail—as if the picture is not a series of cages—and the actor looks away from his accusers, into the dark, and says, "The last man to say that to me was Archie Leach, just a week before he cut his throat."

Every time I see the film, I want to hear more about Archie. The aside says boo! to the dream that a film is for everyone. Movies are made for any idiot with a few dollars for a seat in the dark, while picture people stay up there, inanely wealthy but making *Holiday,* wondering if the suckers will fall for this or that, having fun making fools of themselves. The aside nods back at the very dark this star escaped; it hints at what had to die before he could look so good for the world; and it intersects with *His Girl Friday*'s gallows humor. If it is a throwaway, it is also the moment the film screams, but screams silently, as if to admit that American pictures are commercial lies made by a few to please the masses.

Despite those cartwheels, Grant was no revolutionary. Sadness, optimism and the disconcerting poker-faced smile are all he shows to his or the world's disasters. "Me, the life I want, the house I want, the fun I want"—Johnny's creed from *Holiday,* so lucid but so mistaken as to what he thinks the first sister loves in him—tempts a Hemingway rejoinder, from *The Sun Also Rises,* "Wouldn't it be pretty to think so?" The Archie Leach line is lost in the express action of *His Girl Friday.* You can't get at it, take it apart and ask what it means. The tantalizing giveaway epitomizes Grant's art. It is there if you're not stupid, quick enough to pick it up and sensitive enough to work it out for yourself. No one laid down such drastic standards of intelligence on the screen, or was more scathing of sentimentality. *Who's Archie? Any of you fellows ever heard of Archie? No, I think you've come to the wrong place.*

Only for a few years did American pictures keep that stream-lined grace; *film noir* is the first great slowing in Hollywood, and that is what makes the genre the treat of depressives. By 1952, and *Monkey Business,* the older and wiser Howard Hawks is on to

Grant's mystery, but he tries to spell it out. At the beginning of the film, an off-screen voice speaks to Grant and calls him "Cary," coaxing the actor into the action but rebuking his absentminded prematureness. It's a generous tribute, and another funny film, but just as *Monkey Business* is coarser than *Bringing Up Baby,* so Hawks doesn't realize that Grant needs no voice on the sound-track. He was always going in and out of his pictures—crossing the line, hobnobbing with the camera.

It is only natural that his very best works—his most complex, amusing but unsettling pictures—are both studies in Hollywood fun, and in the particular delight there is (or was) in making films. Isn't screwball usually a metaphor for Hollywood? *Bringing Up Baby* and *His Girl Friday* are checkmates of nonsense and intelligence: *You've got to be very smart and a little crazy to run a screwball.*

The two pictures cherish intelligence, but they wonder if it is not a handicap in the wild world. The further it ventures, the more its advantage looks ridiculous. David Huxley is tops on old bones, and he is doing the infinite academic work that keeps so many wise men out of action—putting together an old skeleton. Walter Johnson is putting out a daily newspaper. He is more worldly than Huxley, as cunning as repressed disenchantment. But what he produces clogs the gutter a few hours after its sen-sational release. The paper challenges ignorance and darkness just as Huxley's hope to name and label parts confronts the animal savagery that prevails in the jungles of Connecticut.

The comedy is rife with desperation. These are portraits of madness and humiliation, corruption and callousness, offset by heroic idealism, a trust in fun and a whimsical nostalgia for order-liness. A kind of demented originality is all that makes life supportable. As if the last razor stroke could be averted, or as if marriage might still be admired, *His Girl Friday* seizes on a last chance in divorce—the ex-husband's fresh opportunity to woo back his wife. He succeeds, but because he out-talks her, outplays her, directs her into something like submission. Romance must arrange itself so wooing never stops. Hildy might as well acknowledge that she will be too busy on the paper to get married, that Walter and Grant, eschewing decent plot, will stand up at the altar and then trip her up on her way back to Mother. *Broken your clavicle? I suppose I'll have to look after you now.* Crisis must continue if this love is to be secure. If Hildy wants Walter— and he does put the onus on her—then she will have to find new Bellamys (cousins to Bunbury) to provoke the ingenuity that is as near as he can come to admitting love. So Grant can honor a woman best of all by thinking fast for her.

Bringing Up Baby is the same legend, a similar chase, even if it is run out-of-doors. No one could hope for a settled marriage between David and Susan; this doctor will be taken over by his wild child. The "fun" he ends up appreciating requires that the night of chasing leopards go on forever. It is not so much Connecticut as a desert island (where Fridays live), a pitch, a court or a board game where you can keep passing Go. "Because Cary is such a great receiver. He was so marvelous. We finally got so that I'd say, 'Cary, this is a good chance to do Number Seven.' Number Seven was trying to talk to a woman who was doing a lot of talking. We'd just do Number Seven. And he'd have to find variations on that. He and Hepburn were just great together."

That's for real; it's Hawks in an interview. But the sublime calling of winning plays is like playing screwball while Munich hangs in the balance. That is not meant to be censorious. Still, screwball coincided with terrifying times, and its stories shout and hurry to shut out the dread. Screwball is a lyric delirium away from responsibility; its fun is made more heartbreaking because the dark eyes of Cary Grant guess how close the brink is. It's hard to believe in a fuller paradise than making *Bringing Up Baby;* the picture and the process could go on forever, the longing in all Hawks movies. That lets us see how far the director is the metaphor for life's most accommodating gentleman, a tactful manipulator whose cut and thrust are made gracious by the revels he designs.

Although his posture in the two pictures appears so different—the whip-cracking center of *His Girl Friday,* the bewildered,

tottering follower of the trail in *Bringing Up Baby*—still Grant
stands for the director. Susan is in a whirl of her own, as pretty
and disruptive as a leopard. David is the white hunter, still aware
of how this all looks and sounds, still trying to recover the situation and his dignity, and drawn to Susan as a lepidopterist might
see a butterfly, its colors and frills all jazzy with madness. *My
word, Howard, look at that one. What a beauty! Look, I'll keep up with
her, and if you can keep up with me . . . Just follow, but walk, don't run.
Got it? Walk quickly, of course. . . . Oh, she's off! Susan, Susan! I'm
coming!*

A director shows us where to look, how to see, when to hurry,
when to stop and think. Grant's perplexed intelligence is always
doing that on the screen: he counts the beat in a double take, he
gallantly shields Susan's silk drawers, he comments on the
action—"It never will be clear as long as she's explaining it." He
is on the screen, in skirts and tatters, or in a hat and in charge. No
matter which, he is also, always, a man in a chair watching the
film, chatting to it, sharpening its edge: *There, now if I trim a bit off
that, and then if she looks in the other direction, and I'll say . . . Oh,
yes, I like that.*

Having fun, perched somewhere between skill and exhilaration, Grant is both the deft director of the circus and a kid in love
with the show. Only such intense pleasure can rise above guilt or
doubt; on the brink, a game may be the best way of forgetting
and being oneself: *Susan, this is a travesty. Now, please, I'll put my
hands over my eyes, and then you go away.* A pause, and there are
Grant's hounded eyes again, wondering if we saw it all right and
asking us if we really intend to take such far-fetched bliss seriously. Only Fred Astaire matches him in the way he grins at us
apologetically, aware that these lumbering, expensive, years-in-
the-making things called movies are really so silly—they are like
a 1,000-franc chip, cold and lost, between the confectioner's custard bosoms of a lady who doesn't know the language. *I asked her
what interest she proposed to pay me, but she didn't seem to hear me.
I believe she thought I was going to retrieve it. . . . I ask you. I'd never
do that. I've made it a policy: I never do that.*

To watch a Grant movie is to be infected with this quick talk. Or, as the Katharine Hepburn character rejoices in *Holiday*, we clap hands because "life walked into this house this morning." One day, Hollywood will be remembered for a perilous line of smart sentiment, and Cary Grant will be known as its exemplar, just as Magritte's bowler-hatted straight man reigns in our dreams.

(1984)

Garbo at 75

Garbo stories are as common as cats sleeping in the shade. I like this one, for it disregards verification or scandal, but gently reminds us of what has become her necessary ghostliness. It occurs sometime between now and 1941 in one of those Manhattan stores where the lady is supposed to walk, as unobtrusive as a spy in a B-picture. A woman notices the passing spectacle of Garbo, and wonders if her suspicions can be correct. She follows her from floor to floor. This is no monster, you understand, not a part for Judith Anderson or Shelley Winters. She would not ambush Garbo, browbeat her with loudmouth flattery, or ask for mementos. But this is a woman who was touched to the depth of her being by Garbo's films in the twenties and thirties, a role worthy of Eve Arden.

Her mind is torn. She knows the legend that this enigma, with nothing else to do but saunter through stores in fedora and shades, has a reverence for privacy. Her heart is beating desperately with the dread of speaking to the goddess. Yet this woman believes in living, and she has not been as moved in thirty-four years.

She stands in the path of indifferent approach, not quite sure that the image won't pass through her, like radiation. Of course, she cannot actually utter the name.

"Are you who I think you are?" she whispers.

"No," comes the reply after the quickest pause has suggested that dark glasses can scan the yearning mind invisible to, say, her husband.

"Thank God," the questioner sighs, and faints in a heap of fur and cologne as the other moves on.

Greta Garbo is seventy-five this year, and I would walk around the frilled shore of Sweden to avoid meeting her. This is not a birthday card or a tribute to life achievement. It may be closer to an obituary. Not that I wish harm to any real woman sequestered in the cathedral called Greta Garbo. But she has existed now for thirty-nine years in a state that we cannot adequately call life. That is why I offer her as a ghost, for ghosts are stranded between life and death, like faces trapped on movie screens. It may be bliss or ordeal for them, and it surely helps us weigh identity to see an image suspended between the two, wistfully looking this way and that, but in the end content to be a phantom. Someone not there, someone less alone than apart, someone for whom reputation and image have eclipsed life.

Look at her face: What is the nature of her beauty? Is it proportion, shapeliness, the absence of flaw? Are we just yielding to the curves of brow, nose and mouth, as if we were looking at coffeepots by Chardin? Must we search for metaphors like "marble countenance," or should we follow the line of her admirers and say, like Robert Sherwood, reviewing her second American film, *The Temptress* (1926), that "there is no room for argument as to the efficacy of her allure"? Can we share Kenneth Tynan's intoxication: "What, when drunk, one sees in other women, one sees in Garbo sober"? Why not, instead, start by agreeing that we are looking at a photograph, not a face? Several consequences spring from that. Hardly anyone writing about her can have seen color pictures of Garbo, let alone the coloring of her face. All her movies were black-and-white, and that face is an arrangement of the "white" that denotes skin and the "black" of eyes and mouth.

In other words, the black-and-white photograph is a scheme

that helps dramatize the impurity of experience that has invaded a face. It teaches us to divine emotion or spirit beneath the surface we can see: at the end of *Queen Christina* (1933), Rouben Mamoulian asked her to think of her face as a piece of blank paper that audiences would sign. Now, if you remember that Garbo was a star at the height of Hollywood's power, and one of the stars over whom the most trouble was taken, then you can begin to see to what extent she may be the model of a particular communicative system.

I am not saying that photography gilded or improved her face—though we know that movies pioneered those skills, and photographs of the seventeen-year-old Greta Gustafsson do show a wholesome, plump and much more ordinary girl. She would have learned makeup in Hollywood, and her mouth was always fastidiously painted: we realize that because it was so often a closed mouth. On-screen, her straight hair was usually curled or waved, and her teeth were fixed in her first year in America. She may not have been the easiest star to photograph. Of her twenty-four American pictures, all were made at MGM and nineteen were photographed by William Daniels. That's not proof of conspiracy, but it reminds us that stardom was the product of certain factories and loyal craftsmen. Moreover, Daniels did concede, "She was always taken in close-ups or long shots, hardly ever intermediate or full figure. The latter do not come out well."

We can return to that "problem" in a moment. It does not jeopardize the possibility that Garbo was the most beautiful Hollywood star of the thirties, however one chooses to define beauty. That is less crucial than the realization that she was more aware than anyone else about what it was to be photographed. She is the greatest movie star because either she has thought or she has been advised about the special romance of being seen as an image.

I say advised because of that early relationship with Mauritz Stiller. It was Stiller who discovered Garbo, gave her that name (it means "wood nymph" in Swedish and "grace" in Spanish) and

put her in *Gösta Berling's Saga* (1924). He took his protégée to
Germany, where she made *The Joyless Street* for G. W. Pabst, and
he engineered her passage to America. There is still some argument as to whether Louis B. Mayer was more interested in the
director or the actress. But numbers tell. MGM hired Stiller at
$1,500 a week, whereas Garbo got only $350 and the command
from Mayer to lose weight.

Stiller is now known as the sad Svengali who was deprived of
his own creation. He failed in Hollywood, and he died in 1928.
Far from guiding Garbo's American career, he was fired from *The
Temptress* by an Irving Thalberg eager to cut down egotistical
directors. There are stories that Garbo was inclined to return to
Sweden with Stiller but that MGM lawyers applied her contract
like a rack. Some say she married Stiller and add Anastasia-like
rumors of a child who died. Others say they were not even
lovers but chaste master and pupil. Garbo's own reticence
ensured that she would become the center of profuse, variant
legends.

That she was moved by Stiller's fate there is no doubt: it
increased her shyness to find Hollywood so cruel. I am more
interested in what Stiller may have taught her. He was very far
from the buffoon humbled by Hollywood. He was a spokesman
for Stanislavsky's teaching, a considerable ironist who influenced
Lubitsch and a man with great insight into the artifice of film. As
early as 1917, he had made a picture called *Thomas Graal's Best
Film,* which is a kind of *8½,* about a screenwriter at a loss for a
subject. He falls for his pretty secretary, and as he imagines her
love life he turns his daydream into a movie. Perhaps the creator
of that could explain to Garbo the way to enthrall a public who
would know her only by pictures. He saw beauty in her, but he
foresaw something more in the photographs.

That's the moral of the story I started with. The star knows that
she is a latent force that works in the minds of audiences she will
never meet. And so she is a figment compared with the immen-
sity the awestruck shopper believes she sees in her. She must be
no one in herself if she is to signify so much to so many others.

Enigma is the most natural role for such a figure: she is like the goddess of some intense cult who only needs to be seen to be believed in. Thus, all her creative energy, all her soul, rises to the level of expressive appearance. And when the faithful look at her, what they call beauty or divinity has the mournful gaze of sacrifice—as if that face looking into the darkness could only feel the absence of herself.

Isn't that the thought in Garbo's face? She has delivered her shell, her look, to us, yet the expression is that of impossible yearning. Time and again, Garbo seems fixed on something beyond the camera, behind or above the other people, outside the frame. How rarely she concentrates on what is being said or done, how often she seems to refer it to that external dream that she can never possess.

The mouth is shut because of that pensiveness, and Garbo speaks like someone reading—I mean that literally: she is saying the lines over to herself, to judge them. There is extraordinary narcissism in that, or the proper spell of a goddess. It is in her prowling slowness, too, which makes everyone wait for her. But it helps explain why Garbo moved from silent to sound pictures—in *Anna Christie* (1930)—with such belated ease. Just as in silent movies there is a rhythm of emoting and emotion with the silent titles, so in her sound films the same slowness applies, and when Garbo speaks it is that inner voice of the reader reciting the line and turning speech into incantation.

Was that skill, or instinct? It was probably both, for we cannot detect any gap between intelligence and feeling in Garbo. More than any other photographed face, she guessed that the secret of the movies is in the face pretending it is unaware of being photographed but offering itself to the fantasy of the voyeur. Her beauty is a matter of resignation and universality. Roland Barthes recognized that Garbo's face was an idea, as opposed to something actual. Study that face again, always looking away from you so that you may be freer to gaze and marvel. It relates to a real woman as the word *love* does to the real thing. All the moods and moments of love are encompassed because the appearance is hollow. We are to inhabit it, to flesh it out.

That's why Garbo was a creature of close-ups and long shots. For those are both measures that increase the majesty of the star and the imaginative complicity of the audience. In the long shot there is only an inscrutable figure, a question mark. In the close-up there is the suffocating expression of exclusive feeling, a gasp or a cry from a head so large we seem to be in it. Between the question mark and the cry, you might propose, there is the matter-of-fact full shot, in which we can see all the figure while being close enough to read the face. That was the normal way of filming most American stars—it is called the "American shot" in France—but, as Daniels noted, it didn't "come out well" with Garbo. That sounds like a ghost leaving no trace on film.

Some said that was because it revealed her physical awkwardness—yet I suspect that is only relevant to the extent that it would have marred the impression of divinity and the pressure of yearning. The pattern of close-up and long shot also bears out the relationship of audience and star—so close, so far. That may seem fanciful for a moment, but it falls into place as soon as one examines the nature of her material.

Just like the lighting and the photography, her plots contributed to Garbo's rarefied status and the balance of appearance and apartness. In fourteen of her twenty-four American films, there are unhappy endings. The enormous stir of romantic possibility made by the story, with stronger sexual suggestions in the silent pictures, is denied by the narrative structure. That there is something fatal or impossible in the liaison at the heart of the film is confirmed either by Garbo's death or by some kind of self-sacrifice.

She perishes in *Camille* (1937), too tainted, too old, too unsuitable for Robert Taylor. In *Conquest* (1937), she must leave Charles Boyer on St. Helena. In *Anna Karenina,* her despair makes her throw herself under a train—and Garbo played that role twice, in 1935 and in *Love* (1927). *Queen Christina* sails into abdication with the corpse of her lover. The ballerina in *Grand Hotel* (1932) will discover only after the film is over that John Barrymore is dead. The title character in *Mata Hari* (1932) says farewell to her lover and goes to the firing squad. In *Inspiration* (1931), Garbo walks out on the sleeping Robert Montgomery rather than ruin his life. For *Romance* (1930), she persuades a priest to give up his infatuation for her, and in *A Woman of Affairs* (1929), she kills herself to avoid breaking up a marriage.

The soulful self-regard of her face required unhappiness. It was her inspiration to linger in our dreams just as much as in Robert Montgomery's. How apt that in the great scene from *Queen Christina*, where she drifts around the bedroom like a sleepwalker, or like an image propelled by the future looking back, touching so many things, she explains herself: "I have been memorizing this room. In the future, in my mind, I shall live a great deal in this world." That may be the strategy that the Swedish queen has set herself, but it is also an inducement to the viewers to carry the imagery home in their heads and relive it afterward. To extend Barthes, the photograph is the idea of reality that permits us to live in our imaginations.

One can see this same impulse and destiny behind her retirement. Indeed, it is less a reason for withdrawing than a majesty that sooner or later will demand it. The most potent star is the one who can go farthest away while still exerting gravitational pull.

There are other ways of explaining what happened after *Two-Faced Woman* (1941). It was a poor film, badly received. Garbo was thirty-six, and she must have appreciated the risk of looking less than perfect. The war had also deprived her of the European following that had always been vital. She was far from the most popular actress in America; some called her box-office poison, and her proclivity for suffering had irked audiences. She laughed well enough in *Ninotchka* (1939), but *Two-Faced Woman* had a strained gaiety. Then again, perhaps she reckoned on a short rest and a short war but found gradually that the chances of a comeback were less easy to arrange while the fear of being rejected grew. You might even let yourself believe that Stiller had told her the very day to withdraw and that she duly carried out his plan.

Her stardom has stayed intact. There have been mouth-watering rumors of return, but what's a rumor if it doesn't make you believe in impossibility? She might have played in Balzac's *Duchess of Langeais* in the late forties: Max Ophüls was to direct, with James Mason as costar, and guess who as cameraman? That was the closest she came to working again, but for at least fifteen years great parts were dangled in front of her, like Fay Wray strung up for Kong.

One was a life of George Sand, and that helped foster another speculation, that she was somehow mannish. Sometimes in her films, that fond, amused gaze that knows how quick and fickle men are takes on itself real masculine decisiveness. "I will die a bachelor," she says gloomily in *Queen Christina,* where she also dresses up as a man. One day during *Grand Hotel,* Garbo met Joan Crawford, held her face in her hands, and told her she was beautiful. Crawford later admitted that she was ready to turn lesbian on the spot. It was alleged that Garbo had not married because she was every bit as interested in other women as in men. That is what makes people claim that she was tall (though she was only 5 feet, 6½ inches), that her shoulders were broad, her voice deep and her reserve strangely virile.

But she was bound to love no one, just as the actress would enjoy pretending to be anyone. Stiller may have been most valuable to her as a way of fobbing off every later man, from John Gilbert to George Schlee, with "I only ever loved Stiller." You can imagine her murmuring it with that same faraway look from the screen.

Some of her friends of the last forty years say that off-screen she is as she was on-screen: ultimately inaccessible. Most of them have honored a pact of silence about her, but who knows whether that has been to protect her or to shelter their illusions about her? She has done little, except travel and be rich. It is not quite existence so much as an obligatory interval, waiting for stardom and death to merge. Joshua Logan saw her East Side apartment once and found exquisite living areas as well as entirely empty rooms.

There had always been a lazy streak in her, not indulgent or slack, but maybe the result of thinness of character. Even when she worked, at MGM, she made twenty-four films in a period when Joan Crawford completed fifty-three. In 1927 an article appeared under her name in *Theatre Magazine* denying charges of reclusiveness but admitting a "Swedish" shyness: "My country, Sweden, is so small. It is also so quiet. The women there are entirely different, so inactive, almost placid, I might say."

Cecil Beaton, another close friend, once described a woman rather closer to Gloria Swanson's Norma Desmond: "She is not interested in anything or anybody in particular. And she has become quite as difficult as an invalid and as selfish, quite unprepared to put herself out for anyone. She would be a trying companion, continuously sighing and full of tragic regrets. She is superstitious, suspicious, and does not know the meaning of friendship. She is incapable of love."

But how could the word *love* actually be capable of love? The sign is cut off from participation. Greta Garbo may be as cold and empty as a ghost—the photographed face is explained by "tragic regret" about the personal failure. Whether we regard her as an actress, a woman, a triumph of the industry or a model of photography, she is bound up with the unattainable— her face conveys the idea of a love that enthralls us, despite impossibility.

George Cukor saw an actress, in *Camille*, who worked in the knowledge of disappointment: "She never saw rushes, and I asked her why. 'I have some idea, some notion of what I'm doing,' she said, 'and every time I see it, it falls so short that it throws me.'" That is an actress who might retire at any moment, the idea is so much purer than the reality. And if that is too ethereal or uncanny for you—so that *you* might faint—then settle for another kind of mystification, described by one of her least likely contemporaries at MGM, Lon Chaney: "I told Garbo that mystery had served me well and it would do as much for her. She is a

clever woman, and she adopted my policy of never having portraits made except in character and never giving interviews—and
look where it carried her!"

I'm looking, but once you've looked at Garbo's face, she is
everywhere, like a watermark in a sheet of paper.

(1980)

The Lives of Stars

The January 22, 1981, issue of *Rolling Stone* can go straight into the capsule we are burying to amuse the year 2081. It volunteers a confession of our absorption in contradictory figments— newsprint reality and imagistic glamour—and all in the cause of that religion for the godless, celebrity. We are mad for stars because photography and the other media have blessed them with appearance without substance. It is living without friction or decay: that's how anyone in a picture is poised between life and death. We call it being lifelike, and we treat it as a way into immortality.

Stars shine light on our lives, without knowing we exist. Their fireball glamour confronts our black-hole anonymity. We behold and they are seen: yet our reverence verges on the hostility that cannot endure the knowledge that it will never be recognized, never have its moment on the screen.

This issue of *Rolling Stone* sings of the death of John Lennon, but it celebrates stardom and the determination of the faithful to maintain the religion rather than examine it. The magazine is giddy with grief and its sense of significance; it cannot be quiet or at a loss; the dynamics of stardom deny and transfigure anguish; the death of Lennon becomes something that happened to *Rolling Stone*. It is as if we had seen so many fictional deaths that we know the sentimental role of mourning too well to experience the grief as a real thing.

This is not simply an attack on the sensibility of *Rolling Stone*. Let me quote a letter in the January–February 1981 *American Film*, from David Kaftal. It reproached me for an article on Greta Garbo that had appeared in the October issue. Mr. Kaftal found that article "to be in abysmally poor taste. The writer is apparently so enamored of his model of Garbo as image that he neglects to consider that she is in actual fact a flesh and blood being, capable of feeling hurt by thoughtless insults." The letter ends with the suggestion that I had used Garbo's "photographic image as a stimulus to mental masturbation."

I don't mean to muffle the criticism by not quoting all of the letter. Instead, I congratulate Mr. Kaftal's description of some cultural consequences of stardom. I do believe that stars are like ghosts, and that the process of photographic reproduction and communication has left a rift between our sense of image and reality. If not ours, then mine. Just the fact that photography is modern and technical does not prevent its fostering of superstition. To believe in faces we never meet, and to let their moods affect our lives, depends on irrational faith.

It would frighten me to meet Garbo because she has become so steady and luminous in my imagination. My fondness for her did not register with Mr. Kaftal, but I accept his charge that once I regard her as an image, I may wrong the real person. This is like Marilyn Monroe being stung by Laurence Olivier's brisk, professional request that she "be sexy." To that extent, I am prepared to admit a small but definite kinship with Mark David Chapman, Lennon's killer. Stardom nurtures a need for insurrection in the viewing mass. That can be all the more dangerous if it has begun to lose sight of the vulnerability of real flesh and blood.

Rolling Stone sees itself as priest or intermediary delivering John Lennon to the public. He was on the cover of the first issue; and he was meant to be on the cover of issue No. 335, inaugurating

a new year and a new format for one of the best-selling magazines
in the world. Lennon is still on the cover. Photographer Annie
Leibovitz was in the Dakota apartment only hours before Lennon
was shot. Being in that sanctum is as much evidence of priest-
hood as Moses going up the mountain. The cover picture is the
kind of religious icon that comes from such privileged access. It
is a vision of intimacy, an embrace between a naked Lennon and
a clothed Yoko Ono. Leibovitz in the magazine says that Lennon
saw tests of her pictures and liked them, and that the day after the
shooting the widow made the final selection of pictures to be
printed.

The cover will sell the magazine in greater quantity than most
other issues of *Rolling Stone*. Even after death, Lennon and his
admirers cannot extricate themselves from the commercializa-
tion of his name and image. After the death, the picture automatically becomes a premonition of the tragedy. Lennon may
have thought it captured his relationship with his wife, but all
pictures are traps for the subjects. Now, we see a Lennon with
eyes shut, body curled up, clinging to an Ono who is open-eyed
and Garbo-like as she looks away, out of the frame, wistful but
enshrined in an eternal mystery of sadness and ecstasy. We have
to know that she chose the cover, for it is a picture of her and of
the way the loss has altered her. She becomes a star now, holder
of the spirit, rather than just the problematic consort to a star.

It is a very romantic picture, yet aren't all photographs expressions of the yearning that imagination is more potent than reality?
And although Lennon was a musician, I doubt if his fame would
have been a fraction of what it is but for pictures. He made a few
films, he was on countless television shows and interviews, and
he was photographed wherever he went until he had to find a
refuge. Most of us never meet stars, so photography must bear
witness to them. It is the essential discourse of stardom.

In which case, it is possible that movies have always been less
stories than offerings of photographed personality. Any film magazine must believe in the worth of motion pictures, in the study

of them, their preservation and the chance that some of them may
be art. We therefore treat films as the natural extension of the
novel and theater, narrative art forms capable of moral significance. But suppose movies are reiterations of the religion of
imagery and glamour.

When we say that the "grammar" of long shot, medium shot and
close-up permitted fluent storytelling, should we add that the
variation of shots also proved the dynamic magic of the people on
the screen? We realize how the picture business accelerated when
the merchants appreciated the selling strength of a name and a
star. Every auteurist knows how often he or she watches a film
because of the appeal of the people in it. Occasionally, auteurism
has given some credit to the creative force of stars, just as the big
studios once searched for vehicles for their famous properties.

But those concessions do not grasp how entirely our pleasure
may rest on vicarious involvement with those photographed
souls. The great popularity of star interviews on television suggests that we might be content with a full-length movie in which
a star was photographed without pretext of plot. *To Have and
Have Not* is not Hemingway or any other plausible or suspense-
ful story. But it is Bogart and Bacall drifting around the screen,
talking to one another as if in an endless rehearsal and yielding
sweetly to the lens.

Today, those exalted figures are covered in so many other ways.
There are biographies of both stars, Bacall's own book *By Myself*
and rip-offs like *The Man with Bogart's Face*. But in their heyday
there were no books by stars, only the fan magazines and the
gossip press to maintain our contact with celebrity. The fanzines
were fed material by the studios, and it was a contractual require-
ment that stars should cooperate in whatever forms of publicity
the studio approved. That was just part of the studio's ownership
of actors or actresses: names changed, noses and hairlines altered,
pasts and presents doctored in the interests of lucrative futures.

Stardom did more than promulgate the language of photographed personality. It institutionalized a tacit prostitution

whereby the performer became a company property and the helpless instrument for millions of spectators bent on the "mental
masturbation" of watching movies. No wonder some stars resented
the system and felt that their real souls had been stolen or warped.
Just as the public is eager for a few stars to be disgraced—so that
the gap separating them from us seems fairer and manageable—
stars had reason to despise the fickle but devouring public taste.

The star is adored but not liked: that is the consequence of a
religious respect that enjoys no ordinary relations with the object
of its desire. Some stars resisted or were hurt by studio control.
Why should I go to the premiere with so-and-so? Why must I
make this piece of trash? But being used cultivates the code that
everyone has a price: that is a legacy of prostitution. And so, in
the extensive library of books by and about stars, it is not easy to
see many that demanded to be written. Brooke Hayward's
Haywire is an exception: it convinces the reader of the author's
personal need to let the story of being Margaret Sullavan's daughter out into the real light.

But most star books were written from a need for vindication,
money or vengeance. The genre only came into being in the
fifties, as stars lost some of their luster. There were pioneering
books by Bette Davis and Mary Astor. But Errol Flynn's *My
Wicked, Wicked Ways* was a landmark in 1959. It was written at
the drunken, debt-ridden pit of Flynn's life, and only after the
publisher assigned Earl Conrad to serve as interviewer, tape-
recording mechanic and "ghost." Occasionally on talk shows
there is a comic meeting between an interviewer (who has not
read the book) and a star (who did not write it and cannot recall
every passage in it). Hedy Lamarr even published an autobiography and then sued the ghostwriters on the ground that they had
damaged her career!

Such books vary in the candor with which they admit literary
assistance. A few movie stars write every word. Some cheerfully
give up their life to a ghost. Others require a great deal of editing.
Sales usually reflect the degree of authenticity as much as they do
the drawing power of a star. But books with the breezy, revelatory

ease of David Niven's *The Moon's a Balloon* and Shelley Winters's *Shelley* have had runs on the best-seller lists beyond their authors' box-office appeal.

Many of these books have no indexes, let alone source notes. Stars' memories are spared doubt or dispute. Not many of them have been letter writers or diary keepers. They have often lived on the run, outside any settled pattern or habit. To most of us the lives look disorderly: that is one of the things that makes them enviable. But, as authors, stars expect to be trusted. This is not a blanket accusation, yet in a short article it can hardly sound less than provocative. Still, I wonder how many stars are reliable judges of what has happened to them. Their life and work are rooted in make-believe. They have been surrounded by flattery and lies, and they have entrusted many parts of their lives to agents, lawyers and managers. To this day, stars are victimized by a gossip press that prints flagrant lies with the insolent legal safeguard of an "alleged" here or there. Yet those victims may themselves write records of the past that are partial, wishful thinking.

Stars seldom supply dates or details in their autobiographies. They feel free to assert and describe without verification, as if they were telling stories. That is what their publishers have advised, and it represents the way many books have been "written" into a tape recorder. Star books meet no greater test of veracity than the qualms of the publisher's libel lawyer. Yet such books do provide us with a profuse, contradictory patchwork of what happened in Hollywood. The film historian has the tricky task of picking out the useful from the specious. That is not a new problem: the historian knows the rubbery nature of any "fact." But show business has few rivals as a setting in which what happened is what people remember or allege. After all, these people are dedicated to the life of the imagination. Actors like being someone else as much as any audience.

At best, star books give a flavor of the personality being described: that's true of Lauren Bacall's book, of *Memo from David*

O. Selznick, and it's what distinguishes the forthcoming *The Quality of Mercy* by Mercedes McCambridge. At worst, they are picture books and showbiz small talk. It is no longer enough for a star to write a restrained account of the good times he had. James Cagney gave us no more than that and everyone felt struck by the contrast between a staid old author and the brilliantly dangerous young actor. To make the lists you've got to dish some dirt. Bob Thomas wrote a discreet, formulaic biography of Joan Crawford which had the misfortune of coinciding with the publication of Christina Crawford's *Mommie Dearest*.

That is a horrendous book: it is badly written and its malice is disconcerting. No reader could trust it. Yet no one familiar with Joan Crawford's films could dismiss it. For it describes a nightmare of flashy on-show surface and private torture that is so close to her movie scenarios. The most convincing things in the book were pictures of Joan with Christina as a child nearly eclipsed by the stepmother's blazing claim on attention.

Mommie Dearest is being filmed. The star books are being fed back into the mass media, especially on television, where the dramatized lives of "real people" were popular some time before that slogan was taken as the name of a series. The confusion is rampant, especially when Sophia Loren plays both her mother and herself in a small-screen adaptation of a 1979 book that had this sublimely contradictory title page: *Sophia, Living and Loving: Her Own Story,* by A. E. Hotchner. In such heady spirals, real life becomes a genre instead of an unshakable experience.

It is as if stardom was itself an overriding mass medium, a mechanism in which the multiplicity of us can look inward and upward and clutch at the straw that we are still a society, a cult or a faith rather than an impossible crowd driven into dead ends of anonymity and alienation. The chief function of a mass medium may be not to inform or entertain but simply to exist as a climate which says to us: "Yes—all of us together—with a center."

Rolling Stone was not the only publication that printed inane or grotesque pronouncements about Lennon, or the only place where the rhetoric of morbidity overwhelmed true feeling. But it had its share of bad moments and strained attempts to insist on the writer's own involvement in Lennon's death. Dave Marsh said that "what we're mourning now is the end of a time when all of us held human life dear." The editor and publisher, Jann Wenner, wrote:

> I cried and cried and went home.
> In the next few days—not able to say goodbye to John— I realized that one of the reasons I felt so afraid and so alone—and unable to face the continuing news—was that I had formed my adult life around this guy in very serious ways.

People were writing too quickly, perhaps, led astray by the hope that turmoil guaranteed sincerity. Scott Spencer, in *Rolling Stone,* recognized that the problem of writing was part of the subject: mourning is a process of self-analysis and retaliation that begins to alleviate the loss we cannot reverse. Spencer described Lennon's achievement in a way that suggests a young movie tycoon telling us what excites him about film. It is also a description that knows the religious potential in a mass medium:

> The astonishing—and, for me, unduplicated—characteristic of his art was that it brought together people who may have had no single thing in common. It was the only true mass phenomenon that's ever touched me.

Anyone reading all the despair in *Rolling Stone's* obituary issue—despair for all our futures, for a church without its god— might have had an inkling about how troubled Mark David Chapman felt. And he is an important part of the tragedy— because Chapman is alive still, because he was the active force in it and because the little we know of him suggests that he was a stargazer.

Lennon had an extreme and popular talent, even if he was not profound. But his most inventive act may have been the degree to which he was able to withdraw from being just a Beatle, though he was not as successful as Garbo. Whatever kind of retreat they found for themselves, they were always imposed upon by their fame. There is an elderly woman "living inside the cathedral called Garbo" just as there was a forty-year-old inside the Dakota cut off from much of life. *Rolling Stone* quotes Lennon commiserating with the performer who played him in *Beatlemania:* how difficult it is to escape from a long and successful run. That fever of stardom brings sums of money and adulation that no psyche can resist. It also undermines the drive for further achievement. There is no rescue or retreat. No artist can endure acceptance; no person can survive neglect.

Stardom resembles death in life, a kind of perpetuity, like the existence of a fictional character. Only the details of the ending remain to be worked out. Then the whole life hangs in the air, no longer a story but a chant or an image.

Meanwhile, some people haunt the dark, teased by the Warholism that one day everyone will be a star for fifteen minutes. Mark David Chapman's act cannot have taken fifteen seconds. But why he acted could be a deeper mystery than any of Lennon's art, and just as much caught up in the urge to be transcendent. We cannot hope to comprehend it unless we see how far photography and its forms have erased the settled distinction of real and fantasy, life and death, by making a religion of the lifelike.

(1981)

James Dean at 50

September 30—At Cholame, California, on the way to
Salinas, James Dean, 24, actor, was killed in a car accident.
His Porsche Spyder struck a Ford sedan, driven by Donald
Turnupseed, 23, student. "I didn't see him . . . I swear I
didn't see him," cried Turnupseed. Dean died from injuries
before reaching Memorial Hospital, Paso Robles. The actor
had made an impressive debut this year in *East of Eden*. His
latest pictures, *Rebel Without a Cause* and *Giant*, are still to
be released.

At least seven newspapers ran that hasty story in different parts of
the world, and Dean has copies of them all. Mourning in English,
Hungarian and Chinese. But the single paragraph just quoted—
it was stop press in the London *Daily Mail*, printed within an
hour of the crash, 5:45 p.m. Pacific time—has been enshrined
ever since in the palm of the artificial left hand which is the most
evident damage to the mind and body of James Dean.

The enigmatic but hugely influential Dean has long since given
up asking fortune-tellers to read his hand. But the chance and
game of death haunt him still. Very few have so narrowly escaped
fatality, or come so close to being the god of a morbid cult; not

many people have seen so many friends and acquaintances carried off in such bizarre and unexpected ways. Yet Dean has a
sense of life that is still urgent and excited, however absurd or
slippery his own existence may seem to him.

He will be fifty on February 8, 1981, and the shy moodiness of
his youth has turned into the rather disenchanted middle age of
someone who seems wistful about having survived. But the new
year must surely present fresh opportunities and risks to James
Dean. No one seriously expects to see him on camera on inaugu-
ration day. But in the storm of intrigue and allegation surrounding
him, who will question the unique access he has to the new president? Plenty worry that his influence could prove sinister. There
are gloomy predictions about further entries in the book of fatality associated with Dean. Reflecting on Edward Kennedy's victory
over Ronald Reagan in the recent election, in a piece to appear in
The New York Review of Books in January, Gore Vidal writes:

> If we can congratulate ourselves on being spared a retired
> actor, accustomed to being told when to smile and frown,
> and when to jump up and down, we must now survive the
> left-handed bonus of a stand-in who has let himself be used
> by an actor.

Of course, the ambulance did reach Paso Robles in time; and later
that weekend, the body—or its bloody bits—was moved to Los
Angeles. There were already such crowds converging on Paso
Robles that police had to close sections of highway to enable the
transfer to be made. For months thereafter, the area around
Cedars of Lebanon Hospital was a battlefield of crowd problems.
Impromptu religious services, the sale of ghoulish souvenirs and
constant attempts to enter the hospital—all required police attention. One young woman went in for an appendectomy in the
hope of seeing Dean, had complications in the routine and
absolutely unnecessary operation and died a few weeks later. The
LAPD later revealed that security measures had cost over $1.6
million by the summer of 1956, when Dean left the hospital.

Inside the hospital, nineteen operations were needed, six of them in the week after the crash. Once the Warner Bros. publicity department took charge of the press releases, we had graphic details of every delicate stage of treatment. Pauline Kael would later call it the "first great hospital soap opera." Dean's head was hanging on "by a string," according to one eyewitness at Cholame, but miraculously the spinal fracture could be repaired and enough blood vessels were intact for the intricate and very painful business of putting Dean back together again.

The eight-day coma that Dean suffered left fears that he might survive, only with brain damage, and Jimmy has ever since reveled in masquerades of mental impairment—most notably in his performance as Benjy in the extraordinary Jean Genet stage version of *The Sound and the Fury* that contributed so much to the street emotions of Paris in May 1968.

The jawline was made again, and Dean and Montgomery Clift were surely brought together by shared disaster and facial reconstruction. But whereas damage preyed on Clift's confidence, a new appearance fostered Dean's fatalistic vision of a mutable, infinite being. Dean did emerge a half inch shorter, with an appealing limp because of the pelvic damage, and minus his left hand. Or was it minus? Grotesque stories circulated that Dean kept the hand, and that Marilyn Monroe once awoke, disoriented, in his bed to find it—cold from formalin—resting in her most tender parts. This is the legend that later inspired Norman Mailer's essay "The Ghost in No Man's Land."

And what did Mr. Paul Newman, 55, of Cleveland, Ohio, think of Dean's protracted recovery? "I had such mixed feelings, I was a mess." Newman now is a successful Shaker Heights automobile dealer, blue eyed and pretty in a way that went out of style in the early sixties. He is being touted as the next mayor of Cleveland— "I should be so lucky," he says wryly—but he lives with the thought that he might have been a star if any of Dean's operations had failed.

Newman had gone from Yale Drama School to New York,

notable supporting parts in *Picnic* and *The Desperate Hours,* and work for television. They made an uneasy screen test together, but Newman lost the part of Caleb Trask in *East of Eden* to Dean. "I could smell that part," said Newman. "But Jim was the country boy they needed, and I came out looking Ivy League." Instead, Newman made one of the all-time bombs, his only picture, *The Silver Chalice,* a cut-price biblical schlepic in which he played opposite none other than Pier Angeli, the tortured madonna of Dean's life.

At the time of the crash Dean had been set to play the boxer Rocky Graziano in *Somebody Up There Likes Me* for MGM. Early in 1956, when it became known that Dean had lost the hand, Metro announced that they would go ahead with Newman in the biopic. Dean's agent, Jane Deacy, said that the decision was "outrageous and inhuman," and a distressed Angeli told Hedda Hopper, "I do not think it is kind to Jimmy." Those protests were nothing compared with what happened at Metro's Culver City headquarters. The studio was besieged by Dean fans, the switchboard was jammed and a petition with 2 million signatures was presented at the Irving Thalberg Building. All over America, theaters playing MGM pictures were the objects of demonstrations. Graziano himself, an overlooked figure in the furor, was as anxious to be played by someone, anyone, as he had ever been to get a title shot at Tony Zale.

On February 8, 1956—Dean's birthday—MGM recovered its grasp of public relations by saying that the Graziano project was on hold, and that the studio was optimistic Dean would be able to play the part. Angeli was said to be ecstatic. Paul Newman let it be known that the movie business was full of shit. And Dean was photographed in his hospital bed (for the first time) with a boxing glove on his left arm jabbing gaily at the camera and the world.

Somebody Up There Likes Me went before the cameras in the fall of 1956. The actor's limp was wonderfully absorbed into the fighting crouch of Graziano. Pier Angeli was cast—in a process of

public acclamation that rode hard on her husband, Vic Damone—
as the fighter's wife. *Confidential* ran an article—"Death and the
Angel"—which implied that Dean could be the father of Pier's
child. The director, Robert Wise, claimed that Dean was the most
creative collaborator he had worked with since Orson Welles (on
Citizen Kane). The MGM studio remained the Mecca of crowds of
young people anxious to see the actor arriving for work. And
when it came to the fighting sequences, Dean never flinched but
used his left as a destructive club. Graziano, visiting the set, reckoned that if he'd had a metal left he would never have been
beaten. Dean also made a famous TV commercial on behalf of
disabled veterans that multiplied by four the annual level of
public donations to the Veterans' Administration.

But MGM paid for all the publicity. While Dean lay at Cedars
of Lebanon, in a coma, *Rebel Without a Cause* had opened. Before
he regained consciousness, it had done the best opening four
days of business for a Warners film since *The Jazz Singer.* It had
also earned a file of reviews that hailed Dean as the actor of his
generation. In the *Saturday Review,* Arthur Knight recognized the
unique affinity among Dean, his part in *Rebel* and the tumult in
the teenage audience: "He projects the wildness, the torment,
the crude tenderness of a rootless generation."

Early in 1956, Dean was nominated for an Oscar for *East of
Eden.* But anyone voting felt the additional force of *Rebel* and the
extraordinary public sympathy for a young invalid who might be
encouraged to get better by the award. Elizabeth Taylor, his costar
in *Giant,* visited him at Cedars of Lebanon in early March and said,
"I hope the Academy has a heart as well as good judgment." The
Oscar was Dean's by power of magnetic attraction, and Sal Mineo
received it on behalf of the actor, giving a long, incoherent speech
of tribute that ended in a tearful Mineo being led from the stage.

The Oscar became another bedfellow for Dean, and from the
table of his private room it must have presided over negotiations
for his future. Dean was under contract to Warners, who had
loaned him to MGM for *Somebody Up There Likes Me.* But with an
Oscar, the box-office success of *Rebel* and expectations that *Giant*

would be exactly what the title promised, the stricken Dean was aware of his commercial power. He dropped his agent, Jane Deacy. She said, "I'm very sorry about it . . . but Jimmy is bigger than all of us." Instead, he was signed up as a personal client of Lew Wasserman, supremo at MCA.

With the decisive maneuvering that had always distinguished his career, Wasserman used the uncertainty about Dean's health and the public demand for him to renegotiate the *Somebody* deal. MGM would now distribute the film, but it was the first production of Left Hand, the company that was incorporated around Dean's hospital bed. Dean was guaranteed $1 million—paid in its entirety before shooting began—against an undisclosed percentage of the profits. Thereafter he would return to Warners to fulfill a reduced version of his original contract. Jack Warner said tersely, "An empire has been born."

There were immediate signs that the empire would be unruly. While *Somebody Up There Likes Me* was shooting, *Giant* was released. Several critics thought that Dean's attempt to show the middle-aged dissolution in the tycoon Jett Rink was less than a success. In an unexpected reaction, Dean said that the director, George Stevens, had "botched" the picture. He claimed that if the film had been made according to Dean's ideas it could have been a masterpiece. "The public goes to see actors," said Dean, "and it's about time we had control of our films."

Metro insisted they were very enthusiastic about the Graziano biopic. Gossip columnists wondered if the Dean–Angeli love scenes were not unusually tender. But after five weeks, Robert Wise and the scenarist, Ernest Lehman, walked off the set. They alleged that Dean had become increasingly tyrannical, and that in one scene he had actually struck Angeli so that she could not work for two days. Wise added that he believed Dean was consulting at night with Nicholas Ray, the director of *Rebel Without a Cause,* and then imposing their ideas on the shooting. Dean retorted that the charge was nonsense, but he added that, in his opinion, "Nick Ray is a genius and Wise is . . . well, Wise isn't."

The picture was completed, but only with rising acrimony after a six-week holdout in which Dean and Wise disputed the final cut. Years later Wise revealed that at one stage Dean had taken over the cutting room, hiring "a gang of toughs" to keep others out, laboring for a week and then quitting in disgust, "leaving absolute chaos behind."

Friends reported that Angeli was "close to a breakdown" in the aftermath of filming. She had married Vic Damone in 1954 after a close relationship with Dean. Angeli made no secret about regrets at having yielded to family pressure. But if she had had hopes of a lasting relationship with Dean, the Graziano picture destroyed them. Her life would be short and tragic, and on several occasions she was rebuffed in efforts to rekindle Dean's affections. "He wants no one he can have," she said once. She and Damone were divorced in 1959; a second marriage, to Armando Trotajoli, broke up seven years later. At that time she told the *National Enquirer* that Dean "is the only man I ever loved deeply as a woman should love a man. . . . I tried to love my husbands but it never lasted. I would wake up in the night and find I had been dreaming of Jimmy."

Pier Angeli died in 1971, weeks after Dean's prison sentence, having taken an "accidental" overdose of drugs. By then, however, she was several names down the list of deaths in Dean's life.

Dean saw many other women, some from show business—like Ursula Andress, Leslie Caron and Jean Seberg. But stories began to be heard that he would pick up anyone on a whim. He settled out of court with a Hollywood Boulevard waitress who said that he had beaten her up when she refused to be intimate with one of his friends.

There were also rumors that Dean was involved in homosexual affairs with Montgomery Clift, Sal Mineo and two of his own bodyguards. Another admirer, Elvis Presley, after a long weekend at Dean's Palm Springs house, said, "Jim isn't real well, yet." Two months later, Dean was arrested in New York for possession of marijuana. He appeared in court, paid the fine on the spot and was jailed for seven days for contempt of court when he tossed the bills on the floor. "This is nothing," he shouted to reporters. "This country is about to come apart."

By the middle of 1957, the press was regarding Dean as a rogue celebrity, carried away by the adulation of the young. Within the industry, however, some people saw Dean as an unconventional but brilliant businessman. No matter how wayward his private life, business found Dean punctual, lucid and hungry. Reviewers were convinced that *Somebody Up There Likes Me* showed all the battles of its making. Bosley Crowther said that "rather than the rough energy of a prizefighter, Mr. Dean gives us the mannered grace of a Nijinsky who has become a gangster." The public had no doubts, and Dean was reckoned to have earned another million from the profits.

Despite the protests of Warners, Dean made another picture at MGM: *Cat on a Hot Tin Roof,* opposite Elizabeth Taylor. It was their second picture together, and Taylor seemed better able to humor and discipline Dean than anyone else. The feverish story was filmed without mishap or problem. Taylor said that she thought too much had happened to Dean too soon, while he said it had been a privilege to work with her on such fine material. Tennessee Williams, visiting the set, confessed that he found Dean "exquisitely churlish, and as blind as a bat."

It was Williams who introduced Dean to Gore Vidal. Apparently in the course of a weekend on Nantucket Island, Dean persuaded Vidal to let him film his TV play about Billy the Kid—*The Left-Handed Gun.* Jack Warner, prepared to lecture Dean on breach of contract, was instead presented with a script, a one-page budget and the package of Dean and Nicholas Ray as director. Months later, when he looked more thoroughly at the script, Warner found that after page 17 there were only pages from other old scripts. But by then *The Left-Handed Gun* had been shot—along with Nicholas Ray.

No one any longer knows how much script there was, or how much improvisation. The veteran photographer J. Peverell Marley said simply that "making it was the worst time of my life . . . and of just about every other life around . . . but, by God, when I saw the thing finished, it was Stroheim, Buñuel, Kurosawa and the Marx Brothers, all at the same time." *The Left-Handed Gun* is regarded by many historians as the start of new American cinema, the first movie in which a classical genre was reworked to express the passion and turmoil of modern times.

Dean's own Billy was nominated, but the film won no Oscars: the homosexual scenes were too direct for the sensibilities of 1958—they were only visible because the censors could not fully understand them. Nor was Ray nominated, though the design and energy of the film were his, until, in the last week of filming, at the height of a murderous argument over how a scene should be played, Dean picked up Billy's gun and shot Ray in the shoulder. "I thought I had the bullets," murmured Ray from his hospital bed. "Jim had been using real bullets all along, and I'd been emptying the chambers." Ray pressed no charges, saying it was the kind of thing that could happen in heat on a movie. Dean later apologized publicly, and never gave up the difficult friendship with Ray.

Dean had made six films in four years, one of which he had spent as an invalid. So he told the angry but helpless Warners that he would take the rest that had been talked about for so long. When the studio threatened legal action, Dean enlisted medical opinion, including the startling verdict of Dr. Harold Strom that "this young man is risking his life. He seems to believe that he can put the long process of recovery aside while he attends to more pressing matters." There was renewed speculation that in the hospital Dean had become addicted to painkilling drugs. This owed a good deal to the death by shooting of Lamar Larrabee, a friend of Dean's, in Florida. Larrabee was found on a drifting motor cruiser that contained traces of a cargo of heroin.

Then another death did something to steady the young actor. He was playing Caliban to Charles Laughton's Prospero in a Santa Fe production of *The Tempest* when Mike Todd was killed in a plane crash. Dean and Todd had not been close, but Dean's devotion to Taylor was something that the husband had joked about. Love or mutual need bloomed slowly in the mourning, and in April 1959 the couple were married in Las Vegas. Liz told the press, "Jimmy has been a tower of strength. No one knows the depth of his kindness." Dean promised that this was the end of his "wild" period. "She is a very great lady, and she is going to look after me." However, Dean seemed amused when a reporter pointed out that he was actually one year older than his new bride.

In the spirit of reform, he went back to work for Warners as Dude, the drunken deputy trying to rehabilitate himself, in Howard Hawks's *Rio Bravo*. As costar he had John Wayne, and from the first day on-set the two actors took a violent dislike to one another. "Picture was meant to be a story about friendship," said Hawks, "but it turned into the most god-awful study of two spoiled brats, needling one another about liquor, women and anything else they could think of." A frustrated Hawks simply filmed one of their arguments—about how to roll a cigarette— and was able to use it in the picture with only minor cuts. Whenever Walter Brennan appears in the film, there is an odd sense of *The Odd Couple* plus one—a kind of *Three Sisters* of the range. Yet again, Dean had drawn the American cinema off on one of its strangest diversions.

Moreover, the proper joys of marriage were undoubtedly threatened by the relationship that sprang up on the set of *Rio Bravo* between Dean and the young Angie Dickinson. When Liz visited the shooting one weekend, it was to discover that Dean and Dickinson had gone to Mexico together. According to an exuberant Angie, "We went to see a cockfight." Liz had no comment, but it was after she had spent an afternoon with John Wayne that the senior actor added something to the stage booze Dean had to drink in one scene. Whatever the addition, Dean's Mexican trip was tinged with Taylor's Revenge.

Was Dean a little bored as the new decade dawned? He faced being thirty. He had proved himself as actor, star and producer. It remained very difficult for him to set up the kind of movie he wanted. If he knew what that was. As a rule, his creativity worked when he found himself in some old-fashioned project which he would try to remake. Rather than an original artist, he was a marauding iconoclast.

So it was, in the spring of 1960, that he took an active part in the actors' strike. Though he had been in movies only a few years, he argued, along with the Screen Actors' Guild, that actors should be paid for all the old movies that had been sold to television. SAG was never a radical union, and Dean was just as willing to chastise the union leadership, notably Ronald Reagan, as he was the studios. At the same time, Lew Wasserman, still Dean's agent, pointed out to *Variety*: "Jimmy should remember that on *Somebody Up There Likes Me* he was himself a producer. And I daresay he will fill that role again." It surprised many when Dean refused to respond to that remark but reduced his efforts on behalf of the strike.

Instead, he threw himself into support for John Kennedy. He was not an adroit public speaker, but he campaigned with a will and may have had some influence with his general theme: "John Kennedy knows what young people want." The Kennedys found Dean a disarming supporter at times. The famous photograph of Dean, Jack, Angie Dickinson and Marilyn Monroe may have lost as many votes as it won, but it did promise new attitudes from the White House. Dean was with the family on results night, even if there was a scuffle between him and Robert Kennedy. A few days later, the president-elect said, "James Dean has as good an understanding of political power as Queen Elizabeth I or Jack Warner."

Cleopatra was a venture that perplexed Dean, perhaps the one thing that has ever upstaged him. The marriage with Taylor was not secure, and Dean's comments on the idea that he play Marc Antony could not have helped. But when Liz fell seriously ill in London during the first abortive shooting, Dean grew weary of another hospital vigil and returned to America. "What will be, will be," he told the press at Heathrow. "I've been through these things before, and you have to do it alone." Reports of that press conference only established that Taylor's dramatic wrath had not been sapped by pneumonia.

There were reconciliations to come still, but no one was surprised when the eventual Roman holiday of *Cleopatra* saw Liz and Richard Burton growing closer. The divorce was a formality, at which Dean guessed that "Elizabeth will make a great empress one day."

And so the terrible uncertainty of the sixties began, for America and for Dean. The details are both familiar and confused. All we can do now is enumerate the highlights, like the cries in some awesome melodrama.

- 1963, *The Moviegoer* is released. Perhaps Dean's greatest film. He had persuaded Walker Percy to sell him the rights. He directed it himself, and played the lead, opposite Tuesday Weld. The picture took the Palme d'Or at Cannes, but it was a failure in America, despite magnificent reviews.
- Within weeks of the assassination of JFK, Dean speaks out in public about the possibility of conspiracy. He gives funds to Mark Lane to assist the investigations into the findings of the Warren Commission. In Hollywood, there is widespread criticism that Dean is out of his depth, paranoid and the victim of delusions.
- Summer 1964, he reveals that he is dependent on heroin and undergoes a six-month treatment.
- 1966, the first rumors that Dean has had connections with organized crime; at the same time, he is seen often with Jacqueline Kennedy, who says of him, "He is a great but troubled American artist."
- He personally produces, directs and stars in *Two Oswalds,* a rather awkward mixture of fact and fiction that purports to show the plot behind the shooting of John Kennedy. But no American distributor will handle the film, and Robert Kennedy disowns it in the course of the 1968 primaries. The picture plays in Europe to mixed reviews, and there are

underground showings in America. Dean loses a great deal of money on the film. Lew Wasserman says, "Jimmy is learning the facts of life."

- 1968, with the assistance of the cinema vérité pioneer Richard Leacock, he makes *Disabled,* a harrowing documentary about Vietnam victims who have lost limbs—soldiers and peasants alike. Dean had always been in favor at the Veterans' Administration because of his commercials for them. But the film is a thorough indictment of the VA, America's policy in Southeast Asia and American neglect of the wounded. It becomes one of the focal points of the American agony of the late sixties.

- 1968, Dean is once more arrested for possession of drugs. It is revealed that his sight is failing rapidly, and that certain drugs had been prescribed as treatment. Other doctors say that that claim is fatuous.

- 1971, release of *Performance,* the film Dean had made three years earlier in England with Mick Jagger, lead singer of Last of East of Eden, the rock group so heavily influenced by Dean's early films. *Performance* is obscure and heavily censored, but the on-screen atmosphere between Dean and Jagger revives controversy about Dean's gay leanings.

- 1971, Dean is convicted on charges of tax evasion and sentenced to six months. He claims that he has been victimized by "the criminals who now run this country." But in prison it is discovered that he is still addicted to heroin. Stories fill the press that he is broke, a discard of organized crime and near death. "I've always been there," says Dean, on the day of his release from prison.

So low then, what a remarkable comeback he has made in the 1970s. And yet, just as until that prison sentence Dean was still a hero to the young, in recent years it must be admitted that nearly everyone views him a little askance, as if recovery was tainted by suspicion and the corruption of middle age that the younger Dean always challenged.

He said in 1971 that he would not act again, and he has not, apart from his wickedly sinister Noah Cross in *Chinatown,* the film he produced with such success. He only took that role because John Huston changed his mind at the last moment. But Dean has been the most creative independent producer of the 1970s. He it was who put together the money for *American Graffiti* and then set up George Lucas for the showbiz empire of *Star Wars.* Today, Dean and Lucas have their studio, as well as three of the biggest box-office bonanzas of all time. No one knows how wealthy Dean is or whether his comeback was assisted by or remains in debt to the Mafia. Lew Wasserman will only say that "Jimmy is still learning." But in the recent actors' strike, Dean was unequivocally on the side of the producers.

That is one side to his life. The other had as its turning point that night in July 1969 on Martha's Vineyard. For hours certainly, for days in many minds, and always for a few, it was thought that Ted Kennedy was driving the car that went into the water at Chappaquiddick and contained the unfortunate Mary Jo Kopechne.

Kennedy's statements were belated and evasive. Then two days after the incident, James Byron Dean called a press conference, said that he had been driving the car and had panicked after the accident. According to Dean, "Ted Kennedy's willingness to take the blame is one of the finest actions I have ever witnessed. But I couldn't let him stand for the rap. America needs Ted." In his turn, Kennedy told the press that, "faults and all, Dean is an American we can be proud of."

Dean was criticized at the inquest but exonerated. *Real Paper* reporters from Boston alleged that Dean had been in Wyoming at the time of the incident and had gone east secretly to save Kennedy from repercussions. Doubts remain: Dean had once called Edward Kennedy "the thickest of them all," so the newly revealed friendship was not entirely convincing. But who can say what lasting damage the affair could have done to the career of the next president of America if the blame had fallen on Teddy? And who knows what influence Dean has now in the halls of government? We face the eighties ready to find the answer to the second question, mindful of Dean's post-Chappaquiddick reflection, "I guess if you have a steel hand, you shouldn't drive."

(1981)

The Shortsighted Voyeur

I live in San Francisco with a view to the south. We are on the third floor, high on a slope, so there is nothing between us and the changing light. Our windows absorb it all, lungs as well as eyes. They are called picture windows, but they amount to a skin we share with the world. I am never sure whether the skin yields contacts or illusions, everything is so spectacular. Even when I sidle up to the dominant glass, feigning absentmindedness, I can never catch sight of anything ordinary. Does the glass promote any sight into a lesson or a drama? Still, I can never tear my eyes away; I am held by both the looking and wondering if it is a show painted on the large glass with all the guileless light shining through.

The sun does its daily melodrama, a blaze of midday airiness separating the sultry convulsions of mood at either end of the day. There are fogs in San Francisco, reliable at certain times, but there are more days when only at dawn clots precede the sunrise, like fruits in a smoky yogurt. It is very still. Stucco columns of boiler smoke seem pinned on the rose seepage in the east. The view is a collage, and the precise rim of Oakland's hills could be a wire embedded in the glass.

Twelve hours or so later, the west has become a Chez Panisse dessert, a sky that changes color every ten minutes as it goes from egg custard to cherry surprise to burnt caramel, until it makes an ultimate magenta like a neon wash. That magenta goes mauve and velvet while you watch, sure you will not see the change. Nature here is as keen to get in the movies as any of us. The light in California is very tour-de-forcey. It's a virtuoso.

Which brings me to the young woman across the way—a petite ghost, all of my own imagining. In San Francisco, you may have heard, the land goes steeply up and down. You could say that a series of hills and valleys are jammed together, but that makes it sound just an oddity of topography. Whereas, the changes of height seldom feel natural; they make an unlikely place for a city where the poker-faced picturesque dares the chance of earthquake to crack up first.

This young woman lives in the next house down the hill. Our small garden shares a fence with the rather larger one of her building. On level ground, the fence and the trees would interfere with vision. In England, net curtains would veil its risk. But here, as in many other parts of the city, I can look down and watch her, as if she was an experiment or a play. Not far, not a full hundred feet away, but far enough to watch in what I call innocence.

This other building is a muddle; it has nothing like our flawless wall of glass. There is a variety of windows, bays, alcoves, nooks and crannies; so it looks like a hiding place with several peepholes. The young woman does not, I think, have all the house—no one can afford that in this part of San Francisco. But she has parts of two floors. I see her come and go, in and out, up and down, like water following a course. She never becomes quite clear; I saw that elusiveness early on. But I never wanted her to be real, and the element of mystery is protective.

We have not come close. I never see her on the streets, at the café, the movie theater or the local market, where everyone knows everyone. We do not acknowledge one another, not apart from that first time. Perhaps we know the sight will only persist if neither of us notices it. So we cultivate our solitariness, though I am very happily married and she has fellows in. They all look alike, young successes, but it is too far for my short sight to be certain.

That first occasion had a peculiar charm. We had not lived long in our apartment. One evening, I wandered toward the window, lost in the difficulty of something I was writing. I cannot remember what it was, or whether I solved the problem. But I daresay I gave the impression of advancing: my mind was elsewhere, but my figure was edgy with the dissatisfaction. She must have seen just that image of action—as if I had noticed her and hurried forward like a guard dog. It was that time of day when the sun was down, and the air was milky gray. There was no light on in my room, yet I must have been plainly visible in the splash of sunset . . . like a peach glaze on vanilla. She had one lamp on in her room, and she was sitting in a chair beneath it, gazing out at the view—which I had decisively filled. Her windows look north, of course, and I have imagined her since then in the cool gloom of her room, enjoying the amber of the opposite shore.

I may have looked fine and golden: this is the hardest thing to imagine without embarrassment. But her right arm went up, as if raised by my appearance, and its small white hand waved. My eyes saw it, and knocked at the door of my closed mind. I was stricken by the simple gesture. I waved back like someone on an island who sees the last ship sailing away. Not quite a hundred feet, but I don't know if I have ever had a stranger sense of remoteness allied to intimacy. It was like seeing my dead mother in a dream and realizing she was smiling.

Had I been bolder with life, I might have opened the window, leaned out and called across the way. Then the enigmatic perfection in seeing and being seen would have been disturbed by untidy words and eager misunderstanding. Sound would have come to the silent movie, showing us what fools we are. We stayed strangers. I came back to the room a few times that evening as it grew dark, and I had the cunning now not to put a light on. I saw that her light burned still, but the chair beneath was empty. An hour later the light was gone; I wondered if she was in the chair looking up at a window as glossy, black and secretive as hers.

After two years, we are still here and there, the two of us. I take her possibility for granted, passing her and the window as if she was a potted plant, not always noticing it, but then stopping to enjoy the fragrance and my own well-being. I have gained no fuller sense of her; she might be anything still; we have kept all story lines open. There are books on the shelves behind her, and I have seen her reading them. Then sometimes I have noticed her face illumined by the blue glow of her tiny television. I have been tempted to warn her: she sits so close, it will strain her eyes.

I have accumulated a series of snapshots: one Sunday morning, my eye was tugged by the drawing of her curtain, and I saw her in a white nightdress in her bed, stretching and yawning as if an advertisement; she does exercises and yoga—with her eyes shut, I think, but I am just too far away to be sure; there was a day when some meal was spread out on the floor—it was inexplicable and extravagant, a birthday perhaps—and she was there in a robe, sitting, with one bare foot showing, and there in the top corner of the frame was a man's lower leg, the rest of him not showing. Then very early one summer day when I had been up an hour to work, and was moving quietly so as not to wake my wife, I came up to the window and saw all of her, naked, cross an open window space and disappear. It was such a brief glimpse, but I believe she was on tiptoe too, as anxious as I was not to disturb someone.

Perhaps she was in bed with her lover and had gone to the bathroom, a sliver of body across the poised rooms, half asleep, a stealthy tinkle, not flushed, its bubbles vanishing as she slipped back into the warm. I am not supposing she leads a wild life; she is demure in the light of my imagining. I am not even sure that she is what you might call pretty or personable. I am too short-sighted a voyeur to establish that, and too dependent a watcher to be a reliable judge. After all, she is the thing likely to be seen, and that has more potent appeal than real features. It seems that my wife does not notice her at all. Indeed, there are days when I have even wondered, as my wife waters the potted flower in our window, and she, over there, trims a geranium, whether she is not the screened projection of my wife's image. I touch my wife to make sure she is real and her face opens with pleased affection— I have decided not to tell her about the woman across the way.

Why should you believe in her, when she might not notice herself in this account? Do we remember everyone we wave to? Is she caught up in composing *her* essay? What is the view like from there? I can tell from where I am that she does not wear spectacles, but I would have to be impossibly close to rule out contact lenses. Perhaps she sees me very clearly and is only waiting for this essay to call the police. I have seen the telephone on her table, and seen her talking to it, laughing, unheard but eating the air, at the delight of some private plan.

I am wondering about the propriety of all this—it seems like a phantom story loaded with implications. And as a moviegoer and a San Franciscan, I have been nudged in the wondering by the reappearance of two Alfred Hitchcock films, *Rear Window* and *Vertigo*.

They have been out of sight for many years, and like anything in circulation but withheld—Howard Hughes or Atlantis, your mother's nakedness or the voice of a woman across the way— they have been eroticized by absence. I knew the films well in the 1950s and '60s, when they were available. I loved them both, and reckoned them the best and most significant films by a master I cannot quite like. It would not have troubled me if the pictures had never been re-released—seeing is always a kind of privilege, and we all of us treasure the things only a few of us have seen. Out of sight, those pictures flowered with desirability.

The reports said *Rear Window* was withheld because of legal problems, and *Vertigo* because Hitchcock disliked it for having failed with its first audience. But I doubted those explanations. Both pictures are so concerned with looking at the inaccessible or impossible. What loss would provoke the voyeur more than that of his spectacles? The true subject of both films is movie itself; in being withdrawn they had attained that acute paradise of a spectacle not quite in sight. "Look," they said, "ah—you just missed them. If only you had seen them. . . ." The films could hardly be more anticipated, more felt; the unlucky asked you to describe them in as much detail as you could summon up. Not in release, they were a definition of desire and of how the greatest satisfactions exist only in prospect.

Back on the screen, the two thrillers surpass most new films, even if exposure has curtailed their highest mystery. We all grow older, and there are those who could have died without ever having seen the films. I would not wish that. Erotic hopefulness will not keep you alive forever.

In *Rear Window*, a man's desire is confined in a plaster cast. He has only a back scratcher that he can slip down inside the plaster to ease its itch. He is a photographer, a man who returns from reality with magnificent moments that deny time or change. He is a kind of thief, yet he may be the victim of his own deceit. There is a photograph in his apartment, of a racing car, out of control but not moving, suspended in the blowup, coming toward (or going away from) the lens. A split second after the aperture gave up its virginity to the light's swift prick, the car hit the photographer. Thus his broken leg.

He sits in his New York apartment, waiting to heal, afflicted by aggravation. He would like to be out and about, snapping the world. But he is tied down by his own ponderously enclosed desire, all the more vulnerable to his girlfriend's plan to marry him. She is the epitome of magazine loveliness, Grace Kelly at her peak, a wave pouring herself on his dry shore, over and over again. It was made in 1954, when such things were suggested, not shown, but the film's irony extends to letting us know how ready she is to be his—preview of coming attractions, she captions her own image, dressed in a bridal nightgown. But cast in plaster, his desire is as forlorn as King Kong's. He will resort to its substitute, a lens turrets. But that is the tool of his trade, an everyday sexual deviation.

The photographer looks out on a courtyard which is really a gallery of screens. Like a man with too many TV channels to choose from, he goes from one to another, briefly interested, quickly bored, longing to be held. He sees several versions of marriage: a honeymoon couple who keep the blinds down; a pair of veterans who have a pet dog as their only offspring; a young dancer with many beaux; Miss Lonelyhearts, a spinster in a green dress with pills in a drawer; and a lonely male song-writer, trying to find the great lyric of desire but short of female company. There is one other couple, a flip-flop of the photographer and his beauty: across the way, a wife is laid up, an imaginary invalid, sex and companionship soured into spiteful hypochondria. Her sad hulk of a husband, fat with undelivered longing, is a jewelry salesman. Every day when he gets home, he must cook for her and endure the abuse we can only see, darts of animosity sticking in his bulk.

The photographer watches; he spies. He sits there in the dark, with his long lens and binoculars. He is chided for this. His girl and the masseuse who comes in once a day complain about "rear window ethics," no matter that their curiosity (like ours) stows away on his lines of sight. He is a photojournalist; all his life he has expected to see drama. And so he fancies that out there, across the way, he has seen the hints that surround a murder. Watching is a vocation: it involves such dedication, such strain-ing of the spirit, that it needs mighty fulfillment. The jewelry salesman has killed his wife, hasn't he? Don't wives provoke that? The courtyard is filled with Hitch's gloating misogyny. Where is she now, and why is he washing out his sample case? Do rubies really bleed?

The voyeur puts a case together on the fragments seen in the movie opposite. We are with him as he focuses his suspicions; and we are as thrilled as he is to spy the inhaling flush of the "murderer's" cigarette as he sits in the dark—scheming, exhausted or peaceful? The photographer's girl goes in by the rear window looking for a clue, the wife's wedding ring perhaps, for no one would go on holiday without that, and Hitchcock needs a ring to round up all his themes. She finds it, but the murderer discovers her in his apartment—another wife apparently, for the cute cover girl has put the ring on her own finger, which now she waggles, sure that the photographer's lascivious close-up lens will read it. But the murderer notices this cocky gesture, and he tracks it across the courtyard, looking at us and seeing the photographer, who is just too late to scurry back into his dark.

There's an ending to be negotiated still, but this is the electric instant, in which the voyeur is as fearful as the murderer, desperate not to be caught. And the true scheme of *Rear Window* is to make us linger with the consequences of inquisitive looking. Murder is no less wrong, say the rear window ethics, if the relentless starer acknowledges his own heartlessness and his responsibility. A subtler film might deal with a possibility aroused by this one: that of turning a blind eye, as if the spy was a priest, privileged but bound to silence. He might even emerge from the dilemma a more humane person than this photographer.

The real plot ends with that sentimental favorite, decisive action. The killer comes at the spy, the image turning into an actual threat. The film is amiable enough to let us settle for that. Unless we care to remember that in the context of its parallel— moviegoing—the people seen can never get at, or know, the watchers, unless one of them comes out of the crowd with flowers or a gun; and the watchers will never meet or know the objects of their gaze, but may dream of them, vote for them once every four years or watch them in the window frame of the television screen, taking cold comfort in the medium's lie, familiarity.

Does New York foster such voyeurism? Visibility is often denied there: people avoid the eye, and windows have blinds or the grimy snouts of air conditioners. I have always felt that *Rear Window* had intimations of San Francisco, the setting for *Vertigo,* a city where appearance is flagrantly incestuous with its own light.

The air here is pellucid and polished, not much less sunny than Los Angeles but so much less polluted. There are vantages from which you can see two or three silver streaks of water—the Pacific, the northern bay and the inner sea between the city and Oakland. You can see two astonishing bridges, you can see the light on Alcatraz, just as not long ago the prisoners and the free could gaze on one another; you may see men kissing on some streets without caution or rebuke; and, with the characteristic disparities of height between buildings, and the bold nakedness of the glass, you may see a nude descending a staircase or a writer cleaning his spectacles.

Vertigo ostensibly concerns a fear of falling, and San Francisco is a backdrop of dangerous steepness. But the screen is still a flat plane, and the film's true peril is not measured vertically; instead, it is the risk of entering that false perspective, of falling into the story. *Vertigo* is a fatal parable on judging by appearance, and on the erotics of seeing without touching. Yet as a film, it can only stroke and shine up the very process of looking that it warns us about.

Its most compelling part is the long, sustained speechlessness with which the private dick follows a woman supposed to be the wife of an old friend, caught up in morbid identification with a woman she sees but cannot meet, a woman who killed herself in Old San Francisco, a hundred years before. It is the breathless tenderness of that pursuit, the eyes always caressing the blonde in gray, that lets him, the audience and the film fall in love with the beheld Kim Novak.

What a fall: the woman is a fake, hired by that old friend as part of a plan to murder the wife. This woman who seems spied on is an actress, sure of being watched, luring the watcher into her beguiling performance. She is so good at it, we know she is a believer, too. Like all film stars, she gives her intimacy to strangers. But she does not look up in anger or alarm. She does not accuse the Peeping Tom. She abides by the eyes' rape; she has that nearly religious grace of a star who knows she has a duty to be photographed while seeming alone and unobserved. It is a trick now that politicians strive for. They all know that looking honest and photogenic depends on not noticing the camera.

The detective cannot prevent murder. At the vital moment, his vertigo keeps him out of the picture. He does not see one gray-suited blonde already unconscious in the arms of her husband, as the other, exactly alike, comes through the trapdoor and onto the stage set at the top of the monastery tower. Several flights down, the detective is swooning. He hears a scream and turns to see a blond-topped gray flash falling to its death. He collapses, and the guilty couple above—lovers we presume—sneak away. The detective has lost his love: he could not fall fully or far enough to get into her picture.

He recovers sufficiently to walk the streets. But he is only look-ing for a ghost, made mad by the cruel construct of the film. He sees another Kim Novak, brunette not blond, coarse instead of refined. It is the same woman, the real fake: he can see well enough to recognize the inner stamp of her features, but he is blind to the context. Like a storyteller or a director determined to rework an old script, he woos Novak back into her former image. This must be what the husband did once before to make her resemble his wife—a character we never think about, too real to compete in this intrigue. We gather she was an invalid.

There's another ending, not as forceful as *Vertigo*'s insistence on the nihilism of film. For surely it is saying the blind would be safer in this treacherous spectacle. Whenever we see and are moved by the sight, whenever we imagine a meaning for it, we make mistakes. Nor are these just comic. In *Rear Window,* a killer is punished; in *Vertigo* he goes free. But there has been no enlight-enment in that relaxation. *Vertigo* ends in despair and an image of crucifixion. It is as if a natural moviemaker, more skilled than any other, was horrified at his own cold power of scrutiny. It is the confession of a chronic voyeur that his mind betrays his eyes.

Rear Window and *Vertigo* are from another age, before Kennedy's debates with Nixon, the shooting by Jack Ruby, the television war in Vietnam. We had not yet seen "everything" then, and we still trusted our ability to decide what we had seen. But they are movies full of foreboding, skeptical of their own medium—the innate storiness of the visible, and the exalted state of the story-teller. For over fifty years, the movies had been confident in the assumption that photographs do not lie. In those blithe days, it

was thought that the only liars were those who chose to manip-
ulate pictures. Now we begin to suffer from the alternative reality
they have provided.

Later this year, the Democratic convention will come to San
Francisco, to its Moscone Center. I could go down there and
battle the crowds. I could hear the amplified boom of speeches,
I might see tiny figures in the distance, I would surely get the
atmosphere of an event now staged and organized for television.
But I will watch on that medium where even I can see the leaders' faces clearly, watch them wait, listen and grow older in those
slow days of TV coverage. There is something more distinctive in
how they let passing time wash over them than in their speeches;
it is a better test of their intelligence—old movie stars know they
had their best moments listening, not talking. I can scarcely think
of anything Ronald Reagan has ever said, but I know how he
manifests thought and timing before he speaks, and, along with
200 million Americans, I could give a passable imitation of him
saying anything. That's what his actorliness has given us, an intimacy with style. I do not mean to call acting a deceit. On the
contrary, actors are those who believe the lie.

Some time before the convention, television will have identi-
fied a winner. I doubt if even the candidates at Dartmouth in the
PBS three-hour show would have put serious money on anyone
but Walter Mondale, alas. Just as *The New Republic* put Gary Hart
on its cover, and a six-page article inside, *Harper's* reported a
poll of leaders of the Peace Movement that asked the question
"Who is most likely to be elected?" among contending Demo-
crats. Hart scored 0 percent. Mondale had engineered enough
endorsements and polled well in advance; he had only to avoid
making an idiot of himself at Dartmouth. That is a top priority in
political discourse now, and one we all subscribe to; for we have
made a silent agreement not to notice idiocy when it occurs.
That is the harvest brought in by Reagan's sincere playing of an
honest fool.

No one now employs the memory that he was an actor. That
charge lurked above him for a while, and it had no sharper

formulation than Gore Vidal's warning that a president should not
be someone told what to say, where to stand and how to pause.
You cannot appreciate the significance of an actor in the White
House unless you see how far the office had already been touched
by theater before 1980. It no longer required a politician. Some
time before Reagan's election, the presidency had found as its new
basis its extraordinary visual links with America. The president is
the man on television, and television is the medium we hardly
watch for seven hours a day. And so the president is the figurehead
that defines the habit of seeing after belief has ceased. He is the
image that reappraises us as dejected viewers, not citizens.

Once upon a time a voyeur was a pervert or felon. He gained
sexual satisfaction by looking, as opposed to doing. That sense of
the word has fallen away from common usage, I think. A voyeur
now is anyone who watches more than participates: thus many
people making love are still voyeurs. Sex is no longer as promi-
nent in the character, because we have realized how all seeing is
erotic, and maybe cleaner, less wearying and more endlessly
renewable than sexual intercourse. The impact of pornography is
that pictures may be better than people. The original sense of a
"Peeping Tom" is less easy to justify when millions "know" Garbo,
Monroe and Ronald Reagan by sight; when our awareness of
news and the world out of sight is constantly supplied by visual
images and when it is taken for granted that we all have fantasy
lives, films running behind our open eyes, which we want no one
else to know, and to which we resort when the real world is
brutal or indifferent.

The desirability of democracy and liberty has been offset by
our furtive discovery that desire dissolves chains, and fantasy is
quicker. We can be destroyed, of course, and there is an uncertain
orthodoxy still that we are worried about that enough to want
disarmament. But I doubt whether many people think a moment
about the end of the world, or are motivated by it, beyond wondering about the special effects. Life on earth is like any other
on-off mechanism. Easy come, easy go, just so long as the off
switch works as quickly as fantasy. The greatest absurdity in

nuclear armaments lies not in overkill or the convoluted defini-
tions of deterrence, not even in the number of concerned orators
who cannot pronounce "nuclear," but in the old humanist homily
that the end of the world is a disaster. That's the myth trashed by
Punk's dead eyes. The fantasist knows the world ends with his
sleep. The voyeur is as skeptical of, but as wistfully attentive to,
lovemaking as a killing. So long as there is a show, our identity is
ensured. Keep the set on, then we know we are alive. We would
rather watch than enter into any more strenuous involvement.

On the one hand, in 1984, a year we have always anticipated
as an ordeal, with stinging coldness in international affairs and a
budget of demented deficit shelved for a year, we have an election
that is best anticipated as a comedy show. Shouldn't we own up
to the glee we felt when Jesse Jackson entered the Democratic
contest? It was as if a famous young clown, Eddie Murphy, say,
had joined a circus old with Hope, Burns and Berle and their pre-
dictable routines.

The election does not matter, and if there is one grim realization in 1984 it will be that this country has a process as vain as
that in Russia or whichever third-world country next concocts a
fair-play picture to get its aid. Apart from that, 1984ism is just
one more of this century's camp playthings, all hype and residuals, the official T-shirt of paranoia, a mercy that will not come.

Reagan will win again. He knows it, and we know it. I am not
sure that even his death would rule out another four years. We
smirk at Russians icing a leader who may be dead. Yet we have
had a cleverer trick, a leader already out on his feet. And in the
United States, if a leader died, we would not make his absence
mysterious. We would rerun the old footage: we have the technology, and audience is often mistaken as an equivalent of
democracy. Indeed, we are close to a new kind of life. It is nearly
possible to put images of a person into a computer and then
have the computer generate lifelike moving images of that person
doing and saying things never actually done or said. For maybe
150 years photography will have been reluctant to lie. Then it can
come into its full nature.

I know that sounds like fantasy—and that is why you will all have understood it. We do think now as fantasists, for that mode is so much more stimulating than reality or humanism. The relationship (or the figment of it) that I have with the woman across the way is very like the political discourse of this country. From decades of watching film, we need fiction in all imagery employing the real. We only tolerate that made as a pretext for fantasy. This election is about stardom and illusion, not simply personality edging out policy or issues, but personality so inflated that there is no room for other considerations. It is a kind of tyranny that will outlive the last sense of freedom and our nostalgia for humanism.

It turns out that *she* subscribes to *this* journal! She read the whole thing. I had imagined that our straight lines had had their one meeting, and were only diverging now.

I was resting when her call came.

"David," she whispered in rapture; the voice could have been beside me—it was clear she thought she knew me. "I can call you David? I feel we're reunited, if you know what I mean."

"I—"

"Now don't get me wrong. I'm not huffy or anything like that. I just looked you up in the book, and I thought why not? Window to window—how about it?"

I can recognize grotesque irony as well as the next man. My wife and I have established in the past that our bed is just below the windowsill. But only a small levitation is enough to peep over its rim. Ghastly with the surety of exposure, I raised my head as far as the white dazzle of the sky. I swallowed and went another six inches higher.

"Hi," dreamed the voice in my ear. "You look like a pumpkin in the window."

I dropped down, but I had seen the petite figure, cross-legged on the floor by her window, her arm coming up before I hid.

"Oh, don't be shy. You're so cute. I know, I've seen you in the telescope."

"Telescope?"

"First purchase I made when I came here from Omaha. I'm shameless. You've got to free yourself, David. What you said is so right."

"I said that?"

"Didn't you say that? Anyway, I look a lot. I mean, a great deal. But, truly, I had never seen *Rear Window,* and I have to thank you for the recommendation. Excellent flick. Such smart people. I always think film reviewers must have a great life."

"Ah," I subsided, feeling worse. The phone was like a sodden towel in my hand. I imagined it bending with this conversation.

"Anyway, listen, it's so neat to be in touch after all this time, and all these views." She chuckled as if to acknowledge the luridness we had both known. "I was going to have a small drinks party next weekend and wondered—"

"I don't think I can."

"No?" It was plaintive.

"Well, we are ships in the night, if you know what I mean. We might shatter the charm. . . ."

"Uh-huh"—she was a shatterer, I knew.

"Better, I think."

"But I can call you?"

"Well . . ."

"I learned so much from your piece."

"Ah—"

"I mean, what you say about the election. Right on. I'm not going to vote, and I know a lot who won't. Except . . ."

"Yes?"

"Well, I hear that the Russians maybe might give in a little on the talks if they think Reagan's a shoo-in."

"Who—"

"And that could be good, don't you think, David? So if too many of us don't want to vote, and the Russians knew about that . . . see what I mean?"

"I don't think—"

"Anyway, on the candidates you were exactly right. I have an argument with one of my friends. He says that after Reagan, it's going to be a lot easier for better actors, like Warren Beatty or Robert Redford, and I think Paul Newman, too—because that man has suffered. But you know what I say? David?"

"No?"

"Michael Jackson. Don't you think? Because the young people love him. Anyhow, for me, it's Michael or David Brinkley. I adore that sad smile of his. I think that says it all. Every time I see him it's like eating Brie cheese, my favorite thing."

"You must forgive me," I struggled to say.

I heard a reverent gasp. "I bet you're writing. Do you write in bed? I know I would. So, look, David"—a gurgle—"and I know you know what I mean by that—I understand your attitude about the drinks. It's wise, really." Then her voice swooped down and I felt her smile stroke my face. "Just look out for me some night soon. Oh, and I love that striped silk robe you wear sometimes."

I could not sleep, but I had a nightmare about a nocturnal street scene in which Michael Jackson kept turning into Jesse as he led all of America back to the thrilling grave.

My recovery was not rapid. I moped around the apartment for several days until one evening after supper I went into the bedroom to find the cards so that my wife and I could play hearts. I looked, and there was a crude orange light in her window. She was as close to the glass as she could get, so close she might have been a moth set in it. As I watched, with her grave aplomb of a supreme actress, she did a sort of spiraling upward movement, her arms above her head, while her flimsy gown shimmied to the floor.

"I wonder if we shouldn't move soon," I said to my wife.

"Keep passing the picture window," she told me. She was used to the blank wall that actually faced our apartment—but most wives know that absent attention in a husband's eyes.

(1984)

Driving in a Back Projection

I would like to say that this piece was composed—written, or dropped into the spirals of a recorder on the front seat—while driving in Los Angeles. But I am not that relaxed a driver, or that good a writer. Let the thought register, however, and try to imagine a traveling inquiry in which the view changes according to what may be our most commonplace magic, driving in the city, handling the wheel and being rewarded with a stream of effortless, unexpected sights.

Of course, I might have managed it, if the car were still, the dangers abstract and the roaming, unstable city just imagery behind me in a back projection.

As far back as the eye can see, the air and place of American movies are California. I am thinking of elements in the picture that we take for granted: the adrenaline light, some sediment of haze and sight's limits that stands for distance, the prickly hump of hill behind John Wayne, the square of receding street seen through the back of a car in which Cagney's fierce but defeated eyes are fixed on "getaway"—fierce because he wants to go, but defeated because this car never moves, no matter how persistently the background assures his escape.

The story's hoodlums did break out, into death or glory. But the actors resided in Bel Air; and if they lasted long enough they noticed that the city's light was growing brown and bitter from the crowd and all the ways it used up freshness.

That perfect light is always there on the screen, even in day-for-night, where it makes nocturnal meetings hot and sweaty; it is one of the abundant natural facilities that made California the home of picture making. The hill has been patient in countless shoot-outs, never once winking at the camera to say, "Don't you *know* who's going to win?" And the street scene was kept in a can for years, available to be unwound behind every rocking but tethered car, a back projection as serviceable as the length of red carpet that travels with the British royal family to ensure that their steps are hallowed.

These are real commodities. Three hundred days of sunshine a year in southern California are no more fraudulent or less photogenic than half that number in New Jersey. The most heavily used back lot may have been trampled flat by the design staffs who erected Shanghai there last week, and Casablanca this, but it can be measured in square feet and property values. Today, pictures can go to Casablanca and Shanghai; they are ablaze with the real thing. But they miss the point, the imperial, storytelling confidence that staged faraway places in Los Angeles. Obviously that had to do with cheerful indifference to the real China or North Africa. But if we scold that too much we may miss seeing a concomitant insight—that L.A. could be anything, because L.A. was not quite a solid "here" or "there," not quite an item in geography.

The back-projection street that goes with Cagney is a stock item, like "excitement" music that could be poured over every "getaway" scene, or like the close-up of Jimmy, so head-on that it must make driving so much more difficult than the idea of being driven. Still, the street behind was, let us say, Wilshire between Vermont and Western on a Thursday morning in October 1934, and there, fifty yards behind Cagney, was Mrs. Koslovsky, going to the market. She turned back to her dawdling boy, Max, just as Jimmy snarled to the air and an audience yet to be, "I'm crashing out for good." Max and his mother were scraps of life in the snapshot, unaware that their midmorning "Come along, slow-poke" would go unheard but marginally apprehended in fifty Warner Bros. tributes to crime on the streets.

The compliant sunshine, the studio props department and the Koslovskys were all Californian; and just because they were all bundled together in the same eighty-eight-minute fabrication doesn't mean that the historian, or anyone interested, should dismiss the evidence they offer. As evidence, I think, it is the more appealing in that it is so casual, so devoid of intent. Movies full of entertaining lies stiff with intent and controlled telling are also spilling over with helpless, neglected phenomena, and the least doctored of those, the most available, are visible background, the presence of California. Examine studio records, and you might ascertain that on that second unit's morning, between ten and eleven on Wilshire, it was sunny. Look closer, with a magnifying glass, perhaps, freezing the frames that want to melt away, and you might see a police car bundling past Cagney (when surely it should be after him), giving dreamy Max a scare and disappearing toward downtown, where—further research discovers—a jeweler's at Third and Miramar had been broken into by toughs who had seen a Cagney picture the night before, for hints and courage.

(Suppose a bystander was killed in the incident at Third and Miramar: imagine your own rage and distress if you had seen that real thing. Now consider the wicked enthusiasm with which you are urging Cagney on in the screen. Los Angeles was a factory city that manufactured lifelike fancies in which our relationship to reality was drastically altered. It may be a more potent invention than any bomb.)

I beg your pardon for the aside, but in driving one cannot help but turn to an interesting face.

We do not have enough historians to check out where everyone in that back projection was going. But we do agree that, more or less, in the ordinary way of hope, every one of them thought he or she was the center of the universe. My Max

Koslovsky is an invention (unless I have forgotten some real Max—his name *did* jump to mind). Still, it seems to me a routine ethnic name, two words a child actor might learn and speak as Cagney's character, rounding a corner, ruffled the child's hair and said, "Hey, kid, what's your name?" But children do amble across momentous streets, and in Los Angeles no one in the last seventy years has ever been sure that a camera isn't watching. Isn't that the drugstore where Lana Turner was discovered? Or is that whole "access to fame" riff a conspiracy among small corner stores, inviting us in because we might be discovered? Is that what the video cameras in the top corners of banks and markets are all about? Mrs. Koslovsky may have been setting out to get a nice piece of fish for Maxie, but in Los Angeles she would never have given up loftier dreams for her boy. "Hey, Maxie, do you know what the mailman said? He said you reminded him of that Leo Gorcey"—one of the Bowery Boys, whose exploits were struck in silver salts in Burbank, Culver City or Gower Gulch.

There are films more deserving of a California historian's attention. When Erich von Stroheim went to San Francisco and Oakland to make *Greed* in the early 1920s, the cities were linked only by ferries. There are moments in *Greed* when you can see and feel the importance of the Ferry Tower Building, though now it is dwarfed and patronized by the Bay Bridge. And there are scenes in which McTeague, the dentist, and Trina, his love, sit on the beach with only pale, desolate water behind them. Their images are lonelier, larger and more poignant because the progressive spans of bridge do not yet contain them. You can feel how in 1923 the Bay Area was not an area but only a number of separate communities and the daunting space of water.

It seems that Robert Altman made his *The Long Goodbye* only yesterday, instead of in 1973; but that is the farewell fallacy. Think yourself forward to, say, 2019, when the true Los Angeles might meet the studio prognostication of *Blade Runner*, a dense plastic and neon burden of metropolis presiding over alley streets where Asiatics serve hot snacks, animals jostle the hustlers and rain makes an undergrowth of trash; and where the burned-out lights of the Bradbury Building give entrance to a deserted cathedral of somber wrought iron, allegedly built for commerce but always more mindful of being available for *film noir.*

In that world, Altman's *Long Goodbye* could seem like an elegy to the deserted village that once was paradise: do you remember when people lived in Malibu, the Sunday beach parties, and those plate-glass facades in which, after dark, you might record in your mind's movie, but not have to notice the reflected image of your husband, drunk, staggering bravely into the waves to kill himself? Remember suicide, and drugs, and those gorgeous cars and the way they seemed to leave an unbroken smear of acid color on the freeways? Do you remember the freeways and the supermarkets, and the morning fog you knew would burn off by eleven? God, the light then, the ease, the jokes. Why, the central character in *The Long Goodbye* teases people all the time, and that's really all he does, imitating actors in movies, and stoically enduring his own failure less than thirty years later to keep up the glamour of Bogart's Philip Marlowe. So he kids himself, and us, for watching. You won't know about kidding in 2019, maybe, but there was a lot of it in L.A. in the 1970s.

I am imagining that teasing will have gone out of our lives, or that it will have become such an orthodoxy, so complete a scheme of lying, that there will be no charm or edge left to it. After all, teasing is a moment in our relationship with reality when we know both the real thing and its awful or delicious shadows, and when, in play, we flit from one to the other to show our grace and our spirit of traveling. It is the irony that can see Cagney going hell for leather from a fictitious crime while real police cars charge in the opposite, "wrong" direction toward an authentic outrage. And it is wondering whether the jewel heist was inspired by a Cagney picture. Even in a fireball explosion, "Made it, Ma, top of the world" is hardly a warning or the urging of civil order. It is the payoff in a joke, for only movie stars truly know the exhilaration of screen gangsters.

How far does the irony cut? Does it make everyone his own actor, and every place just a backdrop? Well, California remains a stirring reality, even if its ecology struggles to keep up with the mythology. It is wild still, in many places; its beauty is robust, not yet tamed by being photographed. It is the desert, the Sierras, the sparkling gray stretch of Los Angeles like glitter in rubber, the model of pride and danger in the hills of San Francisco, the redwood forests, the coast between Big Sur and Carmel, a valley named Death, Yosemite, the vegetable patch around Salinas, the flower festival at Santa Barbara, the coziness of small fishing ports up the coast from San Francisco, the mansions on Sunset Boulevard, the rancid border with Mexico, the sinister aqueduct bringing water to Los Angeles, the wind in Bodie.

I have seen most of those real things and had some sense of how early filmmakers must have hugged themselves. "It's all here, desert as well as milk and honey, box canyons for Westerns, beaches and cliffs for smuggling pictures, wide streets for car chases." And so on. But I had known them all before I arrived in the West. I had seen the desert in *Greed* and *Zabriskie Point,* perpetual moral reminder and harbinger of nothingness to the busy city ants. In *High Sierra,* I had watched Bogart strive to escape into the peaks; in *10,* there was an exquisite view of Los Angeles spread out beneath Mulholland Drive, and the fear that Dudley Moore could fall all the way down. From *Vertigo* I had a premonition of everyone's first alarm at steepness in San Francisco, and in the same film I had seen Kim Novak in the still and gloom of the redwoods, remembering, or pretending to remember, her past as she looked at the rings on a cut tree. For me, Salinas is James Dean watching his beans grow in *East of Eden,* and Santa Barbara is *Cutter's Way,* where death grins through the flowers. I learned how to beware of relaxation at Bodega Bay in *The Birds;* I expect Norma Desmond in every other mansion set back on Sunset; I believe in the border because I have been on Orson Welles's camera in *Touch of Evil,* tracking across it; and I know the additive of corruption in L.A.'s water—I've seen *Chinatown,* and I know there's no sense in protesting.

Wherever I might have come from, there's no place I could have seen more of in advance than California. It is the most extensive emporium this world offers, a shop of moods and scenes.

We are all Koslovskys who have come running to a catalog of real splendor, the biggest back lot in history, top of the world. California was made for movies. Which is a way of saying that, hypothetically, it offers as rich an imagined experience of life as anywhere in the world. Gold and movies started here. They transformed the place into legend. They made the state the most radiant advertisement for the pursuit of happiness: getaways going in every direction; good earth, air and water, space; a stage, a state of mind and becoming, as potent and present in the domestic interiors of *Leave It to Beaver* as in the luxuriant sweep of the Carmel coast where Clint Eastwood played "Misty" for the me in all of us.

Misty indeed, a place forever in and out of focus, our perception always couched in the language of photography. It is the frontier where we step from reality into story. But we are the golden age in a golden state, still aware and fond of the trick, still teasing. The movies are the throwaway art, the souvenir postcards, of that teasing. Camp, but our culture, the fitting, eloquent junk of a place named after appearance, or as Ed Ruscha has it in a twenty-eight-by-forty-inch painting, blackberry juice on moiré, refined and absurd, "A BLVD. CALLED SUNSET."

(1984)

Now it is four years later, and the editor who asked me to write the preceding has wondered if I would look at it again, and perhaps say more, for a collection of pieces about California.* He has asked, also, that I reexamine the essay in the context of others he has chosen for this stretch of the book's traffic. And so I have looked at the Hecht, the Vidal, the Didion, the Buñuel and so on—none of which makes driving less intimidating.

*A shortened version of the preceding text appeared in *West of the West: Imagining California*, edited by Leonard Michaels, David Reid and Raquel Scherr (San Francisco, Calif.: North Point Press, 1989).

But sometimes on the freeway, you do find yourself inextrica-
bly placed between a glossy block-long semi and a blonde in a
convertible. You cannot escape the impacted trio. The road has its
speed, a sort of twenty-four frames per second that cannot be
varied. You are being driven by the road: the thought brings an
unexpected calm, and begins to explain the stunned peace in
the blonde's eyes. The culture of the back projection is here
already, no matter that to stray leftward more than a foot and a
half would be to squeal to death against the sheer, silver wall of
semi.

There is a distress, a bitterness, an uneasiness in so many of these
other pieces about being in Los Angeles. It takes the form of
satire sometimes, self-loathing, wry absurdity or a giving up of
the ghost. There is a shared assumption that Hollywood's L.A. is
an affliction, a place where idiots or worse make rubbish for staggering, demeaning salaries; a place of smog, deceit, vanity,
cultural cancellation, death of the soul, et cetera.

These are all among the reasons I try to assemble whenever
people wonder why I like L.A. Not that I want to offer myself as
just a masochist or a necrophile. Those traits are there, and I
cannot deny the wounded nostalgia that L.A. furnishes for me,
like a fragrance close to decay. That is plain enough in the 1984
piece, which veers too close to being a sleepwalker's rhapsody. But
I also enjoy the weather, the beaches and the driving, as well as
the restaurants, the museums, the Lakers and the people in L.A.
nowadays, all of which have come along since Ben Hecht had
such a grand time being disillusioned and cynical.

The fascination of Los Angeles for me has been that while the
city is evidently so "advanced," so "modern," so "new," so state-of-
the-urban-art, it is also a museum of itself and of the process it
has given us in which reality, substance and the thing itself are
revealed as gestures caught in calm intrigue with image, illusion
and lie. I like it, you see, that Los Angeles has so many charac-
teristics of an anthology of sets, a backdrop, a figment of our
imagination. Whenever I call L.A. Lies Allowed, I do not mean to

stress the lies in moralistic reproach. It is the condition of being allowed that most interests and stimulates me.

For it is exactly in the absence of classical structure, center, stability, tradition and integrity that Los Angeles appeals. There is no need to preach any moral advantage in being fixed or in being unstable. I do not mean to propose Los Angeles for its virtuous novelty any more than I can honestly regret its departure from conventional ground plan, neighborhoods, neighborliness and traditional ways of interaction. Rather, it is that Los Angeles is what it is, changing before your eyes—not out of forced, degraded habit but from nature—slippery, imagistic and imagined. It is so very free a city in that the cults of opinion and fantasy have shaped it.

What Christopher Isherwood calls "impermanence," it seems to me, is a volatility that waits for metamorphosis. The buildings are as solid as warmth requires, but so are sets solid. It is just that every column of stone in a Tudor set today knows that it was Arabic last week, and Tuscan the week before. And it is happy about this in a stone-faced way, not filled with a sense of exploitation or corruption.

This is not meant to excuse the villainy, the crassness or the dishonesty of movie people, all those sins that might make Gore Vidal sigh and give Joan Didion a headache. But I believe there is a way in which all those small, local sins (not really greater than mendacity anywhere) pale in the light that begins to dispense with truth altogether.

It is in L.A. that we may see how far the light itself has acquired the character of a trick, or a service that can be employed and colored for fiction. Whereas painting celebrates light, in a more or less sacred spirit, photography steers it, plays with it and shatters its integrity. Similarly, in L.A. the city manifests itself as the game of so many million art directors—no longer the grim, visionary consistency of planners, architects and those qualified in urban appearance, but available for every whim and fantasy. Of course it looks awful and trashy, if you compare it with Bath, Florence or New York. But the look of L.A. should be compared with other things—a studio back lot full of sets is one example, but something fresher and more intriguing may be multichannel TV.

In other words, it can be anything: if you don't like where you are, travel, change the channel. And if real travel is wearisome, impractical or slow, then let traveling come in the flick of a switch, the work of a cut in the back projection. Let the scene come to you; be the happy client of the Max Koslovsky who grew up to be a maker of TV commercials and atmosphere videos.

As you may have surmised, I don't deplore TV commercials. Indeed, I watch them a lot. Yes, of course, they can be deluding, meretricious, vulgar, dangerous, et cetera. Any fool can see that. But they also seem to me to be beautiful, mysterious and among the best expressions of us now. Where else is there such complete, ecstatic confusion of the real and the fantastic done without guilt, and with a humor all the greater in that we know we need not laugh?

That doesn't mean Max Koslovsky is my idea of the new genius. Rather, it may be that our "great" and "characteristic" works no longer require genius. That was always an implication of the movies that alarmed the Hechts and Vidals, that millions might be moved or tickled without the neodivine thought of a Mozart or a Tolstoy being responsible. But art and its adherents have always anticipated the massive dilemma of what would happen in an age of universal education and opportunity, when art no longer leaned on forms of advantage and superiority. That's one reason why popular movies (and an unpopular movie is not a movie, it's cinema) frightened the elite in the twenties, thirties and forties. That's one reason why some people hate to concede the pleasure there is in L.A. and its tumult of fictional forms, styles and views. It is the first place which has given up the truth and not been swallowed by the earth or a furious god. I know, the earthquake *is* there, an ongoing coming attraction. Meanwhile, Lies *Allowed*.

(1988)

The Towne

It may be the best screenplay Hollywood has seen in the last few years; it may even be the last great classic American script; and it may be that you're never going to see the movie.

The Two Jakes has been in the mind of Robert Towne for a dozen years—since he wrote *Chinatown*. Towne won an Oscar for original screenplay for that picture; he was working with his oldest friend, Jack Nicholson, and for a producer he regarded as a prince among men, Robert Evans. *Chinatown* was a triumph; Hollywood knew it was the kind of thing it did best, a genre thriller, a *film noir*, but lifted higher with mood, lyrical foreboding and a bittersweet nostalgia over the city that the movies and Robert Towne love above all others, Los Angeles.

Chinatown dealt with the place of water in the history of L.A., but like all the best American movies, its doors swung open without urging, revealing metaphor. The film was also about idealism being screwed, about being raped and keeping a straight face. "Forget it, Jake—it's Chinatown," a friend tells Jake Gittes, the private-eye hero, urging him away from the disaster in which a beloved has been killed and an innocent is left in the care of the corrupt tycoon who raped her mother—his own daughter. *Chinatown* was about water in L.A., about America in the time of Watergate, and it was a parable of Hollywood and getting used by the system.

In 1974, amid the triumph, Towne felt he'd been just a touch screwed by another friend, Roman Polanski, the film's director, who had changed a few things in the script, including the ending, and had eventually had to have a distraught Towne barred from the set. So Robert Evans consoled Towne while they shot the altered ending and probably told him, "Forget it, Robert—it's pictures." And Towne took the Oscar, the brief glory and the reputation as the best screenwriter in town. Evans said he'd rather have the next five commitments from Robert Towne than the next five from Robert Redford. Which is the sort of line you know is going to turn sour. But there are linesmiths in L.A. who talk as if there'll be no tomorrow.

No writer in Hollywood has much enjoyed the position; it is a little too much on its knees with its bare ass in the cool air, waiting. And if Robert Towne has been the business's most desired writer, that hasn't made life easy. A writer is like a divorce lawyer or a private eye: when you want him, you have to have him; but later you despise him. If you're the writer, you feel privileged, invited up to the big house, flattered, confided in, given money and the private number, hungered after even, because you can solve the problem. So you solve it, you write it away, and people laugh and say, Why, there wasn't really a problem, was there? Just see yourself out, and count your money outside, not here. You end up humiliated and demoralized, and that's why they call you again. If you think about it, you can see why Hollywood private eyes are as sour and cynical as Jake Gittes in *Chinatown*. They're sick of being taken.

Robert Towne was also, often, sick. People in pictures made jokes about the famous script doctor whose own uncertain health made it easier for him to work at home and in spurts, and only rarely on complete ventures. He is now fifty, tall, a little stooped, his hair gray and straggling. In the few years I have known him, I have seldom found him other than anxious, exhausted and generally jittery that he might be coming down with something or being got at. I'm not making fun of this vulnerability; he is also fiendishly athletic, obsessive and inclined to talk for hours and work all night. It's just that Towne is one of those Hollywood people in whom health, or well-being, is more than merely physical. It also seems to be a manifestation of sensitivity, a way of not trusting the world and a means of attracting attention. The novelist and screenwriter John Fante once described Towne with a blend of affection and guardedness that I share, and cannot top. He said Robert was "a very sweet guy, gentle as a kitten and crafty as a wolf."

The sickness in Robert was a matter of allergies—to the air, the dust and the smog. He has a nose like a divining rod. In *Chinatown,* he dared to slit his male star's nose. "That must really smart," someone murmurs. "Only when I breathe," answers Gittes—and it is Towne and Nicholson talking as one.

Yet Towne lived in Los Angeles, where the nose is regularly in jeopardy. He had been born there and spent most of his life there, loving the sprawled city but seeing it change for the worse. *Chinatown* and *The Two Jakes*—the first set in 1937, the second in 1948—are but the first parts of an intended trilogy meant to describe the modern history of Los Angeles, how it spoiled the land, killed the scent of eucalyptus and peppertrees, and left guys like Jake Gittes suspicious and fearful for their own and their city's health. This has been Robert's song. He can bring tears to your eyes with it, so that you think the smog has crept into the story. He could woo young women with the story, so rousing them that they wanted to console his loss and catch the scent of true nature in his nose, lurking there like Howard Hughes in a penthouse suite.

Well now, wait a minute. I did that?

I'm inventing these italic lines for him; Robert is so innate a story man that one feels him intervening in any story about him. When you talk to him, you can sense him feeling out your structure, giving you quote lines. He writes scripts for more than just a living. Life surrounds him in fogbanks of scenario.

This is all very well, he says, *this sort of diagnosis. But we need some back story.* We do? I say. *The magazine will,* he says. *No one trusts readers to wait. And if I'm a character in this story*—which you are, I interrupt, meekly—*OK, then we're going to need to say why they should care. You can't move people until you've got them caring.* We have to tell your whole life story? *I hope not*, he says. *I think we can do it in a couple of minutes' screen time. Imagine some views of L.A. in the thirties and forties, a voice-over, a breath of swing music and the sound of wind in the palms.* . . .

How he was raised in San Pedro, the harbor city south of L.A., born in 1934, of Russian descent and Romanian atmosphere, with tales of one grandmother fleeing a pogrom and another who was a Gypsy fortune-teller. The name was Schwartz, but Robert's father opted for Towne when he bought the Towne Smart Shop in San Pedro. It was not a dull family. One grandfather contrived to be honorary queen of the May in Santa Ana. "And I had a great-grandfather," says Robert, "I wasn't allowed to meet. He was over ninety, tall, white haired, a writer, and a womanizer of sorts, I hear. My mother has since said she regrets not introducing us."

How Robert knew a rural L.A., the landscapes Jake Gittes explored in the 1937 of *Chinatown*—once loved, never forgotten. How he loved the smell of water coming out of the ground, and how he cottoned to the notion that Los Angeles was really a strange, urban island formed by ocean and desert: "I like islands," he says—"Catalina, Maui and L.A.—because island people are in a certain place that's knowable. It's their secret. And if you love where you live, it's a chance to love life. But in L.A. there's always been the danger of people mining it to death, changing it out of all recognition because they're on the make."

And how he works as a fisherman and goes to Pomona College and does English, spends six months in military intelligence, and joins an L.A. acting class and meets and rooms with someone called Jack Nicholson. This is the late fifties, with everyone trying to be like James Dean. The class was run by the actor Jeff Corey, and it treated acting in the full context of making a movie. Actors and writers worked on scenes together. A rich, new strain of naturalism had its roots in that class, with no finer manifestation than the way Towne could write for Nicholson. "I saw Jack work and improvise two or three times a week for maybe five straight years," Towne has said. "I've seen him work so much that I feel I know what he does well." Jake Gittes, the character, was not just the finest fruit of association; he was the shared ideal of a friendship—shrewd, funny, sad and error prone.

And then how Towne starts writing, because he doesn't quite cut it as an actor or has too little energy for that struggle. So he writes for TV and does scripts for Roger Corman, small pictures, one good horror flick, *The Tomb of Ligeia*—granted it's Poe and Vincent Price and all that lurid period nonsense. He isn't really getting anywhere until he does a Western, *A Time for Killing*, and takes his name off *that* because he loathes the way it's rewritten. But Warren Beatty likes the script (scripts are passed around, like pictures of women), and so when *Bonnie and Clyde* comes along, it's Robert who does the rewrites on the original Robert Benton–David Newman script. Do you see how paranoia and dependency can become like illness in this scheme of sometimes secret, unacknowledged rewriting? How do you know you are not being interfered with? How should you not be awed and resentful of the great and powerful men who hire you and act like your friends?

And how they still argue over how much Robert did on *Bonnie and Clyde*, and how in the end Warren gave him a rare, secretive credit, "Special Consultant," a big credit with only one other name on the screen, in the head credits, mysterious and potent. It was like a nudge, and it had everyone muttering about what Robert had done.

There's more. How Francis Coppola called Robert in overnight to write the final conversation between Pacino and Brando in *The Godfather*. Brando would be off the film in twenty-four hours; Coppola was under great pressure. So Towne looked at a few hours of footage, got the flavor, and wrote a scene that all viewers remember. It is maybe the quietest and warmest stress on family in the picture; it is also a cameo of male friendship. There's no credit for this—a film has many one-night stands that do not make the slow crawl. But when Francis got the writing Oscar, he thanked Robert and polished the mystique.

Or how Robert, coughing and breathless if you like, doctored this and that over the years (*The New Centurions, Cisco Pike, The Yakuza* and *Drive, He Said*—enough for everyone to wonder about the others) and really made it in the midseventies with *The Last Detail, Chinatown* and *Shampoo,* three cool beauties in a row, two of them originals, with no other screenwriting credit, except that Warren shared *Shampoo* because he rewrote it. And Hollywood says this is one of the greatest screenwriters it's ever had.

I think that'll play, says Robert.

Our script now focuses on a man of large and proven talent tempted into being more adventurous and open and being cut down for it. It's full of Towne's dark suspicions about fate and enterprise, which is a way of wondering whether he isn't as fulfilled by the disaster as he would have been by success. To fail in Hollywood is nearly essential if you need to think well of yourself without losing your mind. Visitors to Hollywood appreciated Robert because he was an insider with an outsider's perspective. He knew box-office figures, but he could put them in the context of Raymond Chandler and Carey McWilliams. East Coast editors found him wonderful to talk to: he understood the business, but he was intelligent and well read. And Hollywood got more suspicious, for why should Towne want to waste his time impressing outsiders? L.A. is an inside town.

If you wanted to get into the Towne psychology, with an actor playing Robert, you'd have to ask whether maybe this stress on intelligence didn't court antagonism, whether he doesn't believe so much in "Chinatown" that he insists on inhaling its noxious air. It may be a proof of authorship to say that no one but I will stop or stain my work. And then, if you look at Nicholson's sad eyes and hear Robert's foreboding lines, you are close to understanding one of the great symbioses in American movies. You may even see how inevitable it was that things end in betrayal—for betrayal is sometimes a plot device, a paranoid hope, that simply arranges events, given enough time.

So Robert set out to be a director as well as a writer. This was where artistic authority and Hollywood sexiness lay. He felt stronger: he was getting offers, and he had found a drug that dealt with many of his allergies. It is called Nalcron. But others said it was just success that was encouraging him. He had a great idea for a movie: Tarzan from the point of view of the apes.

Robert wrote a script called *Greystoke;* he believes it's the best thing he's ever done. That may mean it was the closest he has ever come to an obvious challenge—writing a novel. No one, not even Robert, was ever sure *Greystoke* could be filmed.

It was the story of an infant aristocrat lost in the African jungle and raised by apes. I know what you're saying—you've *seen* that film. But you haven't, not Robert's.

He worked on *Greystoke* for years, reading all he could find on the English in Africa and researching the behavior of monkeys. There was an hour at the start of his *Greystoke* with no human talk, just the interaction of apes. Warner Bros. wanted to do the picture, with Robert directing. Who else could? The script was legendary before it had been shot. But it was always going to be expensive, and Robert was never sure if apes could play the apes or if he was bound to use actors in suits.

Time passed. Robert was delaying, or he was taking the proper time to make up his mind—you could take your pick. He passed up other chances—for example, John Fante's novel *The Brotherhood of the Grape,* for Zoetrope and Phil Kaufman. That might have been a fine picture, and it would have been very good for Fante, who was in terrible health. But Robert let it slip, even though he still did a few small doctoring jobs when friends asked—*Marathon Man, Orca, The Missouri Breaks, Heaven Can Wait.*

Then he said he'd make *Personal Best,* a small film about women athletes, while he was making up his mind about *Greystoke.* But *Personal Best* got out of hand. The budget escalated. There were delays, a strike and then a shutdown, prompted by the feeling of the executive producer, David Geffen, that Towne was "overbudget, behind schedule and not in a condition that inspired confidence."

The picture seemed frozen—at least three-quarters shot, some $13 million in the hole, but going nowhere. Towne was frantic in his search for help. With the aid of Allen Klein (once personal manager of the Beatles), he got a tortured agreement whereby *Personal Best* could be finished. The price turned out to be the script to *Greystoke*. Towne said it was the most painful decision he had ever had to make: "It meant for me I had to accept the death of one child to preserve another."

Personal Best came out, and it didn't do well. Geffen was sick of it by the time it was finished. Towne started a lawsuit. The reviews were mixed, and the picture flopped. No one could say it was as sharp as Robert's best scripts—it was sweeter, but less alive. It did moon just a bit over the lady athletes, as if a naturalist were celebrating gorgeous animal bodies. The eye loved it, but the talk was tame; and Robert has never been as good on women as he is with dry, potent men who sniff sex and challenge in the air.

Greystoke did rather better, but its new director, Hugh Hudson, had changed a lot—more than Robert will know, for he refuses to see the picture. A rueful irony had him nominated for an Oscar for it, in the guise of P. H. Vazak, the pseudonym he took in the credits and the pedigree name of his adored Hungarian sheepdog. Vazak didn't win the Oscar, and the dog died in 1982.

At least two other big projects came to nothing in the next few years: *Tequila Sunrise*, a script Towne had written about old school friends who meet again as cop and drug runner. Robert wanted Warren Beatty in it, with maybe Pat Riley, the spiffy coach of the Los Angeles Lakers—that's the kind of off-the-wall notion that can seem like genius or craziness in Robert. But *Tequila Sunrise* hasn't been made yet. Nor has *Mermaid,* a Ray Stark venture he wrote for Beatty and Arthur Penn.

The Two Jakes was therefore a major effort of recovery. The first *Chinatown* was in love with loss—it is haunted by the melancholy of an exploited Los Angeles, the rape of Evelyn Cross

Mulwray and the fate of her child, Katherine. Towne gave the name Katharine to his only child, born in 1978 to his first wife, Julie, the daughter of movie actor John Payne. The picture is a tragedy to the extent that, at the end, you know Jake Gittes is never going to be the same again.

But Robert wanted him to live on. After all, his own *Chinatown* had been interfered with by Polanski. He wanted a chance to have his say, and he wanted to pursue the history of Los Angeles. So he wrote *The Two Jakes*, in which an oddly unaltered Gittes has further adventures, meets another Jake and finds Katherine Mulwray again. Like the ending Robert had wanted for the first film, this one would turn out hopeful, half happy. Indeed, it has one of the most poignant and unlikely of all endings—snow falling in Los Angeles, as it really did in January 1949.

And the picture got set up. Roman Polanski, of course, was out of reach. So Towne, Nicholson and Evans formed a company to make *The Two Jakes*, and Paramount agreed to distribute it. But the picture was not conventionally financed by the studio: the three principals would own the finished picture, Towne owned the script and none of the three would take any money up-front except for the reported $125,000 received by Towne for a sequel fee. Paramount would pay for the production. The three men, all on deferred payments, were making it as something they loved: it was a reunion and the continuation of a great story—that was the line.

The finances are still cloudy, for Paramount and the *Two Jakes* company never quite finalized the monetary arrangements. That's why unpaid actors and vendors took their complaints to Towne and company, and why Towne would consider selling his script (for as much as $2 million) just to pay them. *The Two Jakes* was budgeted at around $12 million, with at least $10 million of the eventual gross earmarked for Jack and the two Roberts. One day the courts may decide just what had been agreed, left hanging or fixed. For now, it is an unholy mess. When the project broke apart, Hollywood was shocked at the unprofessionalism. But it could yet emerge that greed and anxiety about the money were also reasons for halting it. It is not always just a movie that is being made but a deal.

Robert Evans was to play the other Jake, Jake Berman, a real-estate developer who is building on what may be oil-rich land. Evans had last acted on-screen in the late 1950s. No one then ever accused him of being a great actor. In the years since, he had been a producer, a studio head (at Paramount), the best-looking fast-talker in Hollywood, a ladies' man and a cocaine user, though, he said, "It's bad for sex. It also ruins your tennis game, and I like to play well." His last few years had been bad, and on his most recent production, *The Cotton Club*, he had had to go to law to retain a hold on the picture when his problems so inflated the budget that others took it over in desperation.

Why did Robert Towne cast Evans as Jake Berman, a very difficult role in that Berman lies most of the time, seems inept but is really shrewd and strikes up a bizarre but touching friendship with Gittes? Not easy to answer now, except to say that Towne is addicted to the hope of friendship and to glamorous, stylish men who smile with power. It is a movie about friendship, and Robert may have thought to rescue Evans without seeing how that generosity could damage himself. He once wrote, "Bob Evans remains, in memory and in life, a standard for every kind of human generosity, and one I have yet to see matched in this town." There are those in that town bewildered by that line and what it says of Towne's judgment. But if you want to understand Towne, you need to see the romantic view the once fragile recluse kept for his old heroes.

The Two Jakes lined up better than anyone could believe— even if many crossed their fingers that someone would see sense about Evans. Caleb Deschanel was the cameraman, Richard Sylbert the designer. Frank Mancuso, Jr., was the executive producer, and Frank Senior is chairman of Paramount. The cast also included Kelly McGillis and Cathy Moriarty in the two female leads, and Perry Lopez, Harvey Keitel, Dennis Hopper, Joe Pesci and Scott Wilson in major supporting roles. The oil tycoon, the rough equivalent of John Huston's Noah Cross in *Chinatown*, was to be played by Budd Boetticher, a veteran director of Westerns and a whip-smart, gray-haired wolf.

Shooting was set to start in late April 1985. Sets were built at the Laird International Studios in Culver City. Locations had been found all over the city and out at Ventura. I was at Laird one day when Robert was still casting and rewriting. He was with his new wife, Luisa, previously the wife of Piero Selvaggio, owner of the fashionable restaurant Valentino. It was late in the day when a black Cadillac convertible arrived, vintage 1948—Jake Berman's car, a thing of beauty, all set to be repainted celadon. People on the picture were already bidding for that car when the shooting was over. Robert seemed about as relaxed as a nostril suspicious of poison gas.

For a month Towne had been coaching Evans at night, and getting nowhere. A day came for the routine of shooting make-up camera tests—establishing how the central characters would look in the picture. In one smooth morning, tests were shot for McGillis, Moriarty and Nicholson, who had gone into hard training for the film and shed twenty-five *Prizzi* pounds.

The afternoon had been cleared for Evans, but the afternoon was insanity. He needed a haircut so that he might look like 1948. Some actors would have relished going to the barber well in advance. But Evans came to the set in his own up-to-date hair, and as scissors appeared, every kind of fear and panic gathering inside him surfaced. He refused the picture's hairdresser; he wanted his own. He resisted cutting; he wanted the hairs sensitively "tweezed" from his head. The situation stretched on for hours.

At last, Towne announced that he would not proceed with Evans in the Berman role. An understanding had existed between Towne and Evans. If the director thought the actor wasn't cutting it, one old friend was to tell the other. Towne did speak, and Evans blew up. There was a standoff, and as one observer felt, "When Nicholson was looked to as a peacemaker, he said, 'Let's start shooting and see about Evans later. Give him a chance. If he doesn't cut it then, replace him. His scenes don't come up for four weeks anyway.' "

Nicholson's attitude surely had to do with the fact that it was late in the day for a change. Towne, presumably, had had chances earlier, and he had cast Evans. Towne kept hoping. But maybe he put off the evil moment. In his autobiography, Roman Polanski voices a feeling about the defect of Towne's gentleness that is held by others in the business: "Bob Towne is a craftsman of exceptional power and talent. . . . He's also a very slow writer, delighting in any form of procrastination, turning up late, filling his pipe, checking his answering service, ministering to his dog."

For Towne's part, he has always nursed the solitariness of writing. When asked about the difference between writing and directing, he has stressed the distractions on a set and the feeling of being with "55,000 people." He said it was like "going from that incredible silence under water to the surface and that gaggle of sound where it's very fucking noisy."

Some of the actors and crew went out to Ventura on the night of April 30 for shooting the next day. And then, as a witness states, "In the morning, nothing happened. They said the weather was wrong. But you could tell the plug had been pulled, and there was a rumor that Paramount had said not to roll the cameras. There were telephone talks all day with lawyers and the studio, and you heard stories that maybe Towne was going to sell the script and maybe John Huston was going to direct. And maybe Roy Scheider was going to play Berman. One of the problems was that with all the principals getting nothing up front, how could they find the money for anyone new they had to bring in?"

No one moved, and there was no final deal. The sets were struck, the production was closed down, Nicholson went on to another film, cast and crew dispersed and Towne was heard muttering about disloyalty, lawsuits, his resolve to set the picture up somewhere else, and how "this time they aren't going to fuck the goose that lays the golden egg."

As the summer progressed, the picture was regarded as dead, the subject sooner or later of exhaustive litigation. Still Towne struggled to keep it alive. He wanted Dino De Laurentiis to take it over; Harrison Ford was interested in playing Gittes. But Paramount was asking a prohibitive amount for turnaround. Meanwhile, Robert was working far into the night to rewrite *8 Million Ways to Die,* a Hal Ashby picture just starting shooting that would be credited to him and Oliver Stone. I saw him then in his Santa Monica house with that movie tacked up on a board, two hundred or so index cards, each one a scene. He was doing this, in his other crisis, because of friendship, because he needed the money and because it is habit. Robert Towne has been a scriptwriter now for twenty-five years, which means that he's written, worked on or thought of at least two hundred movie ideas, every one of which at some hour of the night he's thought might be his best yet. And so far, he has his name on ten of them.

I was around then because, long before, it had been agreed that I could be on the set of *The Two Jakes.* We talked, but not much about the picture. There was a lot of anguish and confusion to express, but real legal jeopardy if anything went on the record.

And so when we talked, he grew quieter even than is his norm. At midnight, in the silent house, I had to lean forward to hear him. I have noticed this with Robert before. He draws you in by letting his voice become elusive or invalid-like. I've taped interviews and then had difficulty hearing them. And on the phone with Robert, you press the receiver closer and closer to your ear until you need it inside your head. It's as if he might be in bed, not wanting to wake a companion. It always feels like the middle of the night, and it often is.

"So what *can* you say?" I asked him.

"Well," he said, so faintly he might have been dying. "You could say that with my daughter and my wife I'm the luckiest man alive." And he started singing the words "Who Could Ask for Anything More?" from "I Got Rhythm." He had just come from the concert version of Stephen Sondheim's *Follies* in New York, and he was tired and exhilarated enough to ruminate on how bad Hollywood can get:

"I was doing this rewrite once. It had a confrontation scene between a cop and a bad guy. And I had done the scene in such a way that, when he was attacked, the cop had to pick up a rocking chair to defend himself. That's all there was. And I liked it because it was absurd but true. And so they took the scene and they shot it. And apparently they said, 'This is silly. This couldn't happen.' So they changed the rocking chair to a baseball bat. I ask you. It's always a baseball bat. And in life, people do silly things. They pick up what's there. But that's movies now—the baseball bat!"

He has great fears of conglomerates making it impossible to produce interesting movies; of a Hollywood beset by rumor and paranoia; of lawyers taking over the business: "We all live in an endless slough of not just despond but renegotiation. There are people now trying to renegotiate the facts. They're so dependent on appearances, they think they can change the facts if they alter the appearance. And they have the nerve to say that appearance is illusion. Whereas illusion is the most precious thing—it's what an artist can make—and it's a very real thing. And it's what movies can be, could be."

Then he feels the risk of becoming gloomy, and he admits that for a long time his life was a mess, too much work, not enough sense of relationship: "But there's never a day in my life now I'm not happy, because of Luisa. I can be sad and angry, but I'm still happy, and I think she and my daughter can see that. There's something Mandy Patinkin told me, and I think it's vital—that the best thing you can do is show your children you are happy."

No doubt Harrison Ford could play a detective in the Los Angeles of 1948, with Kelly McGillis as his love. But could that private eye be Jake Gittes still, and could McGillis really be the Katherine Mulwray we last saw in Noah Cross's terrible, enfolding arms? *The Two Jakes* is a tremendous script, yet it always had a problem. For, on the one hand, it requires a knowledge of *Chinatown*, a film now nearly as old as the heart and soul of a movie audience that shows no special sympathy for middle-aged failure and regret.

And on the other hand, if you know *Chinatown,* you wonder why this Jake Gittes of 1948 comes on as slick and sardonic as he was in 1937, before his first disaster. You see, Robert, I think the first film was so good, and Jake so stricken, that he has to be darker now—maybe too twisted to be the lead in a big picture.

By September, an agreement seemed possible for a new *Two Jakes* as a Dino De Laurentiis production, Towne directing, with Harrison Ford and Roy Scheider. But it could not now be known as a sequel (for legal reasons), so Towne would have to do a lot of rewriting, turning his script into something more self-sufficient, free from the memory of Nicholson. Shooting was expected to start in the summer of 1986.

Then, on the evening of September 18, Robert called me. He sounded energized; I thought the news would be good. "The negotiations to save *The Two Jakes* have broken down irretrievably," he said. "Dino has been wonderful. But Paramount and others want too much. It would have been at least a $25 million movie."

I said I was sorry, but I did think he sounded relieved. He talked of getting on with other things. *The Two Jakes* may therefore be dead—but can Hollywood let such a property go?

So, cross your fingers, we may see it. The question then remains, Does the climate exist now for a picture as good as *Chinatown?* And does Robert Towne have the stamina in crowded, crazy, vexing circumstances that it would take to get this picture done? He may be too much an islander. I do think there is something in his very attractive, eloquent but crafty nature that could slip from being the uncredited master on other people's films to the thwarted author of unmade masterpieces. It is all part of the inherent tragedy of being a writer in Hollywood, of acting cheerful while being sick. And in Robert's case it would be more of a loss because he has occasionally broken into the kind of descriptive prose that shows what *Chinatown* and the Jake Gittes story could be—a book.

In 1983 the script of *Chinatown* was published, with an introduction by Robert. He talks about a night on Catalina Island when he was writing *Chinatown* and he felt the breeze stir the air, the foliage and the hair on his sheepdog Hira's back:

> I can't honestly say the air helped straighten out many plot points. But I can say there was never a moment where some errant breeze didn't bring me something that made me care, made me feel it was worth trying to straighten out the story, all the horrible melodramatic machinations that remove you farther from detectives and human life than any cross-word puzzle.
>
> It brought me back to saying, these things, dead and dying that still linger in the air, had more joy in them than I could have known, and this tepid, deft, adroit, dry breezy collaborator of mine, rustling thru weeds like a child wearing a sheet, this air was worth grieving over more than I ever supposed. There's no other word—'Chinatown' is a sort of eulogy for me.
>
> It is a eulogy I'm afraid for things lost that would concern others about as much as a missing button or a dead mouse. Easterners, for example, have often tended to be a little snide about the tepid weather and negligible change in seasons—things I have loved perhaps the most about L.A. I've loved the first hint of October nipping thru the sunlight after school, New Year's Day, chilly and clear as crystal as tho someone put the sun in the freezer overnight, the February rains that came with Valentines and would flood intersections with muddy waters rushing around stalled cars, vacant lots in March that overnight sprouted thousands of sharp green spears you could pull and send with a clod of dark earth hurtling at another kid, little ponds of black polliwogs squiggling like animated commas—and then spring and summer with the smell of pepper trees mentholated more and more by eucalyptus, the green lots turning to straw leaving foxtails in your socks and smelling like hay in the morning, the Santa Anas progressively drying the city into sand and summer smells—and best of all then you could

stand on the Palisades overlooking Portuguese Bend and
have all the dry desert breeze at your back abruptly
splashed with salt air from the sea crashing on the rocks and
swirling tidepools a hundred feet below. Well—time, smog,
and development have virtually obliterated these pastel sen-
sations for pastel sensibilities like mine—but like most
things I truly value, the weather, along with love and health,
are more keenly appreciated by their absence than by any
dramatic and pushy presence.

That piece is as sad as the thought that somewhere in the
Paramount vaults there are a few hundred feet of Jack Nicholson
ready for 1948, lean, soulful and a private eye again, and somewhere there's a Cadillac convertible maybe half black, half
celadon. It makes me wish Robert would try the Chinatown
novel, even if he has to drag himself away from Los Angeles first,
from the money and the intrigue, the sexy telephone calls and the
slippery frame lines of loyalty.*

(1985)

Tequila Sunrise was made in 1988, with Mel Gibson and Kurt Russell. Robert
Towne's *The Two Jakes* was never made. But in 1990 Paramount did open a film
under that name. Its Jakes were Jack Nicholson and Harvey Keitel, and
Nicholson was its director. Towne retained screenwriter credit, but he and
Nicholson were by then hardly on speaking terms. Since then, Towne has
cowritten *Days of Thunder* (with Tom Cruise) and *Love Affair*, for Warren
Beatty—an experience that ended their friendship—and been one of three writers on the Tom Cruise movie *Mission: Impossible*. He is now making *Pre*, about
the distance runner Steve Prefontaine, with Cruise as his executive producer.

Not Available for Interview

The Selznicks had told me stories about Joan. She was the "difficult" one in the family, they said, the willful outsider. She had married as soon as she could, to get hold of her inheritance and be rid of the family name. I was left to ponder whether it was the worst idea if you were a Selznick to take the money and run. The family said Joan was a recluse, beyond reach or reason. No one ever considered that she might be lonely or in trouble, longing to be called back. The family had not heard from her in thirty years. That long ago, in 1959, Florence, the mother of David O. and Myron Selznick, had died. Florence, the grandmother of Joan. But Joan had made her final gesture by missing the funeral. Or had she? Irene Selznick, David O.'s ex-wife and Joan's sometime aunt, did tell the story of how a large, veiled woman seen hovering in the background at the funeral *might* have been Joan. Of course, Irene had not been there herself. The story had the mixture of hope and unreliability that the Selznicks cherished.

So I waited. I was writing David O.'s biography, and I hoped to talk to this Joan, the only child of Myron Selznick, one day. But there was time, surely, for this interview. Joan was in her late fifties only, and my meetings had so far concentrated on people twenty years older.

Her relatives had made Joan seem forbidding. The closest I
came to facts was that she lived in a gated, guarded mansion,
somewhere around Laguna, south of Los Angeles. She did not see
people or answer mail. But in the last resort there would be one
sure way to her, I was told by Jeffrey Selznick, Joan's cousin, one
of David O.'s two sons. She had a lawyer who received the royalty
checks from MGM, or whoever owned that company this year.
For there was one exceptional, Selznickian thing about Joan—she
was the only family member left who still received income from
the bounty of *Gone With the Wind,* that gold mine opened to the
public fifty years ago by David O. Selznick.

Then came word, in March 1989, that someone who might
have been Joan Selznick had died.

David and Myron Selznick were the sons of Lewis J., a giant of the
early picture business, a rogue and a publicity genius who jostled
Adolph Zukor, Carl Laemmle, Louis B. Mayer, Samuel Goldwyn
and all comers from about 1915 to 1923. Then he went completely bust and the family was reduced from fabled wealth to
Micawberish optimism. The sons of Lewis J. vowed to make the
name of Selznick great again. David would become the producer.
He married Irene, the daughter of Louis B. Mayer; they had two
sons, Jeffrey and Daniel; he made *Gone With the Wind* and
Rebecca; and he was divorced by Irene, whereupon he married his
discovery and the star of most of his subsequent pictures, Jennifer
Jones.

Myron became an agent, a revenger who would bleed the
moguls who had humbled his father. He did just that, and then
seemed bored or used up once he had succeeded. He was a man
who did not care enough about life—and his daughter, Joan, was
left to inherit his wealth and his cynicism. For he had pioneered
the power and the threat of agents. He was a tough little man,
with the look and manner of a gangster. He held the studios up;
he boosted salaries out of recognition; he dictated brutal terms.
And he was so quick and natural a business executive, for years
he could get away with being a drunk who downed tumblers of

Scotch before lunch. He was screwing the studios, and killing himself. Nothing deterred him from self-destruction. Maybe he was depressive; maybe he envied David's creative glory and the intelligence of David's wife Irene. Myron married a meek, pretty movie actress, Marjorie Daw, and straightaway lost interest in her. Their daughter was born in 1930. Myron said he would have preferred a son. But perhaps a pretty daughter would have sufficed.

Myron had none of David's romanticism. He took all the women he wanted, but never fell in love with them. He was the man who brought Vivien Leigh to the set the night they burned Atlanta, when David still hadn't got the magical Scarlett O'Hara he needed. And Myron had a small holding in David's company, Selznick International, and thus a piece of *Gone With the Wind*. By 1942, David had sold out, swept off his own feet by success, money, opportunity and indecision. Between drinks, Myron told the kid brother he was a chump: *Wind* had lots more left yet. So, when Myron died, in 1944, aged forty-six but looking twenty years older, his estate had 6.77 percent of the producers' share of *Gone With the Wind*. Agents like to get as much 10.00 percent, but who needs that much when the net rentals are $800 million in the first fifty years?

Late in March 1989, Jeffrey Selznick had a call from a friend at an L.A. radio station. A woman had died in Laguna Beach, a woman named Frances Whitcomb. But locals were saying she might have been a niece of David Selznick. Jeffrey and I agreed to meet in Laguna Beach. There was a chance that we could get into the dead woman's house, and there were reports of papers inside. Jeffrey was already being drawn into what promised to be a complicated estate; he might be among the next of kin. I was in search of materials that no one in Hollywood had ever been able to trace—the office files of the once great Myron Selznick Agency.

"Well, it's no mansion," said Jeffrey, when I met him that first night in Laguna Beach. We drove past, though the alley was narrow for the ponderous rental car Jeffrey had acquired at LAX. Indeed, it hadn't at first seemed possible that there could be buildings between the Pacific Coast Highway and the sea itself.

But there was a row of stucco boxes—Gaviota Way, it is called—all perched on top of the cliff. Joan's was one of these, tied up in sealer ribbon from the office of the public administrator of Santa Ana County. We couldn't get in that night, but we had to behold the very reduced reality compared with the legend. If this was the house of anyone from Hollywood, then it would be that of some retired makeup assistant, an old lady struggling to survive on scrapbooks and savings.

There were days to wait before we could get in the house. The legal web was extending all the time. An old friend of Joan's had come forward with a will in which the friend was the beneficiary. But the will was twelve years old and the friend had not seen Joan in a decade. There were other aspects of the will that raised doubts and promised contest. Furthermore, it was emerging that Joan had died wealthy, far richer than the plain house led one to expect.

As we waited, we explored Laguna Beach, not much liking the place, with raw-colored housing developments wedged into every available slot of ground. It didn't seem a comfortable place to live, yet Joan cannot have realized that, for the local estimate we heard was that she hadn't been out of the house in twenty years. We were picking up information from a few people who had done errands for her, delivering vodka and sandwiches, getting cat food in by the carton and sometimes going to the bank to cash checks. Her eccentricity was coming into focus, but these locals told us to expect something worse in the house. They worried about how a cousin might respond.

Had anyone really known Joan as a person? we wondered; instead of just doing her bidding? One name came up, and we sought out this woman, the mother of the man who had done a lot of the deliveries and who had found Joan dead on the evening of March 28. So we called on this woman, hoping for insight. And we began by asking her when it was that Joan had started to put on a lot of weight.

"Oh, I never *saw* her," said this woman. "We only ever talked on the phone." For twenty years, this "friendship" had gone on, never more than small talk. What was talked about? Well, it became clear that Joan the estranged Selznick *had* sometimes talked about the family. Some had known nothing about the association. But others had heard old Hollywood stories about Uncle Bill Powell, the Bennett sisters, the beach house in Santa Monica, and sentimental imaginings of those Selznick cousins, Jeffrey and Daniel, who supposed she'd given up the name and atmosphere of "Selznick."

I'm not identifying these locals because most of them would be alarmed to be named in print; because the estate is still in dispute and because Joan was worth so much it defies belief in how she lived. She was careless, fatalistic; she did not much trust her lawyers, one of whom had sought to have her taken into care— and been fired for his trouble; there was little sign of doctors having been called as decay set in; she may have paid exorbitantly for company, inconsequential talk and for take-out meals she hardly touched.

She lived like a bum, yet she was richer than David Selznick ever managed. There was something stranger than movie craziness here, something against nature. Yet outside the house it was still possible to regard Joan as a wayward recluse, some kind of Norma Desmond, tragic perhaps but fit for a story.

There are disasters that shame story, and human depths that do not photograph. Not that we lacked recording machinery when we got into the house: there was a private investigator hired to be present with a video camera to establish the exact state of the house, in case of future argument. There was a handful of people there in the end: Jeffrey Selznick and I; the woman who has a will and her legal representative; a man from the county to undo the seals; the couple from the next-door house who had done some of Joan's work; the investigator; the woman from the Bank of California who was likely to be appointed administrator to the estate. And last, but not least, by the kind of coincidence that only a Norma Desmond could swallow, Mrs. Mary Rechner Hawk, a resident of Laguna Hills, who forty-five years ago had been Myron Selznick's secretary, maybe the last person to have kept his filing system.

We were so many people, with such interests and suspicions, it was a wonder we ever allowed ourselves inside. Perhaps curiosity overcame all legal caution. No one of the group is ever likely to forget the hour and a half that followed.

There were cats around the house, lean, ragged creatures that came for food the neighbors put out—or because they knew what a lure for rats the house must be. Joan had entertained cats; no one knew how many were hers and how many took advantage of her. But this house we entered stank of cats. The video would not show that—unless you understood the occasional shudder in the cameraman.

The door had to be pushed back against weight and stagnation. The three rooms on the ground floor were spaces joined by the flood of trash, clutter and debris that rose to somewhere between the knee and the thigh. One room was a kitchen, without sign of being used as such. In another there was the bed on which Joan had been found dead; it was rotted through in places from her own waste. The third room was what realtors would have had to call the living room. There was a tiny bathroom too, an explosion of tissue paper, powders, cosmetics and the forlorn array of lotions that indicated the abandoned wish to be beautiful.

What composed the undergrowth on that floor? I was only there an hour or so: I cannot describe all the layers of archaeology, the sediment of twenty years. But there were unopened fifths of vodka, the supply for a large store; there were the packets of mail-order foodstuffs, Pepperidge Farm by the gross—less rotted, it seemed, than fossilized; there were stacks of Polaroid photographs—many of a gaunt-looking man, asleep apparently, who proved to be Joan's second husband; there were jars of decomposing purees brought in by another local, the only food Joan could manage as her teeth fell out; there were storybooks and novels—the name Frances Whitcomb had come from one of them; there were handfuls of canceled checks, telephone bills, the summonses Joan had been served for local complaints and which she had simply paid, rather than face the challenge of a court; there were exercise book diaries, handwritten over the years, and books of her creative writing; there were stuffed brown trash bags—it was reckoned by locals that Joan had a fearful way of hiding valuable jewelry in some of them, so they would all need to be emptied out and sifted through. There were those of us in the house whose purpose it was to look for wills or for evidence that might discredit wills.

In a corner of the bedroom there was a collection of the robes and caftans Joan had worn, anything, it was said, to conceal her size. They were in garish, girlish colors, helpless on hangers. If these clothes were a mark of her "taste," this was borne out elsewhere in the objects and ornaments she had, the sorts of things you might win at a fairground and toss aside before you left. There were soft childhood toys, stuffed or burst open. There were magazines and more books, too, macabre popular studies on health foods and rejuvenation. There was even glory and nostalgia, for there, like a raft floating on the sea of disorder, was a copy of Ronald Haver's coffee-table volume, *David O. Selznick's Hollywood.* It was tipped a little so that its lipstick red jacket caught the bitter yellow light inside the house and made the eye wince. Joan had had heavy white blinds, always lowered, closing out the nearby Pacific, the sunlight and the prospect of geographical location.

The staircase was shelves for more vodka bottles, more brown bags of things not to be thrown out. Joan had been a squirrel, burying herself. Upstairs, there were three rooms again, one unspeakable, where the cats had reigned. Another was bare. And in the third were the drab green filing cabinets that had come from Myron Selznick's office. There were his client files: the deals, delays and bickerings with Merle Oberon, Fredric March, Loretta Young, Vivien Leigh, Olivier and so many others. There was material on the early life of Lewis J. Selznick that made my mouth water. And there was another thing from Myron's allegedly businesslike office: the heavy white crib that Joan had when she was born. Nothing here was disturbed; Joan had been too obese to climb the stairs.

Our inspection was over after ninety minutes. No one could stand the place or believe that the smell of the cats was not human. There was also a worry that, as more things were found, it was easier maybe for "evidence" to be destroyed, or even furnished. The lawyers conferred, and it was agreed that we would all leave. Bank personnel would come in on the following days and begin to remove the profusion to the bank so that search and discovery had a decent chance. Thus, gradually perhaps, an outline life of Joan could be arrived at, along with the inventory of what she owned.

This much is known already: she owned her house and the next-door one at Laguna Beach; they are poor houses, but the site stares into the Pacific sunset; one could erase the flimsy structures, burn the ground free from cat and put up a weekend cottage fit for Merle Oberon, say. Myron Selznick had a ski lodge at Lake Arrowhead, famous in show business for its prolonged parties, romantic escapes and its twenty-four-hour catering—Joan owned it still, and paid caretakers to look after it. The Myron Selznick Agency had stood once on Wilshire Boulevard at Roxbury: in its day, the building was as celebrated and as modern as the I. M. Pei–designed CAA, a few hundred yards down the street. The Selznick building was torn down, but Joan had kept the land and leased it to Neiman-Marcus. There are three properties in Hawaii, one in Michigan; there may be diamonds in the detritus of twists of hair and the wraiths of what were once Pepperidge cookies. And there is the percentage of *Gone With the Wind*.

It was because of that consideration that Joan had had the files brought to her house. For forty years, they had sat at a Bekins warehouse in Los Angeles. But a few years ago, Joan had entered into a dispute with MGM. She believed the distributor might not be reporting her full earnings on the picture. (There was that much old Hollywood wisdom in her still.) So she sent a man and a truck and the files came home. I doubt she looked at them much, but there was a settlement with the studio—on just the alleged arrears—that was a six-figure sum. Over the years, Joan probably made $7 million on the film.

Whatever her dreams for rejuvenation, she seems to have allowed no photographs of herself. The few people who went in the house recalled her taking their pictures, but she was as shy as she was huge. This reticence stuck in my mind a few weeks later when I made one of my visits to Austin, Texas, to the Humanities Research Center, which houses the 3 million pieces of paper in the David O. Selznick Collection, where I have not yet discovered a hint of shyness.

There are photographs in Austin that show the child and the young woman Joan. You can see why other Selznicks called her no beauty—and like Hollywood people, they did expect that in a woman. In one picture, the solemn child is caught in the curiously untender act of lighting her father's cigarette. This is a picture taken in his last year, with Myron in the pajamas and robe he favored. The father's head is lowered over his light; the girl's life does not seem noticed or hopeful.

Then there are pictures that Joan paid for, a series in which she acts out the pose, the costume and the ardent, bitter waiting she had seen in glamour stills. But even in her early twenties—in her prime—the face stayed her own, sturdy, plain and resistant, not available for fantasizing. Were these pictures taken to show around, to impress Uncle David or to torture herself? Or because she was already at a loss with how to use her money?

When Myron died, his estate was left in trust to Joan and her grandmother, and Uncle David had the key role of trustee. Why not? He was a producer, a big businessman, and he was already mortified to see MGM making off with *his Wind* like bandits. He also took it upon himself to advise Joan through her mother, Marjorie. He wrote twelve-page, single-spaced, 5,000-word letters of comment and counsel, insisting on how little he meant to intrude. Joan resented the endless, articulate, self-justifying nagging, and she began to get a notion that David was quietly milking Myron's estate. I think that was wrong, but it was only being true to the family to start mistrusting relatives.

In 1950, she married Louis Grill, an older man with children, a housepainter, largely to come of age. The movement away from the family began. Somewhere along the line, impetuous independence and the fear of interference turned into solitude. Booze and Myron's melancholy asserted themselves.

Those who saw Joan at all in the last years say she was cunning, sweet, fey, evasive and paranoid; she was beyond them. That must be why no one sought help: she was evidently in decline; but, as she made clear, she was rich—she had the means, so let her decide. Those visitors stress that she had charm, that she was generous with gifts; she kept authority and the certain knowledge that if her funds were draining away, still her assets were steadily replenished by interest and inflation. They all add that they never truly knew her, or knew what to do about her. She was out of control, out of reach.

It makes you realize what a tidy, purposeful, actorly recluse Norma Desmond is in *Sunset Boulevard*. Her house was poised like a trap, waiting for melodrama to begin—it's as if Norma can only escape by committing murder. Joan Grill, Joan Selznick, Frances Whitcomb lived in a limbo, in a surfeit of disorder where only the sweet dream of vodka-and-suspicion told her she knew where the bracelets, the letters, the wills might be. You'd suppose she must have been crazy, but a "crazy" now is a character, informed by roles like Norma Desmond. Joan had slipped away from narrative or story long ago. She was not camera ready or fictionally coherent. There remains a mystery, as powerful and movie-proof as the odor of cat shit.

(1991)

Perkins Cobb

ONE

I gave up the thought of writing about Perk Cobb long ago. He had caught on to the idea that I might be imagining writing a book about him. "One of those movie lives?" he wondered. This was in the early eighties, when he was roaming around, dropping his money as tidily as possible, and always seeming to be caught between some Tuesday Weld, Graziella Ortiz and Lady Antonia Fraser. *Vanity Fair* was calling him "Percolating Cobb," and young journalists were out to "find" him. He was still colorful and vaguely active, and he could see as well as anyone that he was "good material."

So he shut himself down, all in a matter of two weeks. He quite simply gave up on doing things. It was as if he was determined to fold his "life" up like a blanket in which he happened to be sleeping. Or a shroud. So I took the hint and I dropped the book thing. But now that he is dead, there are a few things that need to be said.

There was a time when I would not have needed to supply the back story—of how Perkins Cobb, of Escalante, Utah, had fallen upon the film program at UCLA in 1970 like a serene scourge and a lethal visionary—the best anyone could dream of, a kid who could "do" Buñuel, Bergman, Von Sternberg or

Arthur Hiller at the drop of a hat, and who came with a hat. There would have been no need to reiterate how, while still at UCLA, he had in a single weekend done a brilliant, uncredited polish for Peckinpah's *Bring Me the Head of Alfredo Garcia.* ("It was a polish without a script," he claimed, "just a shine hanging in the air.") Or of how, in 1977, he made his first and only film, *My Sweet Dread,* that hilarious, yet unnerving, sun-drenched *noir* that starred Warren Oates, Jean Seberg, Claudia Jennings and Armand Croixant. (Within just a few years, all four of these actors had passed on, leaving *My Sweet Dread* oddly impervious to researching interviews. Thus its legend grew more lurid, fed by extant tales of fights, fucks, spur-of-the-moment improvs and relentless off-camera melodrama on its Mexican locations.)

Though only a small hit in the United States, *My Sweet Dread* was huge in Europe and monstrous on video. There is a graffiti subculture that still talks in its lines. Critics were ecstatic. "Here is a moviemaker," said Pauline Kael, "who leaves us hardly caring what he does—what the pretext is for his camera—so long as he does it for us, to us, now." Vincent Canby said, "This is a debut such as deserves to be ranked with *Citizen Kane* or *The Night of the Hunter.* It is breathtaking to behold so complete a talent come from nowhere." Richard Corliss wrote that the picture was "both nifty and swell, in a rhythm that resembles the roller coaster of your dreams."

The kingdom of Hollywood was Perk's for the signature. He was twenty-six, tall and rangy, with that consumptive cowboy look Calvin Klein had not yet hit on. He could put words together in any way that was required—he once did a panel with Roland Barthes and Jacques Derrida ("Le Signe et L'Abysse"), talking his best southern Utah French—and he knew how to say nothing with force in studio meetings. Then he could wind sentences around women as unbroken and sweet as strands of hot butterscotch sauce.

Jeff Berg was his agent, and ICM was ready to package for Perk. There are pictures I know he declined, or dodged or acted stupid over—*Heaven Can Wait, The Postman Always Rings Twice, The Right Stuff, American Gigolo, Heaven's Gate, The Natural, Atlantic City, Ragtime.* But as Berg told me once (for I was one of those the agent used to rally Perk), "It isn't what he turned down. For three or four years Perkins Cobb could have done anything he cared to name or to invent out of nothing. He could have proposed novels by Robert Musil that didn't exist—*The Novel Without Writing*—and we'd have been in development. The career we could have had! The course of American movies would have been different. I would have broken the skulls of the business for Perk Cobb."

But to it all, Perk offered the wayward, amiable and gentle back of his hand. Warren Beatty was after Perk for years over *Reds.* Not that Warren risked frightening him off with anything as barefaced as an offer. But Perk outpaused him on the phone and steadily missed a series of meetings until finally Warren had nothing left to do but send Perk a cable: "Will you direct John Reed? Or play John Reed? Are you there?" And Perk just sent back another cable, "I would prefer not to." Warren called me up and said, what did I think it meant? Was it a ploy? Was there a subtext? I had to tell him that it was only Perk alluding to the Herman Melville story "Bartleby the Scrivener," about a clerk who stops doing anything. Until he dies. Warren found the story, and he liked it, and he asked Perk to do *that*—write it, direct and play the lead. And Perk just sent another cable: "Ditto." The last I heard, Warren was still fascinated, and Robert Towne had done a script that had Bartleby as a realtor in Laguna Hills. A month before he died—we were in Ely, Nevada, passing through—Perk said very casually, "Beatty's getting awfully pushy after *Tracy.* I may have to check out to get rid of him."

Of course, the great rage for Perk Cobb did not last. You can be a silent sensation for only so long. Perk had known the bright, busy world would go away. "I have made my picture," he said, "and I do not intend to make it again."

"But," I tried to argue with him. "A career—?"

"There are no careers anymore," he told me. "Just one-shots . . ." He took a swallow of Henry. "And flashes in the pan."

It was not Perkins Cobb's way to need to explain what he was doing, or what he was not doing. No, he concentrated on doing it, on doing as little as possible. He had all the single-minded recessiveness of a light in a fade-out. He avoided statements or interviews, any of those formal opportunities for presenting his antagonism to Hollywood as a system for others to emulate. I saw a good deal of him, here and there, but we spent most of our time going from one Best Western motel to another, driving, finding dusty, empty bars for beer and a little pool on parched, humpy tables the color of old money, small-talk flirting with waitresses and watching ball games on the motel TV. Perk had become an Atlanta Braves fan, he was that close to giving up the ghost. (The Braves were purgatory then.) I can see now that he was only patiently waiting to intersect with his end. (I might as well say—not that any biography mentions it—that Perk went over the script of Antonioni's *The Passenger.* I know because I was there—in Roswell, New Mexico—in the Best Western where he did it. I can hear the quiet, tidy blitz of his pen as he took out lines of dialogue. That film would not be as mysterious or laconic as it is, had it not been for Perk.)

Still, over years, I got some idea of why Perk would make only that one startling, lovely and dangerous film, and then do nothing else. It doesn't amount to anything so grand as an explanation. I simply believe that Perkins Cobb was a man, unlike most others, founded in both adventure and boredom.

He was the child of a Mormon preacher and a lady gambler—make what you will of that clash of salvation and uncertainty. There was an incident in his boyhood that now seems more easily "read" as true to Perk. One blazing hot July when he was eight, Perk went missing on a wild trail near his home in Escalante—the Burr Trail. He had walked the trail, sixty miles that took him five days, in heat and desolation, with snakes and countless ways of getting lost. He had a bottle of Dr Pepper and some fried egg sandwiches, and he had made it through, burned black but still as philosophical as ice cream out of the freezer. Some local press had asked the child—I looked this up—"Will you be an explorer in the wilderness one day?" And the boy Perk had hesitated, puzzled to think of America in those terms, and replied that no, he had done the trail, and he was ready for the city now.

So that combination of achieving great things and being unimpressed by them was there very early. Perk Cobb didn't much like to do anything once the world was watching.

"I was a sleeper hit, you see," he told me, referring to *My Sweet Dread*. "That was my trick. And I just got out before anyone caught up with me." There was more to it, but keep in mind that I am putting together odds and ends of what Perk said over many years. He would never have endured making himself this coherent.

Perk had a notion that Hollywood had ceased to exist as a worthwhile business or creative enterprise once the contract system went to hell. And it was Orson Welles, he claimed, who was the "single most effective assassin of the contract system. Because he had a contract, there on paper, that gave him such liberty. The first absurd document in Hollywood."

Perk was all the more admiring of Welles because the Kenosha Kid had gone to work with everyone watching and eager to laugh at his failure. Welles had known no discretion and had never tolerated modesty in himself—that was the secret to his "inhuman genius" as Perk saw it.

"And the picture," Perk said, still jubilant at the flagrant ease of *Citizen Kane*, "it just looked forty years of the business or the art in the eye and said, 'Fuck you for trying to pretend this is difficult.' Welles was insolent, he couldn't wait for the hacks to destroy him, because he insisted not just on making the best ever picture but on doing it in a way that said, This is so easy, isn't it? He made his movie the way John Doe takes a snapshot of Junior."

Perk had known Orson a little in the great man's last decade, in his lavish decline. Not that anyone could ever really get to Welles or penetrate the many layers of the act that left him so large. But Perk's view of Welles was that the man had lost interest after *Kane* yet gone on because he delighted in the self-abuse of being famous as a betrayed genius and a ruined hulk.

"American film," Perk might have said (I have memory, but no notes), "has a series of great one-shots, moments of amazing force after which the genius could only wait to die. Griffith with *Birth of a Nation,* Chaplin before his features, Selznick and *Gone With the Wind,* Dean in *East of Eden,* Terrence Malick with *Badlands* and Laughton in *Night of the Hunter.* Some of them did other things; some of them did a lot of other things. But only with pain, dismay and a certainty about the passing of time. The urge to make a film, the excitement, comes once only. It's like losing your virginity, or watching a movie. You can only get the power in a great picture once. Looking at it again is feeling your own aging process."

This theory lingered in my mind. I sought to argue with Perk about it. Weren't there good or great directors who went on and on? Talents that developed? He allowed that there had been some in the contract system because then there was a climate of slavery that kept desire sharp. But once directors won power, they faced instant gratification and the sudden termination of longing. I pointed to the modern era—to Scorsese, to Coppola, De Palma, Altman . . . to David Lynch.

"Look, old bud." Perk sighed. "Marty made one beautiful thing. *Taxi Driver* was his shot. And he will go on forever, sickly but surviving, making the same film about a guy who is so scared of life he makes himself act tough. That is his one chance of keeping hold of the excitement. De Palma had his rush in *Scarface.* There are lots of De Palma films, but only that once did he really vomit in the public's lap the way he wanted to. As for Francis"—and Perk said this before *Godfather III,* so help me— "he will wander around until he finds the Corleones again so he can get off on destroying his family. He is a great dark-souled bastard with just one movie in him."

Perk could make this case for nearly anyone I mentioned. "Making a movie is so fucking unpleasant," he argued. "And the success is harder to take than the failure. Who has the heart to do it more than once? There are kids coming into the business now who are just crazy to get the fame, the money, the women and the drugs. Sweet kids—they're satisfied after a couple of years. They come and go now like actresses!"

Fumbling obituaries alleged that Perk Cobb "grew melancholy" in his last year, as if some failure had kept him from his true calling. Not true. He was a cheerful vagrant with but one cause left: he wanted to get into the Paramount vaults to destroy the negative of *My Sweet Dread*. He took a meeting with Frank Mancuso as a way of getting onto the premises. Once he even wrote a letter to *The New York Times* rebuking an article in which Martin Scorsese had urged more money for saving and restoring old films. Perk wanted to be certain they would perish. The *Times* would not print the letter.

Lynch was the last topic we discussed. Perk had loved *Blue Velvet*—it was his kind of picture, and he laughed and shuddered at the same time. "The guy did it," he rejoiced afterward. "He blew it all open." Perk felt that cinema was a citadel which needed the regular outrage of desperate newcomers such as Lynch. But then Perk submitted to *Twin Peaks* and estimated that Lynch was "trying to throw the curse. He's making dumb shit. Wants to erase himself. But the public won't have it. They say it's genius. That Lynch is in trouble."

Wild at Heart was the last film Perk saw. He didn't say a word about it. But he went out and hired a white Cadillac Seville and drove east out of L.A. until he made it to Utah. He drove the car off the road in Capitol Reef National Park and drove until the ground stopped beneath the car. It was a six-hundred-foot drop and a wicked, pretty fireball, even if no one saw it. The solemn press he got spoke of suicide and a dissatisfied mind. But I am here to tell you that Perk Cobb was lucid enough to know he preferred not to make something like *Wild at Heart* next.

(1991)

TWO

When I offered my obituary thoughts on Perkins Cobb exactly one year ago, it was with a rather weary reluctance. Over the years, I had determined *not* to write about Cobb. He had made it clear that he hoped I wouldn't—he showed every sign of wanting to vanish. It was only his death last summer, and the remorseless requests of *Movieline* editors, that made me yield. And even as I wrote, I had my doubts. Indeed, there was an odd feeling of, as it were, auto-autopsy.

Still, I did want to give at least a nod of respect to that lost and golden age of the 1970s, when difficult and private, but beautiful, films were made in America, films that stirred up the dark of our souls and our nation. I don't mean just my friend Perk Cobb's one and only picture, the arresting *My Sweet Dread*. I mean Malick's *Badlands*, Penn's *Night Moves*, Toback's *Fingers*, Rafelson's *The King of Marvin Gardens,* and the movies of Monte Hellman, not to mention films that were more glorious at the box office but still somehow seemed aware of our darker secrets and felt mixed feelings of awe, pity and, yes, dread for them: *The Godfather, The Long Goodbye,* the first pictures of Scorsese and the inescapable *Chinatown.*

A lost age of marvels. And haven't attempts at sequels helped us see how completely the edgy moment has disappeared? Yes, I wanted to honor that decade of mavericks by writing about one of its most elusive casualties, a filmmaker who lost faith in the medium, an obsessive who saw through his own excitement, a pioneer who covered his tracks.

There were some friendly remarks made about the piece. One or two people who remembered Perk called to say it had been well worth doing. Of course, *Movieline* was blessed to discover that the photographer Sandra Johnson had known Perk too, and had snapshots from over the years (though none of us in the circle can quite place the very pretty girl in the two Big Sur pictures). Younger readers complained that they couldn't find *My Sweet Dread* at their local video stores—as if those grim, threadbare parlors were reliable repositories of our film heritage!

In any event, the piece appeared, and passed away as pieces do. Then one night, three or four weeks later, as I was drowsily watching *Point Blank*, I got a phone call. The film was ending, and Lee Marvin was resolutely preferring not to appear one more time. At first I thought it was a phone ringing in his story, but it kept ringing. It was a little after eleven. There was no introduction or prelude, just a woman's husky voice straight into my ear: "Did I ever know you? Did you so much as see me, apart from photography? You don't know enough about your precious Perkins Cobb to *begin* his story. I'm not going to talk to you. Hello . . . ?" And then, as I struggled for "Yes?" the phone rang off—it sounded as if it had been dropped back in place.

I hardly slept the rest of the night, alert for a follow-up call, trying to gauge the unstable mix of intelligence and nerviness I had heard so briefly. Was this what one is supposed to call a crank? (The concept seems less viable these days, when one can hardly ask directions without meeting an unreliable narrator.) But how had the voice found me? And what did it mean that this woman had called me to insist she would not talk?

Some superior knowledge in the caller loomed over me. Had she known "my" Cobb in ways I could not dream of? This was likely. There had always been women hovering at the edge of Perk's shadow, liaisons that curtailed phone calls or poker games. There were times when Perk's number had changed—and I now wondered whether I might end up having to do the same if that jittery, unarguable voice roused me again at three or four, improving on nightmare. I remembered something Perk had told me about his Hollywood: "You reassure crazies. You stroke neurotics. You feed other people's bad habits. The lies are not just allowed— they're damn near expected. A few years of that and who's fit for human company? When you're lying, you see, there has to be a script, you need to be a character, so as to remember what to say. Nobody talks naturally anymore."

And I had added, "It could make a person give up on talking."
Perk had nodded and grinned. "I tried that once and liked it
fine. But then it began lending me a kind of magic. The less I
said, the more they asked. Drove girls wild. Couldn't take it
after a while. That's L.A., though. Gets to you some way, sooner
or later."

The best part of another week elapsed, and I was forgetting
the call when the phone rang again. This was a little after ten on
a bright, sun-wiped morning. A brisk secretarial voice asked for
me, and then said she had Graziella Ortiz on the line. I *had*
mentioned Graziella in the piece—as one of Perk's famous lady
friends. Yet, truth to tell, I knew very little about this woman
apart from a montage of reckless yet imprecise press stories, a
few remembered shots from *Vogue* and *Elle* of that stunned, staring face and, of course, the unfortunate Catalina incident. I
wasn't entirely sure that Graziella Ortiz was alive still, let alone
around.

"Mr. Thompson?" It was the same voice, albeit recast from
late-night unease into a tone more suited to fresh-air business.

"It's Thomson," I replied "No *p*."

"Ah," she said. "Right." And there was a trifling laugh. Some
people think a proper taste for detail is amusing and consti-
pated.

"Look," she began again. "I am interested in having a piece
done."

"A piece?"

"Uh-huh. I'm making a return, you see. And I love your
stuff."

"Please," I protested. My heart was beating. Writers are such
helpless idiots over praise—we never trust a word, especially the
words we want most.

"No, really," she told me. How did I know she was grinning at
her secretary?

"How did you like the Perkins Cobb article?" I thought I might
as well take the lead.

"Did I see that one?" she asked the air. She could have been speaking to that droll secretary as the girl repaired her carmine lip gloss. "Anyway, I thought we should meet."

I knew this was a perilous opportunity, even if I couldn't tell whether to be warned or beguiled. I will do anything not to be afraid, or not to have it show. So I said, "Why not?" She gave me an address up above Sunset, and instructed me on how not to miss the concealed entrance. "Come around four," she said, "and we can swim."

My destination was a narrow, winding lane just below the Hollywood sign. The property was cloaked in flowering shrubs, so close to the city yet poised silently above it. The paneled door to the house stood ajar. The interior was Spanish, with bare white walls and just a few pieces of outrageously sparse modern furniture. There was a painting on the wall, one of James Stagg's night scenes, with a yellow cab making a U-turn like a smear of mustard. Doors opened to the patio and an intimate oval pool graded in tiny tiles of every shade of blue and green. There was a gentle noise of swimming. But it was not Miss Ortiz in the water. Her Afghan hound—Laura, I learned—was doing patient laps, her hair spread out like fine fronds, while Graziella, supple and thin, sat curled in a metal chair feeding herself blue corn chips with savage appetite.

You may be interested to know how the briefly fabled Ortiz looked after several years of rest. There is a photograph from the afternoon to satisfy your curiosity. Not that I had made the trip with a camera. Miss Ortiz had one, which, before anything could be said, she held out to me: "Here. Take me. So there will be no doubt."

I could not imagine what suspicion worried her, but I soon discovered there was no measuring her feeling of order breaking down. I did as I was told and took her picture, and this simple absorbing of her appearance seemed to soothe her, in the way a handful of peonies might have charmed another hostess. She made me finish the roll, though she did not bother with other poses or attitudes. There was no vanity in her submitting to the lens. Indeed, she regarded the camera with the inquisitive disdain of someone quite ill inspecting an alleged wonder drug but used to many frauds.

I held the film in my hand and told her, encouragingly, "The first step in the comeback."

"I'm forty, Mr. Thomson. At that age in this city a woman is expected to do the right thing—like Captain Oates, walking out into the blizzard."

A little daunted, I tried to compliment her on the jewel-like appeal of her home.

"Oh, I don't live here," she said, exasperated with my misunderstanding. "I couldn't *live* here. You don't really *get* anything, do you? Those writers with the big opinions—they never get anything."

"Well—" I began.

"Writing all that stuff, and not knowing a damn thing!"

"To write is to seek," I supposed.

She would have none of this (though giants of Hollywood have gathered around the same triteness as if it were a Francis Bacon). She stood up, and her sandals snapped at the pool's surround. She lit a cigarette and picked tirelessly at blooms in the foliage behind her. After examining each flower's head, she dropped it in the pool until her dog was surrounded.

"You people who write about the business, you're so innocent! Especially when you try to be insiders."

"I am not sure readers want this kingdom to be real. They like to believe the best and the worst."

She stared at me now, as if actually weighing what I had said. I could see the youth still in her, or maybe it was just a David Bailey 1/100th of drop-dead affront, hands splayed to guard her breasts—you know the shot. "Perkins Cobb used you" was all she said.

"Perhaps, but amiably."

"Amiably?"

"We were friends." I hoped the humble claim might put off her belligerence. A part of me did not want Perk—or my faith—ruined. Yet some curiosity was ready for the rumor of any evil.

"He was an operator," she said. "He did lots of things. He was always doing things. You think all he did was *My Sweet Dread*—that's a joke. He'd do anything for money, power, knowledge. Anything that got him inside. God, he knew the real stuff! Freddie Katz—did you hear that one?"

"I don't know a Katz."

"That was Perko's real name. He was never from Utah. He was raised in Ventura. He kept Utah for that splashy death scene."

I had noted, in fact, how oddly Perk's farewell had anticipated the last automobile vault into space in *Thelma & Louise*.

"A movie's the only fit place for that kind of death," she said, and she looked at me forlornly, searching for a sign of intelligence. Then she clicked her gaunt fingers and Laura came up out of the pool, water tumbling from her lean sides.

"We can't stay here."

"But we've just started," I protested.

"Do you have a car?" she demanded.

I told her yes, but how was she without transport or luggage if she was staying in this house? As she hurried me off the premises I wondered if she had not simply walked in moments before I arrived.

The dog soaked the upholstery in my car, and Graziella smoked all the way to her next residence—the only person who has ever smoked in that Corolla. The Clark Plaza Suites, between Beverly and Wilshire, is a sedately gloomy place in a placid, residential area. When we entered, Graziella had to announce her name, leaning across me toward the speaker, before the gateway to the underground garage would grind open.

"Gray Opper," she said, her mouth inches from my ear. When I kept a very still head, she added, murmuring, "My real name. I abandoned it when I was hot. Made people think of rabbits."

Her suite at Clark Plaza was chaos. There were clothes, books, papers and tapes, pizza boxes and corn chip bags on every possible surface, and over everything there was Laura's fine blond hair. There were file cabinets, leaning piles of old, stale newspapers, clippings, every sign of someone struggling to swim in the world's seething information. It reminded me rather of my own apartment, so she and I may have grown closer there because of the disorder. We made a kind of remote love (this was only proximity and narrative availability) and, when I woke, I found a cassette wedged between my toes.

What did she tell me about my hero, Perkins Cobb? That he was a scoundrel, a traitor and a fraud, and that she adored him still and could not accept that he was gone.

"Off a butte in Utah?" she asked me. "In a white Cadillac? What was the body like—do you know that?"

"Battered," I seemed to remember, "and burned a good deal, but—"

"Cobb Salad Crisp?"

"—they were confident it was him."

" 'They' would be. Cobb knew 'them' inside out."

I have to say, the possibility appealed. Perk was too playful just to quit.

I visited Graziella several times in the next few months, and the tirade never faltered. She told me Perk had done many movies besides *My Sweet Dread,* or parts of movies, or parts of projects. He had been a "doctor," she said, whose presence let others know they were ill. I cannot name all the pictures involved—there are legal difficulties. But she showed me a videocassette in which no less than Laurence Olivier was shown reciting a verse for children by Maurice Sendak. "I told you once/I told you twice/all seasons/of the year/are nice/for eating/chicken soup/with rice!" Graziella told me this came from a children's book with a verse for every month. Perk had filmed the whole book. She had seen some of the months over the years—Cary Grant had done May and Louise Brooks (sitting up in bed, coughing) September—and she believed that the other contributors had included John Cazale, Paulette Goddard and Truman Capote.

"Where is the whole film?" I longed to know. "It must be a marvel."

"Don't know," she said, staring at me askance. "Don't you get it?"

"What's to get?"

"Why would a man do that?"

"As play?" I surmised. "Or—for a kid?"

"Exactly," she pounced. "And no one knows where the kid might be—or who its mother was."

"Not you?" I inquired, as tenderly as I was able.

"Bless you for asking" was all she answered.

I gathered from Graziella—and I do not know how much to believe—that Perk had been an agent of certain police forces, in L.A. and perhaps farther afield. She maintained that the police had early on seen the wisdom of keeping files on potent figures in the entertainment world, so there had been opportunities for insiders with dope on the past and other guilty secrets. Perk had been a home-movie maker at many parties—Graziella alluded to the homes of Warren Oates, Norman and Dana Chase, Barry Diller and the Dunlap sisters—and no one knew what had become of the footage.

"This is mere speculation," I said, for I had begun to sniff Peter Lawfordism in the air.

"And don't think there weren't people who wondered what he'd seen, or recorded."

"It could be fascinating material," I admitted—I myself had long been on the trail of Hollywood home movies of the thirties. And now, in the video age, with astonishing low-light capabilities . . .

"But dangerous."

It was her conviction that Perk had somehow gone too far, that he had betrayed trusts and that what I had taken for his own resolute quietism was something far more sinister.

Graziella was always jittery. She seldom slept for more than twenty minutes at a time. She had a terror of being doubted—and to treat her fears she had only cocaine, occasional carnality and the flaking mirrors of her suite. She sat for hours repairing age but spying fresh eruptions. Her concentration wavered, and there were stories she gave up on in midstream. For instance, I never found out what "the James Toback tapes" might be.

There was so little hard evidence supporting her Perkins Cobb conspiracy theory, apart from the Olivier–Sendak material, and the five other pictures on the roll of film I had finished on her, apparently views of some desert ghost town—real or a set, who could say? Otherwise, there was only the mess in which Graziella was always searching, and the rising whine of her innuendo and dread.

And so gradually I withdrew as 1991 came to an end. There were calls I did not return, or lingered over answering. Then one day this January I was told at Clark Plaza that she was gone. I wondered what had become of all her papers and possessions. And what about that faithful Laura?

There was no mention of the dog in the report of the accident. I only noticed the small, inside story days later, how at Alden and Palm in the early hours of January 7 there had been what appeared to be a hit-and-run accident in which a woman, Grace Opper, had been killed. In the picture that accompanied the article, I saw the pattern of Graziella's flowered skirt. I went to check out the body—too late, it was cremated. But there was a morgue shot. Graziella looked peaceful.

The papers said nothing about the accident victim having been Graziella Ortiz. It was as if the wondrous face of the seventies had been a ghost all along, and actual death the final proof. I inquired, but I have had no answers. I went to Alden and Palm late one night. It seemed to me that for a vehicle to have hit her the way it appeared in the *Times* photograph, it would have had to have been going the wrong way, or . . . And how was there a picture in the first place? The police denied taking it.

Sometimes around seven on these early spring evenings, as twilight creeps in, I do wonder about the traffic in this L.A. of ours. Is it a mass of private purposes seeking their own routes, or is there a pattern, a single force for which every turn and tremor is known in advance? I have been happy in this city over the years, loved its light, its dusk and the movies that play with both.

But now I begin to wonder whether there is not a fatal design. And if I pass this on, for whatever it may be worth, I do ask myself whether I am known and watched and waited on because of things I have learned, and because of what strangers wonder. I look at the pictures of that ghost town—did Cobb hide out there? Or is he down the street in that gray Cutlass, waiting for me to pause and dream at the curb?

(1992)

Suspects

TONY MANERO (John Travolta in *Saturday Night Fever*)

In the late seventies, Tony was a big attraction in Brooklyn discos; people would come over from Manhattan to see him. He had never believed he could have a career in dancing—he was too shy, he didn't really enjoy being up there in front of people. The thing about dancing that he liked was the precision, the control. The way you could count on it, and count yourself through it, and feel good about yourself. He did floor plans for dances—the placing of the feet. He liked to work them out on paper first and then do them. But he always had trouble finding girls who would study. They said they liked to dance the way they felt it at the moment. But Tony knew it could be an art and a science; that you could dance in your head.

Still, he was noticed, and he went along with the offers: he was passive about it in a funny way so that people liked him but took him for granted. He didn't have a lot of personality. He had a featured spot in Shirley MacLaine's one-woman show that got good notices. Shirley took an interest in him. She'd talk to him, give him notes and lend him books—she was very generous and eager for him, but it left him a little daunted.

"Tony, you have a talent. But you make it look easy—as if you weren't working."

"Oh, really?" he said. He liked that; that was what he wanted.

"Show them it's difficult. Sweat a little. They want to see you trying."

He nodded. It was funny: he liked Shirley, but she was consumed in her own effort, and he found that a touch oppressive, or unhealthy even.

"Well, you know," he said. "I'll try." And he giggled in that soft way he had.

He got his own show, *Satan's Alley,* but it was a terrible piece of shit. "Tony," Shirley warned him, "you have to protect yourself with the right people. You're too polite. You yield. You're grateful to these deadbeats. You should fire them. Tony, you're judged by the company you keep."

He agreed with her, but then he went straight back to the theater and agreed with the deadbeats. He didn't like to make himself difficult; he'd just as soon not get into conversations.

The show closed after eleven performances, and Tony was at a loose end. He took the first offer, from a Las Vegas hotel. He had never been to Vegas, never been out of New York State that much. He wanted to travel a bit. But in Las Vegas, the stage for the floor show was the wrong dimension for the routines he'd worked out. He needed another seven feet in width, which he explained to the management.

"Tony," said the foreman of the maintenance crew, "that's a hell of a lot of work."

"But, you see, I need the room," said Tony.

"What is it, it's just a few feet—am I right?"

"You put one more section in, over there, that'll do it."

"Tony, I gotta get that made. I don't know about the lumber— this is Japanese maple. Then we got to let it settle, and the varnishing! Tony, do you—"

"Well, OK," said Tony, and he let it go, and the second night he ruined his knee. The cruciate ligament, they said in the hospital. His leg was never the same again. Not that he minded so ultra much—after all, dancing had never been the most important thing to him. But, as he rested in the hospital, he wondered sometimes what was.

Travel, he supposed. He had liked just being in Vegas, seeing the desert, Hoover Dam, the lights on the Strip. He liked the way the city had been put there. The world was amazing. So when he was able to, he took a flight to Europe. And he appreciated it. There was something very tidy about being in a foreign country. Tony didn't know foreign languages, so that kept what he said very simple. And what he thought. Which was pleasant. He got confused and unhappy a lot less.

In Paris, he met this couple, a girl and her lover, an older man. Her name was Anna, and she acted like someone on smack, but Tony found she was clean—it was just her nature. They could be together for hours at a time and hardly say a word, and it felt very nice. The only thing she liked him to do was give her a foot rub. Tony knew feet, and she had the coldest, cold enough to chill his hands.

But he liked the look of bliss in her eyes as much as anything he'd ever liked. Anna's lover never had a name; she called him Minister, which was like a joke, yet she never laughed. The man was something in the Thatcher government, and insane over Anna. But she took it all very calmly, and Tony wasn't sure that she didn't want his foot rubs most of all.

"Tony," she said, one day.

"Yeah." He was always ready to serve her.

"When he comes tomorrow."

"Yeah."

"When we're in the bedroom, you know?"

"Uh-huh."

"He'll have a briefcase. There will be a file in it—brown color. Take it down to the copy shop, OK?"

"Yeah."

"Copy it. Put it back."

He did as he was told, and she intimated that she had passed the file on to others. She gave him five thousand francs. Which was all right, because his money from Broadway and Vegas was running out. And it had been very simple, in and out, copy the pages, put them back. He was a deft worker.

Things developed from that. He got an apartment in Paris, and Anna had other jobs for him.

"It's like being a detective," he said. "Right?"

One day, she introduced him to an Italian, though he talked American. And the man was looking to explore other opportunities. Things with cars, for instance, and then carrying packages to Amsterdam or Rome, or even Casablanca.

"Wow! Casablanca!" said Tony.

"You get your passport looking like a stamp album," said the man.

"It's drugs, isn't it?" said Tony.

"As a matter of fact, Tony, yeah. Carrying Camembert to Casablanca does not pay in the same way."

"Drugs are bad, right?" Tony had always heard that.

The man studied him and reflected for a while. "Try some," he suggested, and he gave Tony—who didn't like to say no—some cocaine, and it was sensational. He felt very, very clean and together with it.

"Why'd they say it's so bad?" he asked the man.

"Killjoys."

One day, they wondered out loud if he'd ever killed anyone. Just asking. Turned out he had a knack for it, a way of expressing himself artistically—so long as he could plan it. He drew diagrams and time charts. Then he did it—in and out. Tony's passivity made him a very good killer.

"My man," said the man, about a year later. "They are asking for you."

"Yeah?"

"You have a very solid rep."

"Who's asking?"

"People in Los Angeles."

"I was only ever there at the airport once."

"The airport is nothing."

"Really?"

"It's your sort of place. Behave yourself, you could be in a lot of demand."

Los Angeles, or Hollywood, or Bel Air, or Lies Allowed, has always liked
to see itself as a place of enchanted houses and great monsters, where one
kiss from the prince may restore youth and that thing called happiness.
An advertisement for Jurassic Park – The Ride, and a moment from *Sunset
Boulevard* (1950), with Gloria Swanson and William Holden tango-ing on
the brink of fantasy.

Some views of Mulholland Drive: the Spanish mansions and the modernist spreads wedged into the soft hill-sides – see the dry undergrowth and feel the risk of fire. The houses are best seen from above, where they flash that copper sulphate signal – the pool – that ensures passover. But the Drive is real estate, too, and the selling signs stand patiently beside enormous trash bags waiting to be collected.

The Chateau Marmont Hotel, on Sunset: not the best place in town, but one with history. James Dean lived there once, and he and the director Nicholas Ray had a bungalow there where they worked out much of *Rebel Without a Cause* (1955).

Women in Los Angeles do not have much power, and that may be because they are so revered as images. At Armani, on Rodeo Drive, the intimate magic occurs (plastic gets silk) and so transformation is licensed. And also on Rodeo, girls out together, looking for outfits and hoping to be seen. Can they be Michelle Pfeiffer one day, the most widely honored icon now, seen here at her beginning, in *Scarface* (1983)?

Street scene: New York, early 1900s, but it's actually the Fox lot, 1997, off Pico Boulevard. Question: is the guy in the doorway a lost tourist, or someone dreaming the set into life? Next, in Brentwood, up for sale – a place or a set – a once-upon-a-time restaurant, Mezzaluna . . . you know the rest of the story. Meanwhile, in Century City, at the multiplex, between shows.

The Stone Canyon reservoir, a holding ground for Bel Air's precious water. Then, Faye Dunaway near the close of *Chinatown* (1974), the movie that taught us how little small stories of iniquity mattered compared with the sweet flow of water. Finally, a producer's office, a leather couch, a low table; and outside, the surreal legs that are part of a poster for *The Seven Year Itch* (seen on the Fox lot).

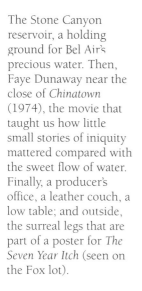

As a young woman, Joan Selznick could hire studio photographers to make her look glamorous – it was a way of trying to get work as an actress. Today, as big as the side of a building on Sunset, Robin Williams in *Flubber*. The idea of coming attractions smooths over all previous disasters.

"That'd be cool."

"It's where the action is, Tony. A hit man essentially, if he's for real, he has to do it in America. Change your name."

"Yeah?"

"Sure. I mean, you had a career there once. Not a lot, maybe. But I'd change your name. It's cleaner."

He liked that idea. It made him feel good to be someone quite new and different. Like starting again. It took him five months to think of the right new name, Vincent Vega. He said it fast so that it sounded like one word, the name of a car.

But, back in America, it wasn't quite what he expected. Europe had been very efficient, very smooth. America was a riot now, as if it had forgotten what America meant. There were absurd fuck-ups that made him ashamed. The boss was a big black guy, and the boss's wife was this white chick with evil eyes who said she was sure she remembered him from somewhere.

He had to take her out one night while the boss was out of town. And she insisted they go dancing. What did she know? He hadn't danced in a long time, and his knee was shot so he could only go through the motions. But she was a wild one, with a lot of funny moves and Egyptian arms. She told him, and she sort of sneered at him, that she had grown up in Las Vegas, where her dad worked for one of the big hotels.

"So there," she said, and then lowering her voice, making the name sound like a mockery, "Vincent Vega."

If he hadn't fallen straight in love with her, he'd have known the safest thing to do, then and there, in and out, was to make a plan for offing her.

ELLIOTT (Henry Thomas in E.T.)

"I would just like for Elliott to be normal again," said his mother.

"Again!" scoffed Gertie, and she chuckled proudly. "He has always been weird." That thought made her feel better about life.

But the government, and especially Mr. Keys, was very sincere about wanting the best for the boy. So this is how it worked out. Elliott and his family made an undertaking not to talk to anyone about the whole matter. In return, they were paid an amount of money that would take care of the kids' education—and then some, so the mother didn't feel left out.

Of course, a lot of people in Orange County had heard the story. You couldn't stop the rumors. But Keys had this idea that, he said, might "deflect the flow." "I always thought," he told Elliott's mother, "that this was Steven Spielberg stuff."

So a deal was done, three-way, the family, the government and Universal (which was Spielberg), to make a movie out of the incident. "And you should feel free," Keys told Spielberg, "to do it your way. Build the story as much as you like."

"I feel I've always known the story," said Spielberg.

You don't need to be told about the movie, or what happened with it. Of course, they altered a few things: after all, there was no way a family entertainment could do the real alien, so they created this little guy that everyone loved. They couldn't handle the real creature's drinking, or his foul mouth—and Steven decided that his interest in magic tricks just wouldn't play. "He *is* magic," said Spielberg. "He shouldn't *do* tricks."

The picture was so big that Keys proved right. In a few years, everyone regarded *E.T.* as just a story, a modern myth. There were people who would tease Elliott, in a good-natured way, about his having made up the whole thing for the movie. And he knew he wasn't to argue. It was easier, too, because with all the residuals they moved out of Orange County and went up to San Francisco, where Elliott's mother bought a mansion in the three thousands on Pacific. And no one in San Francisco believes anything out of Los Angeles anyway. So the whole climate shifted in just a few years. And even Elliott, sometimes, would wonder if it had happened—or if it hadn't been as sweet as the movie.

There were therapists who wrote in out of the blue to say that Elliott was surely going to need professional care sooner or later. Spielberg and Keys offered to be helpful. But the matter was complicated by the return of Elliott's father from Mexico. He had only been away on a spiritual search, he said; he'd never meant to end his marriage. So Elliott's mother had to move for divorce, and the custody settlement became a complicated thing because of the sums of money floating around.

"It's absolutely clear," said Elliott's father. "The boy needs a father. Making imaginary friends is the proof of that. He just wants his dad."

"Who needs the money," said Elliott's mother.

"But if Elliott gets him back," said Gertie, "don't I, too?"

"Naturally," said Elliott's father. "That too."

Spielberg, entirely of his own volition, offered a large cash payment to the father to quit all claims. But the rentals on *E.T.* never faltered, and there was the video to come. So the father said this offer was a shocking and cynical mockery of the nature of parenthood.

Elliott went to a lot of different schools. The family moved several times—to Santa Cruz, to Aspen, and back to San Francisco again. There were court battles all the time, which were expensive, and Elliott had seven therapists over the years—for his mother, his father, for Universal, court appointed and so on. His files grew large, and he got into the habit of saying less and less, for fear of causing trouble.

By 1989 he, his mother and Gertie were in San Francisco. He had finished high school but showed no urge to go to college. In fact, he spent most of his time trying to look after Gertie. She had got into a drug habit in school, and she spent a lot of time with their father in Las Vegas, where he owned a large video outlet—Elliott Video.

On October 5, 1989, Elliott woke up, knowing there was going to be an earthquake. Nothing like this had ever happened to him before. He hadn't had "visions" or anything like that. Some of his many teachers had known him long enough to see that he wasn't a very imaginative kid—it was as if he'd grown to mistrust his own thoughts. But his dream was very clear. He saw fires in the Marina, he saw the Cypress Freeway collapse and he saw the section of the Bay Bridge give way so that when the video footage first came through he was not surprised at all. The stuff had run already in his head—even the angle was the same.

He didn't know what to do. He didn't believe in dreams—not even his own. But this had been so direct, so pointed. It was as if someone was warning him. He felt the responsibility. So he told his mother.

"Elliott," she said. "Honey. How would that be?"

"Well," he said, "aren't there earthquakes in San Francisco?"

"That's why you dreamed it. You had it in your mind. Don't you think?"

So he told Gertie, and she said they would have a party in Alta Plaza Park so that they would have great all-around views. "What day will it be?" she asked.

"I don't know," he realized.

"You don't know!"

"I know it's a beautiful, still day."

"That's something," she sneered.

So when October 17 came along, with the World Series at Candlestick, and the weather so perfect everyone was talking about it, they went out to Alta Plaza Park with a picnic. Gertie was high, despite her promises to him. They were bored and sleepy, and they had finished their picnic when at 5:17 p.m. Gertie said, "Fucking A, Elliott, you are a trip!"

Of course, Elliott wasn't surprised. But he was horrified when he heard the number of people who had been killed. It wasn't just live action-cam material. That was when Gertie got him on marijuana first of all; she said it would help him relax. And before long, she was helping him as much as he was helping her. They became like Hansel and Gretel lost in the dark woods.

In the early nineties, they decided to move to Los Angeles to get back to their roots. They bought a house together on Westgate in Brentwood. Elliott was not in good shape, and he stayed home a lot. But he didn't like television, and he didn't like sleeping: he was fearful of any experience that was close to dreaming. So, just to fill his time, he got into drugs and health simultaneously.

He was doing a lot of cocaine, and he spent two or three hours a day at the gym. And, in the way of things, he spent time with the young set in Brentwood, working up a sweat and then having arugula salad and watching the cars slip by. It was an aimless life, but there was so much money, and Gertie was with him. They used to sleep together, literally, not that anything ever happened between them. It was just a way of masking the lack of anyone else in their lives.

One day in the summer of 1994, Elliott came home late at night after jogging. Gertie was watching the tape of *E.T.*—she loved it, but she turned it off when Elliott came in.

"Where d'you go?" she asked.

"Did my circuit," he said.

"See anything?"

"Why d'you ask?"

"I don't know, Elliott. Just to talk."

"I saw this guy."

"Which guy?"

"He came running past me. And he was taking off his sweat top as he ran, bundling it up."

"Why was he doing that?"

"I don't know."

"So what's so special about it?"

"I didn't say special." He warmed down. "But it felt bad."

"How was that?"

Elliott paused. "Know what he said? He was saying it under his breath as he ran."

"What?"

" 'O.J., phone home.' "

The next day, Gertie woke him up.

"Did you dream?" she asked.

"I don't think so."

She told him what had happened on the TV and just a few blocks away, and she asked him what he was going to do.

"I'm not saying nothing," he told her, and he never has.

JESSICA
(Kathleen Turner, Amy Irving et al. in *Who Framed Roger Rabbit*)

"You know, I bet you could make it as a crossover," he told her one day. This was after he'd just sat there for what must have been twenty minutes, taking her in, studying her. He had a way of looking at her that she could never resist. The longer he looked, the more she knew she was his. Nothing had to be said or done about it. What could be done?

"It's true," he said, reading her doubts. "I could go downtown with you on my arm, go to all the good places—no one would notice. No one would close the door on you."

She didn't know what to say, or how to handle it, so she laughed that rough throaty laugh which she knew he enjoyed. "Except me, sir. I happen to be a happily married woman."

He nodded, without bitterness. There was something about it that simply intrigued him, in the way a chess puzzle might hold your thoughts all day. "That's true," he said. "And he's a nice guy, a lot of fun."

"He makes *me* laugh," she said.

"And you've got a great laugh. All your own." He grinned.

So that was that, but she thought about what he said. After all, no one like her had ever crossed over before—even if Jerry had gone to the dance once with the Irishman. The truth was, she loved her husband, always had, whatever anyone had thought; no matter that he was, well, on the homely side, while she was—she didn't bother with false modesty—a knockout. No matter that everyone thought her husband was a great guy, kind of foolish but good-hearted, while she was . . . well, she had a bad reputation. "But if you've got my lines," she said to herself, looking in the mirror, "a lot of people are going to think the worst of you."

No, it had nothing to do with her husband. She'd always love him—that was written—in the stars and in the script. But crossing over was something else. That was more than love or money. That was no-questions-asked magic. And it was irresistible. There was also the fact that the other guy, the one who'd said she could do it, him with the way of looking at her . . . Well, a woman knows when she's admired, and she's bound to respect it. When a man's like a blunt pencil for you, sometimes you dream of sharpening him a little. So she couldn't get the possibility out of her head. It doesn't really matter which side of the line you're on, possibility is like that—it's the thing you never forget.

Maybe she could go downtown and get in at the best clubs without being turned down flat. Hadn't he said he'd take her? Have her on his arm? Holding hands at midnight? But if she could fool him, too, so that not even he knew she was crossing over . . . Because he couldn't tell the difference. Because he thought she was just the most adorable, ripe-bodied creature he'd ever held. Oh sure, he looked at her for twenty minutes, knew every inch and curve, knew she was his—even if he'd never touched her. But men get cocky. They think they know it all, and then they stop noticing.

Suppose he was hers, too. She'd seen it coming for months. He was pie-eyed in love with her, even if she was the wrong type of woman for him, and married to a swell guy that she loved. He was just dreaming, What if? She could see his sad eyes full of it. He'd stopped seeing her. It was possibility again—people go blind from it, even people whose business is looking.

So she made herself a plan, and she called him up on the telephone.

"Oh, hi," she says, doing things with her voice a little in the way of disguise.

"Who's that?" he asks. She can tell the voice has got to him.

"You wouldn't know me," she says. "My name's Aimée Lapine."

"French?" he asks.

"Only in a manner of speaking," she says.

So they small-talk it a while and she's getting quite a thrill and she says, "Look, I'm here for just a day. Day and a night, actually. And I heard that you could take a girl downtown. Go to the hot places."

"Who told you that?"

"I swore I wouldn't say, but the review was four stars."

"Really?" he said. He was tickled pink, just as if she had a hand in his pants.

Well, they made a date and she got herself up in her best Aimée Lapine style. She did her hair differently. And the clothes were much more sophisticated. She went for the Edith Head look, as opposed to good old Frederick's of Hollywood, the way her husband liked her—and the way he'd always seen her before. It was a terrific new look, sort of a cross between Grace Kelly and Anouk Aimée.

But he told her, "I'd have known you anywhere," when he met her in the lobby of the Beverly Hills.

"You would?" She was ready to be crushed, pancaked. But he rallied her spirits. "I mean, I was trying to imagine the woman— the body—that went with the voice on the phone."

"And?"

"Just what I pictured."

"Don't get too satisfied," she told him.

But he'd been right. She passed. She crossed over. They went to Spago, and they got a great table. Tom Cruise came over during dessert to beg an introduction, and she could tell Tom was bitten. Then they went to a club and they danced, and when she felt his arms around her that's when she knew it had worked. He could feel her, all right. And she could feel the feeling.

They went down to the beach in the moonlight, and then he took her back to his place. It was a mess. There were drawings on every flat surface, and most of them were of women like her. The guy was obsessed.

"I wonder," he said, "would you be averse to my taking off your clothes?"

She could hardly breathe. The clothes felt like paint on her, stifling her. "How're you going to do that?" she asked.

"Eraser," he said, with a smile. And she knew he knew. The trick hadn't fooled him.

"How did you know?" she asked.

"Jessie," he said. "I drew you. Remember, I drew you bad."

"So it's hopeless," she said. And she was so horny.

"Nobody's perfect," he said. "Then again, nothing's impossible."
He was smiling at her in the nicest way, even if it was wicked,
with her a married woman. And he had an airbrush in his hand.

SUSIE DIAMOND
(Michelle Pfeiffer in *The Fabulous Baker Boys*)

It was about six months after she gave up on Seattle, when Susie
was singing in a bar in the Valley. The job was Thursday through
Sunday, two sets a night, a hundred a night and her dinners—if
you could eat what they served there. Nothing was right about
the job. The manager evidently supposed that in hiring her he
had rights, including advice on what she should wear. The trio
they had there were only kids and didn't know the songs she
wanted to sing. So first she had to teach them the songs, because
only one of them could read, and they made a lot of kids' fun
about the lyrics. Plus, it was a dive, and all of L.A. then was
having hard times. The manager used to do simple sums for her
on how many drinks it took to cover a hundred a night. And she
had to listen to him, and stop herself from talking back. "Be a
sweet kid," he told her.

Then one night, after her set, a boy came up to her, a child
even. He didn't seem more than seventeen, and he was as clean
and sparkly as fifties TV.

"Miss Diamond," he said, "that's a terrific act." She had done
"Night and Day," "I Guess I'll Have to Change My Plan" and
"Every Time We Say Goodbye," and she had felt especially right
on the last one.

She didn't say anything. She just wanted to get off.

"Here's what I want to suggest," the kid said.

"What *you* want to suggest?"

"Right. Monday morning I want you to call my boss—Griffin
Dunne. Here's his card. Say Stanley told you to call—"

"Stanley?" She never could help herself with the tough, hostile
attitude.

"Right." Stanley was blushing. She was sure it was all a joke. "What the fuck is this?" she asked him.

He was grinning and nodding, as if, yes, he got this a lot. "It's authentic," he said. "Griffin Dunne is CAA. You have heard of that?"

She didn't say shit. He really couldn't have been more than twenty, and he was hardly shaving.

"Just call him. No promises. But I will speak to him and give him my thoughts. I'll tell him you're a hell of a singer and a pain in the ass. Right?" And then the kid just turned and went away, leaving her without a finish.

She waited until Tuesday to call, and Dunne was in conference then. But he called her back Thursday.

"You didn't call Monday," he said right off, after his secretary placed the call.

"I was busy."

"What were you doing?"

"Maybe I was doing my nails."

"That's neat. So, you want to come in?"

"I guess so."

"No one's forcing you. I don't as a rule have to beg for business."

"That's my job," she said.

"You're funny. I like that. I'm going to give you to Denise. Make a time with her." And, again, she was left without an answer line.

It was eleven days before she got her appointment. She had felt challenged by Dunne, so she made a tape one night after work—on a good machine, giving the musicians twenty dollars each to stay late. She did "Every Time We Say Goodbye" and "More Than You Know," which had been her lucky song since the Baker audition. If you could call it luck.

Dunne wasn't there at first. He was "in with Mike," Denise told her. So she waited, and at last he got there. He acted as if he couldn't recollect her name.

"Stanley saw me," she said, clutching at straws.

"Stanley's at Paramount now," he told her.

"Yeah? By the way, how old is he?"

"Twenty-six."

"He looks a lot younger."

"That's his charm. Whereas, yours is you look older. How old are you?"

"Thirty-one," she lied.

"You look thirty-five." She didn't have to ask whether that had any charm.

"So, I'm out of here?" she said, getting up.

"Don't you know where you are?" He waved his hand to indicate not just the room but the building, the enterprise and scope of CAA.

"I'm talking to an agent who tells me I look old."

"There are people out there who would die, who would kill, to be in here for two minutes to . . . show themselves."

"You mean you want to see my tits?"

"I think I can imagine them, Miss Diamond. Your tits are not a lot."

"And they're thirty-five," she added.

"And you," he said, "expect to sell your weary, unimpressive tits to America?"

"Why am I here?" she asked.

"Why do you think?"

"I'm a singer. I have a tape. You want to hear it?" She was ready to unpack the recorder from the extra-large but elegant bag—she had bought it specially.

He indicated assent.

She put the recorder on his desk and turned it on. Now she heard only the noise and the amateurishness of it all. He listened to twenty-four bars and then indicated to her to turn it off.

"You're a terrific singer," he said, without excitement.

"So?"

"So, when did you last see a picture where someone sang well?"

Susie thought awhile. She hadn't thought about it before, but it was a good question. "*Yentl,*" she said.

"My point exactly." Then he waited.

"So?"

"So pictures don't sing songs. That's not why you're here. I could get you maybe eight bars singing something torchy in the bar in a Jeff Bridges picture. You don't want that."

"I don't?"

"Know what you haven't done since you came in here?"

"No."

"The one thing."

"I haven't sucked your cock." She made a little-girl thing of saying it, as if realizing she hadn't tied her shoes.

"You'd bite it off. I wouldn't let you near it. No, the one thing is you haven't smiled."

"There hasn't been anything to smile at."

"There never is."

"So why smile?"

"To be nice, be pretty, be available."

"Uh-huh." She shrugged. She had heard this before. Baker had always told her she didn't know how to milk applause, make it build. She hadn't made people want her.

"So, I'm out of here," she said. And this time she stood up.

"I'm serious, Miss Diamond, and as a matter of fact I am brilliant. You can read about it. You not smiling is why you are here."

"A novelty act?"

"It's different. That's what Stanley said. He said you are a great singer, that you are terrific looking—"

"And thirty-five."

"That's the point, fuckhead! You look that old because you don't smile. Thirty-seven," he added.

"That's different?"

"It might be interesting. There's a part in the new De Palma film. Gangster's wife. You want to go read for it?"

"She doesn't sing?"

"And she doesn't smile."

"Fuck off," she said and left him there. She got the last line.

When she got back "home," to the room in Culver City, there was Baker on the machine, in L.A., at a motel. She called him back.

"What are you doing?" she said.

"I'm drinking again," he said. "And I'm doing piano next week on a commercial."

"I thought you weren't going to drink."

"I knew I wasn't going to drink. What are you doing?"

"I'm practicing not smiling."

"You don't need practice," said Baker. "You're a natural."

"So?"

"Why don't I come over there, wherever it is, and we get smashed together?"

"Why not?" she said, and she saw the grimace on her own face as the golden stuff went down.

ELVIRA MONTANA (Michelle Pfeiffer in *Scarface*)

They needed Elvira to identify the body.

A handsome, sleek-suited assistant D.A. came to collect her at her house in Cocoanut Grove and drive her downtown to the morgue. He was all over her with solicitude and the hush of morbid celebrity.

"Mrs. Montana," he said, "it's only humane to warn you. Your husband's body was extensively . . . abused. After death."

"Let alone before," she muttered. The guy was fidgeting and giving off sensitivity so much she had been getting the creeps. But her remark stilled him; after one sudden, mouth-open, sidelong look at her he shut up.

Tony was on several tables, like a jigsaw, the head here and the body over there, fragments they were working on.

"The head," said the young man, "was . . . er, defaced. Now, any time you want to pause just say, will you, won't you?" And then the guy fainted with an aftershave-fragrant swoon, like a heavy curtain subsiding on the floor. So Elvira roamed around the room: she felt the chill on her bare arms. She did a line of coke on a marble morgue table, and waited patiently for the papers to sign. She was impressed with the job the Colombians had done on Tony: it was vivid, expressive work, like their paintings. Elvira was always interested in the cultural links you could find.

Then two days later, she had Alejandro Sosa on the phone with that grave, seductive voice of his. "Evvie, you didn't hurry the divorce?"

"I never did, Sandy."

"That was smart. Tony's will has been found, I hear."

"Maybe you left the will in the house," she wondered out loud. "The one thing there that wasn't shot or shat on. Do you know, they killed the tiger Tony gave me?"

"Elvira," Sosa complained. "I have good news, why quarrel? You knew he was a pig."

"Maybe I would have liked to do it myself."

There was a brief pause, then, "If I'd known, I could have given you a turn. Anyway, Tony's heir was his sister."

"And he offed her."

"So it seems," Sosa agreed. "Which leaves you as heir, sole heir, of the Montana Realty Corporation, the Cuba-America Friendship League and something called Our World, Inc."

Elvira wrinkled her nose. "What's that?"

"That's our enterprise. But, of course, at the time of his death, Tony had substantial obligations to us."

"I thought you collected at the house."

"There wasn't more than a mill in the house. No, Evvie, what we're looking for, what I'm hoping for, is some mutually comfortable settlement."

"Like what?"

"We could make you an offer. It would be a very fair offer. A nice, tidy buyout."

"Like?"

"Five mill. Deposited in whatever banks you nominate, whatever currencies."

Elvira let a couple of clear beats go by. "It's a sound business, the cartel?"

"It's the best. I don't have to tell you, Evvie, the stuff makes people feel good. There's no way in a free country they're going to stop that."

"Partners."

"How's that?"

"I'm the new Tony."

Sosa chuckled. "Elvira, it's a tough business."

"Sosa," she said. "*Tony* was your partner?"

"Of course."

"And Tony was an idiot, an animal, a liability. Tony was good business?"

"Tony was erratic."

"But Tony could shoot people."

"He did that."

"I can do that. And I can think, right? I did two years' business studies at Florida State before Frank Lopez, you know that? I'm not a fucking Cuban, Sosa. My family is from Baltimore. My father ran a hardware store."

"This is fascinating," said Sosa, "but—"

"You want I look for other partners?"

"No, sweetheart, no one wants that. Look, it's charming. Why don't we try it?"

Elvira didn't even have to shoot anyone to prove herself—not for years, anyway, and when she did it was Sosa, who was in bed with two analysts from Citicorp, and she shot him up a treat without getting more than the spray of blood and membrane on the howling girls, who were by then shitting in the bed. Elvira helped them take a shower—they were so shaky—and called up a car to take them home and told them never to say a word because no one would believe them, and she would come anni-hilate them. She *would*, she said, because she was a junkie, and nice straight girls like these from Citicorp knew junkies might do anything, didn't they?

Long before that, Elvira had transformed the business and

collateralized it in D.C. There was a day in that town when sequential clandestine arms deals were done and when the guy who purported to be from the NSC gave her his terrific grin and said, "Mrs. Sosa, someday this story will be told—and this country deserves to hear it—how right-minded business opportunity protected America in its hour of challenge." There were eagles perched on his sentences.

"Colonel," she began, "we don't need this shit."

"Oh, ma'am, I mean it. You do not know the relief it is to be dealing with what I think of as solid Yankee acumen. I mean, the people down there, well, you know, they're loose cannons—you're always compromised. But you came to us—"

"It's business, Colonel," she said gently, but with fatigue. "I'm using you."

The colonel had a sad, boyish face, and he nodded somberly as some automatic trick behind his eyes converted the mechanics of intrigue into honor.

"We've got aircraft," she explained, "empty aircraft going back down there. It's utilization."

"Right, right."

"And it gets the IRS once and for all off our backs."

"All agreed. You know, Mrs. Sosa, I dream of an America where the Revenue is just a piece of paper."

She smiled. "That's nice. But until then I'd just as soon fix it."

MAEROSE PARTANNA (Anjelica Huston in *Prizzi's Honor*)

The first time it happened, Maerose waited loyally. She was sure it was one of Charley's long-winded jokes, that he was just telling her the whole dumb story about the Basilio brothers again because the third time he told it there'd be a variation punch line, so Charley could settle in for one of his twenty-minute chuckles. But the third time came, while Charley was still on his second serving of cannoli, and it was word-for-word the same. So it made her sad because talking to Charley, after all, had become a whole lot better than the other, not that the other had really ever been more than another of Charley's twenty-minuters. But Charley was a generous soul when he was amused.

So, the next morning, at breakfast, when she was doing a plate of *linguica* the way he liked, she told him the whole Basilio brothers story—and by then she nearly knew it by heart herself.

"No!" said Charley, laying down his fork slowly and solemnly, like it was a papal seal, so astounded that Maerose could have wept. "I never heard that," he said. "Would you tell me that again just so I know I'm not dreaming?"

Maerose knew what she had to do. She knew there would be no getting Charley to any doctors, even supposing there was anything they could have done, and Maerose had read that Alzheimer's was a fate. But she knew there were things Charley knew—about the Prizzis and the Partannas and the way things had always been done—because he'd been a part of it since he was a boy. And Charley was of the old school that believed you knew it all in your head and never put a thing down on paper. You had accountants sign the checks, you had a wife write the birthday cards to your kids, and if you doodled when you were on the phone you hired a doodler. Nothing on paper was the rule, which was why none of the kids was ever pushed in school, unless they were girls, and that's how Maerose had the Latin, and the history and the calculus. So Maerose took Charley off for a vacation in Acapulco—he had always appreciated it there, liked just saying the name—and when they weren't eating and being on the beach or doing the other (and sometimes even when they were), she was pumping him, begging him to tell the old stories. And, of course, once he got started, he usually told the old stories so many times she thought she would scream. But she was doing it all to remember them, so she couldn't really complain.

And one night when they were in bed, and he was in her like a hippopotamus in water, he got to telling her about Connie Corleone.

"You know her, Maerose," he said, "you met her at—where was it?—Tahoe once. Wonderful witch of a woman. Well, let me tell you, she's been there since the beginning, and she used to just sit in the corner of the room like she wasn't there, but she was, and she was listening. Tahoe, you met her at Tahoe. And, you know, the Corleones didn't take their women seriously—they're really Sicilian like that—but Connie was something. She was as smart as you, Maerose, and not a lot less of a doll."

"Charley! You were romantic with her?"

"Me? She would have devoured me! She went after a lot of guys after she was a widow. With complete discretion, you understand?"

"Like who?"

"Like Frankie Sinatra."

"Oh!" she cried sarcastically, egging him on. "Are my nipples hard yet?"

"OK then," said Charley, aggrieved. And he named the governor of a significant western state.

"You're kidding."

"I wouldn't do that."

"How long?"

"Long enough. What I heard was she showed him the door and he was so messed up over her he killed the death penalty."

"Charley, you're a wonder," said Maerose, and she felt him moving in her. "Charley!" she said. "We already did it."

"We did?"

"Don't you remember?"

"How was it?"

"It was like custard, Charley, just like custard."

"I don't recollect," he said, and she had never seen so ghastly a look in his sunken face.

"You can trust me, Charley," she said, and she kissed him. So there was a sweet, vacant stare in Charley's eyes as he fell asleep saying "Acapulco."

Maerose therefore began to be the possessor of serious and delicate knowledge, and it was good for her; it watered her fertile mind. She had always felt that knowledge was worth more to a woman than beauty or honor. She handled Charley's problem with a grace that all the other men and their insecurity respected. She would be there with him at meetings, prompting occasionally, and moving the agenda on before Charley's repetitions set in. Maerose had the art of never seeming to take decisions; rather, she noted them. No one could mistake her kindness to Charley; no one regretted the new speed and directness in meetings. And Charley was delighted, for he was left with time for golf. The more he played the better he became—he had a natural swing—and so he was more able to accommodate the decay in his own thinking. For there is much in golf where thinking is an enemy.

Maerose never claimed position or powers. She was always acting for Charley, even when he stayed on the golf course rather than take the meetings. People understood. No male privilege was threatened; no advantage was stolen. "After all, it's his own wife," people said, "who's known him since she was a girl." And Maerose was very intuitive. No one ever needed to say, or even think, that she was cleverer than Charley. But her ability eased away any feeling of loss.

It was in the order of things that she came to sit in for Charley at higher council meetings. Those dons were understanding; it was an acceptable arrangement, even if Charley had never, not even at his best, mustered Maerose's succinctness. Further, Maerose was a match for that other exception to all the rules, Elvira Sosa. The women were company for each other, so that the men on their long weekend retreats to rural hotels could the more easily relax with cards, the specifics of slaughter and women they would never think of introducing to their "ladies."

CONNIE CORLEONE RIZZI (Talia Shire in The Godfather films)

As she had grown older, Connie Corleone, or Connie Corleone Rizzi, as she insisted, had improved or intensified her looks. Her hair had taken a little gray, to be sure, but it was the hue of steel. The bone structure of her face stood out more forcefully than ever, and her dark brown eyes appeared black to all except those who got very close. Not too many got close, or dared to examine her if they did. For she was resolute and fearsome, composed yet coiled. If she had been a man, either someone would have had to kill her or she would have run the world. "How are you more beautiful every year?" one of her feeble lovers asked. And she raised herself above him, looked down with those terrible eyes and said, "Because every year I have to see more weakness in men."

Above all she despised her brother Michael. For Connie had made great concessions in her mind to Michael. After all, Michael had had her husband, Carlo, killed. It was true that Carlo had betrayed Sonny, so that he had been murdered; and Carlo had beaten Connie when she rebuked him for having other women. Still, Carlo had been hers, and she his, and Michael had had him strangled; yet Connie had found it in herself to understand Michael because he had done it for honor and order and because he was the head of the family, and because someone had to have that authority. And Connie had never beheld a wisdom like Michael's, so that it moved her even if she loathed him.

But then Michael had changed and made a mockery of her faith in him. He had persuaded himself that he was finding a way to respectability and redemption. He had turned to Rome, and if at first he had done so out of calculation—looking to turn gifts into opportunities and status—still he had listened to the timid prudence of priests and their whispering, and he had become afflicted with prayer. As Connie saw it, Michael had been tempted to give up the power of a great armed city to be the United Nations. She scorned him, and she saw a black justice in the way he had lost his beloved daughter Mary because of his own weakness. And then Michael had been stricken, gloomy, sorrowful and withdrawn. No one had been left in the family fit for power except Connie, so she took it as if it had been a sword put in her bed. And she ruled in the old, strict way, with Sonny's bastard, Vincent Mancini, as her instrument. There were those in the organization who took pleasure and comfort in seeing the old traditions restored. And Connie was more handsome than ever, though there was not a man in America who dared touch her, or be touched.

She held court at Tahoe, and among those she received were Elvira Sosa and Maerose Partanna. They honored her, without flattery or pretense; for they knew how much she knew and had digested. And Connie would advise them on the proper handling of Miami and New York so that they were able to have the loudmouth Gotti put away. But Connie did not understand the two younger women: she could see that Elvira was always thinking of heroin again; while Maerose mourned unduly for her stupid Charley. As Connie saw it, Partanna now, playing golf and repeating himself eternally, was barely less intelligent than in his prime. But then the two women agreed to an article in *Vanity Fair,* a very coy piece on how women were making their mark in the most unexpected businesses. Connie knew that was vulgar and left them looking as pathetic as movie stars. And she began to feel a tightening in her body, as if muscles not known before were making ready. There is a puberty in murderousness.

Her son, Michael, was sent to school at Dartmouth. That was where her brother, Michael, had been, and of course he had become a benefactor of the place—he had helped build the Hood Art Museum—so there was no difficulty getting the young Michael, Michael Rizzi, into the school.

It was at Dartmouth that Michael formed what Connie regarded as an unsuitable association with a fellow student, Vivien Lewis. But if Vivien was wrong for Michael, she might be just what Connie needed. Vivien was a little older than her class. She had gone back to school after what she called "life experience," a part of which involved marriage to the financier Edward Lewis, whom she had met in Los Angeles and seduced, so the legend went, at the Beverly Wilshire Hotel. In return, Lewis had sponsored her in society and undertaken her education. But Vivien learned faster than anyone anticipated. While she was still a sophomore at Dartmouth, Lewis divorced her—he claimed that she had committed adultery with a man named Thompson, formerly a hotel manager. Vivien's settlement remained secret, but it was enormous. At Dartmouth, she lived not in student housing but in a small mansion on Ridge Road, with three servants, one of whom it was said wrote all her academic papers.

Moreover, Vivien had apparently used her house—with Thompson as manager, and Michael as agent—as a place of prostitution during the college's class reunion period, hiring women students as her girls. This would have caused a far greater scandal if the reunion period had not broken all records in terms of donations to the college. It seemed that Vivien had a special aptitude for business, and that's why Connie invited her to Tahoe the following summer.

Connie was vexed. Elvira Sosa, in Miami, had an elaborate plan for humanitarian aid to Latin American countries. It was a laundering scheme, of course, and the numbers were impressive, but Connie found the political jargon odious and she felt nothing but distaste for the attempt to finesse a decent criminal enterprise back into society. Connie was stalwart: outlaw meant what it said—society was to be defied and drained. Maerose Partanna was Elvira's aide in all of this, and she was a sentimental favorite with the New York boys.

"What does Charley say?" Connie asked Maerose.

"Mrs. Rizzi, what Charley says is neither here nor there. It's all Acapulco to him."

Connie nodded. "My Frank is the same way now."

"No, really?" said Maerose. Mrs. Rizzi seldom alluded to her fabled past. "What a talent!"

"What a prick," said Connie. "I hate to see a man lose his edge." She shuddered.

"So, anyway, Mrs. Rizzi, Elvira and me, we'd love to have your blessings."

"Listen, it's not my business. Nothing I understand."

"But you wouldn't oppose us?"

"Cuba! What's the point?"

"The Corleone family had interests in the old Cuba."

Connie waved that past away. "You get socialism in a country, it's ruined for a hundred years. So, how is Elvira?"

"Oh, she's fine."

"Really? I heard that maybe she was on smack again and needed to go to that clinic of hers." Vivien had given Connie the exact information, the dosage, the room number.

Maerose did her best. "She's tired is all."

"Uh-huh. Tell me, Maerose, if someone that tired should just drop dead?"

"Yeah?"

"Would you want to go ahead with her crazy ideas?"

"Mrs. Rizzi," Maerose whispered. "I never thought about it."

"Think about it."

After Maerose left, Connie called Vivien in. They looked on the map where Elvira's clinic was. And Vivien explained the chemistry to Connie and how one simple, undetectable injection could be sufficient.

"You're not to be incriminated," said Connie. "I need you."

Vivien giggled. "No one will know a thing."

Connie sighed. "Sooner or later," she said, "you gotta take someone out. You don't, they say you're soft. It's a pressure. You know what, Vivien?"

"Tell me, please"—with such wide eyes and wider mouth.

"This is a wicked country. Soft, rotten, like old fruit. Someone has to stand up and crush the rot. It's a duty. Someone always gotta be the angel of death, put the fear of God into them. They think the business is just the money, you know?"

"Yeah?"

Connie considered. "They're wrong. It's the fear. The respect." She looked at her hands in her black lap; they were an old woman's hands. "Fuck the injection. Strangle the bitch."

(1995)

Big Bend Story

It began with a coincidence; or what I took for one at the time. Yet I'm not sure that any of us has the right to trust that sort of innocence in events. I never found coincidence in the Constitution.

Anyway, just recently I was away on my own, doing some driving and some thinking, and I was down in the Big Bend, that part of west Texas that juts into Mexico. There's not a lot there except for mountains, great stretches of highway and sudden views of the Rio Grande. It's country where once outlaws would have gone to hide; nowadays, it's favored by stricken hippies and motorbike gangs who want to go roaring over the scrub ground. There's an annual chili-cooking contest in Terlingua. And there are rattlesnakes.

Not too far from Terlingua, I'd parked the car, and I was walking in that semidesert. I wouldn't say I was exactly lost in thought but—

"Hold it right there, sir, won't you?"

A thin man in jeans and white shirt was twenty yards or so off in front of me and to my right. I did stop. He had an automatic pistol in his hand, though he wasn't pointing it at me so much as where I was headed. There was a snapping noise—not loud or menacing—and a few steps in front of me the head of a rattlesnake came apart. I saw the snake's mean eye and then a spray of pink in the air. Funny what bullets can do.

The man ahead chuckled casually. He took out a red handkerchief and blew his nose. There was nothing threatening about him.

"Saw him there," he said. "Saw you coming."

I thanked the man. We shook hands, though we didn't exchange names. I said I had been stupid: I knew there could be snakes in this country. Not at all, he said, no, you wouldn't expect one out there, not at that time of day. He was gracious about it. But I might have walked into the bite. So I went back to my car, thoughtfulness scattered.

I drove on and did not stop until I got to Alpine, which must be ninety miles from Terlingua. That's ninety miles of very little in the way of habitation; still, ninety miles can put you in another state of mind. So I was startled to find the same man in the bar attached to the motel where I chose to stay. (I had no reservation—I hadn't known where I would stop.) The man did not seem at all impressed, and he resumed our talk in that easy, empty way that strangers can share in the West.

"See any more?"

"Not a one," I told him.

Of course, I bought him a drink. He was a kind of rancher, he said, from Del Rio. His name was Blewett, Edgar Blewett. We got to talking and had the steak dinner together, watching Atlanta lose to the Phillies. I don't know how the conversation turned that way—we were knocking down Coronas together—but a moment came, it being Texas, when we reached the shooting of John Kennedy.

"Lord," he said, sadly, as if the pain would never stop.

"I was walking through Chichester with my wife-to-be," I told Blewett. "That's a cathedral town in Sussex, in England. It was dark there—I suppose it was six or seven hours ahead of Central time. So it was after seven o'clock in the evening there." I nodded, remembering it all, holding the hand of my wife-to-be in the cold and the dark. "And we got to a friend's house, and she had the television on, and the news was coming in. It wasn't clear at first, whether or not he was dead."

Blewett smiled; he was a gentle listener.

"What about you?" I asked him. After all, he was Texan.

"Me?" His pale blue eyes gazed across the room, searching the stucco wall for help. He sighed. "When was that?"

"November twenty-second, nineteen sixty-three." I had the date as easily as my own birthday.

He shook his head: I might have been referring to an old dog from our childhood. "Don't recall that," he said. " 'Sixty-three?"

"Yeah."

"I was out of the Army then. Which means I was here, in Texas. Not here," he added, laying his brown hand flat on our table. "I would have been in Austin then."

"You don't remember where you were when you heard?"

He grinned happily—as if not infected, or whatever. I should add that Blewett was plainly in his fifties. In other words, he would have been somewhere, and old enough to remember.

"Long time ago," he said. "Long time to recollect a particular day."

"Everyone I've ever talked to," I said, "has known where they were. How they heard that news."

"Well," he said softly, and I felt he was being kind with me, "I was fair busy in those days."

I was ready to let it drop. Perhaps the man had been in prison, or hopelessly drunk, or running something across the Rio Grande. There were plenty of reasons why someone might not want to recollect, or talk about, that one day in November 1963. Even I was a little jolted to think how much I had loved that wife-to-be then. There were other things about that night in Sussex that I wouldn't want to talk about, and that I likely wouldn't know but for the shock in losing Kennedy, that familiar stranger.

"I could've been with Tip-It," he said. I nodded, for I had no wish to embarrass or pursue this man, this Edgar Blewett. He had only done well by me, and I could have been sitting there alone in that bar in Alpine without him. And I heard Tip-It or Tip It. I concluded that he was talking about some Texas garbage company he had worked for then.

Well, I went to bed, and it wasn't until next morning, in the shower, that I suddenly said to myself, "Tippit." Officer J. D. Tippit was the Dallas policeman shot dead by Oswald, after the Kennedy murder, as Oswald walked from his lodging house to the movie theater where he was later arrested. That was all I knew about Tippit. Not even the name would have stayed with me, I suspect, but for its palindromic form. In 1963, that prettiness had stuck with me—I liked word games and acrostics. In 1963, in Sussex, I used to do the *Guardian* crossword puzzle.

And now I write stories. As I was driving back to California from the Big Bend country, the stories crowded my head. "I could've been with Tippit"? I tried to recall Blewett's manner as he said that. Was he just a guy trying to scrape up a stray memory, mindful that the man he was talking to seemed to reckon it was bizarre and even un-American *not* knowing where you'd been that day in November 1963? Or was he some wondrous, level, Texan deadpan, looking me in the eye, teasing my boots off?

I was a couple of days in the car, going across spectacular, desolate and altogether suggestive parts of New Mexico, Arizona and Nevada, before getting back to San Francisco. The mind can really cruise, hour on hour, at eighty, eighty-five, with more bugs bursting on the windshield than cars coming the other way.

I got to thinking about a man who might have something like my odd experience in west Texas, who drives homeward and begins to meditate on the sheer unlikelihood of anyone old enough not knowing November 22, 1963—but not just the unlikelihood, the profound suspiciousness of the claim. Why, the man decides, driving faster and faster in story's excitement, if there was anyone who didn't remember then it's possible that that man was *involved* in the crime. That would be the giveaway. He stops at a motel—I stopped at Kanab, just over the Utah border—and calls his wife, laughing, telling her the story.

"Wait a minute," the wife interrupts him, unclear over the phone. "Is this a story you're writing, or did this happen?"

"A bit of both"—that's what I actually told my wife.

"Uh-huh," she says—and said.

The next day, going across Nevada, on what the signs call the loneliest road in America, he sees miles away, following him, a white car. It proves to be a white Cadillac, and it takes half an hour to close on him. Then it waits behind him.

The man never gets home. He is found dead in his crashed car by the roadside. The police will never be quite sure what happened. The movie—and I think this is a movie—is about what the wife does, wondering, inquiring, following. The wife could be Jessica Lange or Debra Winger—no one's going to mind having a wife like that, even if he is dead.

I got home to San Francisco, on 80. Coming in from Reno, I dozed for maybe a second and nearly let my car go off the road. That could have set God knows what in motion. No one followed me that I could see, beyond the inescapable obligation of most vehicles on the highway to follow and be followed.

And I laughed when I told my wife the story, and I said that surely the whole thing had been a coincidence.

"Sure," she said. "Tip It—I've heard of that. That's a typewriter eraser ribbon. Isn't it?"

"I thought that was Lift-Off."

"Well," she said slowly, "maybe, but I've heard of Tip It, too."

"Anyway," I reasoned, "how would Blewett have known I'd be at that motel in Alpine?"

"Was it the Best Western?" she wanted to know.

I looked at her. "I believe it was."

"I'd have known that. You always stay at Best Westerns."

"I do?"

"Haven't you noticed?"

Later on I looked at the map, and there it was—the one road, the only road, in and out of Big Bend, stopping at Alpine. Maybe that second meeting wasn't so hard to contrive or predict. But why contrive it? I had told Blewett I was a writer. Was "I could have been with Tippit" a desperate signal from within the conspiracy, the hope of rescue or having the whole story told? But

Blewett only said that at Alpine, so how did he get there except by blind chance? But then again, what was he doing out in that open country with a gun, except waiting? For me?

I was mocking myself as these thoughts mounted. For I am not a conspiracy buff, not by any means, even if I do notice palindromes. I've followed the story of the assassination, and I happen to have thought soon after it appeared that the Warren Report was too quick, too careless and none too smart. After all, it was a government report. My estimate has been that if there were others who were part of the killing, then by now they would have come forward for the talk shows, the book deals and the movies.

It's part of the nervous system of a country where anything can be believed that nothing is kept secret. There's so much airtime to fill. Nothing but that vacancy really explains the hysteria of Oliver Stone's *JFK* (I am two thumbs down on that one). My wish is that as all the sequestered files in this case are released, Stone should be required to read them and make regular reports to us. All of them, until there's nothing left.

More than that, I am sufficiently devoted to the principles of independent endeavor and enterprise to believe that one man, with some luck on his side, could have done it. Isn't that part of the American dream?

Still, as I looked over the few assassination books I seem to have accumulated, and as I checked that it was T-I-P-P-I-T, I found the suggestion that frightened witnesses believed there had been someone else present, with Tippit, or with Oswald, at the moment the policeman was shot. There's hardly an instant of that Dallas day for which there wasn't at least one account that has some extra, unknown person there—like a ghost.

Now, as you may have surmised, I have been leading you on. I haven't been in the Big Bend country, not in several years. Even if you find a Blewett in Del Rio, I deny categorically that I ever met such a man. But I do have a wife in San Francisco, I did have one once in Sussex, and I do like to dream up stories while driving in the deserted places of the West. I think of stories like that, and I fancy that since November 24, 1963, it's been easier for all of us to credit those winds of rumor. We are ready to think the worst, ready to put two and two together.

The 24? Yes, two days later. The death of Kennedy was a swooping down of tragedy. It left everyone amazed and ruined. But two days later, Ruby walked up to Oswald and pushed a gun at him—as if he were plugging it in. That's when we felt we were watching a show, or a story.

(1988)

Gone Away

Where are we when the story begins? At which port on the edge
of northern Africa are we arriving? Neither the book of *The
Sheltering Sky* nor the movie feels the need (or the hope) of
naming the place. The characters argue over being tourists or
travelers, but they are already on their way to being lost in a
blank state where the gazetteer is heavy luggage waiting to be dis-
carded. After all, our hero, Porter Moresby, is known as Port
Moresby, which is also a harbor in far-fetched New Guinea. It is
a droll name, one to find inside the pith helmet of a humorless
explorer in, say, *The Road to Morocco,* that Hope and Crosby quest
from a few years before Paul Bowles wrote *The Sheltering Sky,* in
an age when Arabs were Anthony Quinn.

In the novel, Tunner, the Moresbys' fellow traveler, is said to be
"astonishingly handsome . . . in his late Paramount way." And if
the novel is not quite knockabout, the film makes grotesque
comics of the Lyles, allegedly researching a guidebook for those
English mad to test the fly-dark nadir of mid-Sahara. Is a publisher paying for their white Mercedes trip, or are Jill Bennett and
Timothy Spall just Furies sent to conduct the Moresbys to hell?
There is an airy amusement in the film's unfolding and the forlorn
stance of its brave fools—that way in which vacant, smart
Americans get more than they thought possible. John Malkovich's

Port gives some hint that he may manage to faint before he smiles at the joke.

Not that talk of comedy can minimize the death of Port, the shall-we-say rape of Kit or the larger disappointments in their vacation. Still, it is important to Paul Bowles's tone that tragedy never takes over his story. When Port arches in the spasm of fever, the film's gaze stays calm; it does not pretend looking can share the pain in the scimitar curve of his back. The human figures feel odd, remote, valiant and doomed, and even the failure of the Moresby marriage is incidental to the infinite perfection of the dunes and the black horror that the blue sky is holding at bay. The humor lies in the itch of people to take such things as their marriage, their death, or their satisfaction so seriously. The desert is straight man to their petty humanism.

The movie begins with a sequence sweet with comic displacement. It shows not just what Bertolucci can do but how movie can work. In the novel, when the three characters disembark in North Africa, the dock is empty. Bowles moves on in a single sentence. But Bertolucci takes the moment to inaugurate nearly all his visual and spatial themes. He gives us an event in which the elements of experience are the movement of the figures and the camera, as well as the occasion of arrival and a few words of talk. Hardly anyone else working today makes movies in this sensuous fashion: it is a scene that has to be watched and yielded to. The script has been inhabited, not just executed.

We see an edge first, the oblong of the quay above which three heads rise—Kit, Port and Tunner—like balls rolling up for play. The camera pans and cranes to trace the fatuous crocodile of their luggage, and it continues to soar, slowly, on the balmy air of arrival. To say the camera is coming closer to the sky is too portentous—there is a weary gaiety in these travelers, and their air of discovery is faintly mocked by the vantage above the dock. Distance lets us register the inane prettiness of the color scheme—one in white, one cream and one gray. The trio is gathered in by kids and carriers and borne away to a hotel. The arrival is not Bowles, but it is complex, ambivalent and melodious in its playing with space. Port, we learn, is a composer and the group's gesture toward a leader, as well as the mind most cut off from its own life. Being musical, he may feel the most loss for that sepia, winter-evening New York they have quit, where the notes of Lionel Hampton's "Midnight Sun" fall like snowy blossoms.

That glimpse of Manhattan beneath the titles is inspired, wickedly accurate in its postwar bluesiness and—again—not Bowles. It replaces what could have been pages of explanation, and sets the mood for some misguided but inescapable journey. Why give up that enchanted New York? Why leave its sophisticated mix of cool and warmth? (Truly, in 1946 that would have been a tough question.) The descending melodic line of "Midnight Sun" is a lesson in despairing hope.

The movie has begun so well—I cannot recall so much early achievement in a recent picture. For if the "language" of Bertolucci at the quay is more romantic or voluptuous than the stricken aloofness of Bowles, and even if the mere fact of photography carries the innuendo of a *Vanity Fair* fashion shoot in the Moroccan magic hour, still, unmistakably, we are being asked to measure feeling and content through the movement of pictures. That is the first debt of honor a movie has to a well-written book.

There is also great promise in the people. Campbell Scott's Tunner is so in awe of the others, and so driven to please: he wants to screw Kit to flatter Port's half-forgotten taste. Bertolucci has called Tunner the friend the couple brought along "so they'd never be alone." Yet he is also a busy, prompt third party whose unblinking gaze fixes their isolation. He is there because the Moresbys need some proof of inner torture. Tunner is their loveless love in fine fettle. They bring him along to try to lose him. Tunner is a stooge, but Campbell Scott seems very happy to have the opportunity.

In the novel, Kit is *not* like Jane Bowles: she is blond and "saved from prettiness by the intensity of her gaze." Whereas, I think of Debra Winger as "kept from" prettiness by her daunting stare: there is a frown of bitterness, as if she had grown up intending to be beautiful. That is a large difference, one that concerns the hopes and ideals a person is looking at. Winger's angriness is a little lightweight, or hollow, next to the placid and brimming looking away in Jane Bowles's photographs. Actresses do expect attention; but women in books may have given up the ghost of it before the story starts. Debra Winger looks terrific here—we get ready for her best performance yet (and wonder if her discontent won't harden more at being so good in another commercial failure). She has worked to get the shape of Jane Bowles, and we feel a depth of commitment: a few years ago Winger was trying to do a film about Libby Holman (a close friend to Jane Bowles). But Winger has the face of an actress, a protagonist, a person to whom decisive things will happen. And it is a supreme, submerged point of Paul Bowles's *Sheltering Sky* that what happens to Kit does not much matter—at least not in that way the ambition of actresses requires.

It is in just that gulf that John Malkovich is remarkable as Port. He is not my image of the character; I was thinking too much of Paul Bowles himself, tall, trim, sandy, self-effacing, a touch closed. Port has to be American, yet he could have been Edward Fox. William Hurt was Bertolucci's first casting, just as Melanie Griffith was to have been Kit. So we have reason to feel fortunate as we first see the characters (and to regard Griffith as the new George Raft of woeful choices). Malkovich has the "slightly wry, distraught" face Bowles imagined on Port. But he has a greater facility. Bowles wrote obliquely; he was flat descriptive, with little metaphor or bravura; yet gradually we feel the rhythm of things not quite mentioned. Malkovich is a master of such ellipses: we seem to see him considering and abandoning things to say or believe, and his dreamy malice and hopelessness is not just Port, it is what *The Sheltering Sky* is about—the uneasiness that comes from description, the plague of doubt (which is what really kills Port). With Malkovich, Port is so gentle, so weary, so sad. Time will close his dread-filled eyes. Yet this ghost is the unsteady measuring stick of comedy and bold desert venture, not so much an accidental tourist as an accident hoping to happen.

Then something goes awry. We are in a café in the port before
the interior journey begins; another encompassing camera movement relates the crowd, the space, the light and our trio. It has
begun not on some incidental nothingness but with the ancient
face of Paul Bowles himself. Very shortly, we hear his voice on the
soundtrack, reading his own words, watching his characters
and—whether he intends it or not—being an Omniscient
Narrator.

The screenwriter Mark Peploe told *Movieline* he believed "there
were a few things that could not be explained without narration." Whatever these were, they are not what Bowles says in the
film: his few observations sound as stilted as old quotes—they
might put a stranger off reading the book. At first, Bertolucci
resisted any narration, but then he relented and had what Peploe
insists was "a very good idea."

He asked Bowles to be the narrator. This suggests that anyone
possessed with genius for realizing events on-screen should shun
all ideas.

There is a documentary about the making of *The Sheltering
Sky—Desert Roses,* directed by Gabriella Cristiani—in which
Bowles discredits the "idea": "I felt I shouldn't be there. Who is
this person watching? Bernardo said, 'You're watching your past
life.' He thinks it's autobiographical. It's no use telling him no.
There's no way of denying that successfully. So I don't try."

Bowles is shot more intriguingly in the documentary than in
the film; he talks more naturally and delivers better sense. Indeed,
the Bowles who puts no hope in explaining is a surer guide to his
own novel than the weathered moon of a face in the café. Far
more deadly in the device is its insertion of ultimate wisdom in a
study of implacable solitude. For these people, the sky is the
only shelter—albeit a deluding one—and it is a dire error to put
a guru on-screen. Moreover, once Bowles has been enlisted, the
film is obliged to keep him around. Thus the stupefying ending
is in prospect already.

As the movie progresses, its departures from the book become
harder to bear. When Port goes off to encounter the Arab whore

in the novel, he never pays her. Nor is she the sumptuous odalisque Bertolucci has hired. Their embrace in the book is brief and conventional—it is more crucial that Port has set out to provoke danger. He dares his luck by not paying. All is softer in the film—despite the fine placing of the whore's lamplit tent on a downslope beyond the edge of the city. Port pays, and defeats a further attempt to cheat him. The woman is amazingly endowed for this obscure camp; she should be in another desert, in Las Vegas. And Bertolucci has invented her arresting urge to push a breast into Port's open fly. Thus their film encounter leans toward sexual novelty, and the disquiet in Port's marriage is rather trivialized. But faced with so little action in the story, Bertolucci has reverted to his own schemes and found an excuse for sexual discovery. This whore opens more than Port's fly; she enlarges his numb expectations.

When Kit and Tunner take the train south, the movie omits the begging scene in which Kit comes upon the squalor and chaos of the fourth-class compartment. This is the first demonstration that she is a traveler who will go deeper into the unknown than Port; indeed, that she will stumble into the abyss his laconic pessimism anticipates: "for the first time she felt she was in a strange land," and so the ache in the book rolls from one side of the marriage to the other.

On the page, Kit is so afraid the smell of champagne on her will offend the Moslems, she rubs perfume on her face and neck. Her hand "felt a small, soft object on the nape of her neck. She looked: it was a yellow louse." The reader's blindness is given such a tingle of discovery. Kit presses deeper into the throng of Arabs, until she comes upon "the most hideous human face she had ever seen." It is a man with a cavity where his nose should be; she wonders why a diseased face is more alarming than a whole one. The train grinds on, but Kit is transfixed by several horrors: "She was not conscious of time passing; on the contrary, she felt that it had stopped, that she had become a static thing suspended in a vacuum." Eternity has entered into her; her on-the-beat New York identity has faded.

Bertolucci does not show this. He told the *Time* critic Richard Corliss he had filmed the scene but "it played like a catalogue of monsters, a Westerner's condescending vision of Third World squalor." I do not know how such things should be filmed—or why intelligent filmmakers try. Yet there are other passages in the film where Bertolucci comes close to the same insight by expanding on hints from the novel. The scene on the heights above the desert where Kit and Port try to make love is much fuller than in the book. This is not just Bertolucci's atavism for sexual pathology. He has also found a perfect place—a terrible, serene brink of topography made more auspicious by the rim of sunlight on the crest and the promontory of shadow on the plain far below. But the effect has as much to do with the floating camera, the desperation of human gesture and the wounded cry that comes up out of Debra Winger's Kit.

Bowles did not think to show this lovemaking, or did not think of failure consisting of anything so short-lived or intimately particular. But the film's commanding vision of one broken act in the faultless desert is akin to the prose of the novel. For we have been led to the realization Bowles is seeking:

It was such places as this, such moments that he loved above all else in life; she knew that, and she also knew that he loved them more if she could be there to experience them with him. And although he was aware that the very silences and emptinesses that touched his soul terrified her, he could not bear to be reminded of that. It was as if always he held the fresh hope that she, too, would be touched in the same way as he by solitude and the proximity to infinite things. He had often told her: "It is your only hope," and she was never sure what he meant. Sometimes she thought he meant that it was his only hope, that only if she were able to become as he was, could he find his way back to love, since love for Port meant loving her—there was no question of anyone else. And now for so long there had been no love, no possibility of it.

I have to add that, by the time I had written that out, I felt closer to believing there was never much prospect in filming this book—though directors, from Aldrich to Roeg, have dreamed of it for decades. How does film accommodate such shifts of vital thought? The best scene in the film concludes where Bowles begins: Bertolucci sees the failure of two lovers, whereas Bowles wants to convey the unreliability of association. These movie appearances are so much less than the minds in the book; we are distracted by the visibility of even uncommonly effacing actors. The camera can only try to peer at the interaction of breast and fly, the friction of limbs and the procrastinating ardor of corpses-to-be. But the novel deals with the caresses of thought. Even done well, doesn't the movie present a shallower person?

The fallacy of the film comes to a head when Port has died and Kit is on her own, freed and abandoned. In the novel she attaches herself to a passing Tuareg caravan; two Arabs have sex with her, repeatedly, though the book offers no arousing description. Film, on the other hand, can hardly sniff sex without arousal—but without much else. Is Kit raped in the novel? I do not think the word is sufficient. She no longer has enough self to feel simply violated. Things happen to her, in the way the wind reshapes dunes in the Sahara. She has entered into the state where things do not matter as much as "rape" usually matters to us. She is as much without will or identity, pain or pleasure, as anyone horribly wronged in, say, eighteenth-century New Guinea. The world has too much pain for history, Bowles suggests: look at the sky, instead, and admire its deep, forgiving and dishonest blue.

The film is kind to Arabs—I don't know how else to put it. There was Bertolucci's fear of offending on the train—so much more sweeping than Kit's use of perfume. Mark Peploe in print and Debra Winger on NPR have said Tuaregs do not rape people—Paul Bowles got it wrong. The delicate indifference of the novel's sexual traffic was lost to political correctness. Belqassim becomes Kit's lover and sexual liberator, as well as a role for the charms of Eric Vu-An. As soon as Belqassim has a face, the sex has to take on value and affection. In their silent, rapt rapport there is neither consent nor objection exactly, but Kit is thoroughly fucked; she is helped to come, to see bliss, through cunnilingus. Things dour Port never dreamed of are exploding, and Eric Vu-An seems ideal casting for the magical houseboy in such citadels as Beverly Hills. We assume Winger is satisfied the Tuaregs had acquired French oral techniques, and wait to see whether Paul Bowles will amend his novel to accord with the fresh intelligence.

Bertolucci cannot bring himself to have Kit stay with Belqassim—did he poll Tuaregs to test that ending? Or does he know it's too close to novelette fantasies? But he begins to pretend he is going to give us the ending Bowles intended. Kit is expelled by the women of Belqassim's tribe and brought back to civilization. We are not hopeful: Kit has frills of tattoo at her wrists, and Winger's face is sunburnt and blasted into perilous vacancy. We can believe a final silence has fallen on her. A woman from the American consulate is there to see she is shipped home safely. "It's funny," Bowles has this Miss Ferry say. "The desert's a big place, but nothing really ever gets lost there."

In the film, the consular official tells Kit the dogged Tunner is waiting and excited to see her. She leaves Kit in a taxi outside the hotel and goes in search of Tunner. When she brings the still handsome, unmarked man outside, the taxi is empty. There is a brief exhilaration to think that Bertolucci has just gone away, with the book. It does not last. For Kit has veered back to the café, more pilgrim than outcast. Paul Bowles is there still, waiting for her, inscrutable yet quite evidently the answer.

"Are you lost?" he wonders of Kit.

And someone replies—I feel it is more Winger than Kit— "Yes!" with mighty, trite satisfaction. She is close to being saved; an actress, at least, has come home. The elation is very silly, even if, after the filming was over, the impressionable actress remained in Africa awhile to be among the Arabs. (The waywardness of players is often more interesting than the madness of scenarios. There is a moment in the documentary when, skylarking, and playing with the thought of a scene being dangerous to do, Winger cries out, "If I don't come back, would you make sure that my parents don't get Noah?"—her son by Timothy Hutton.)

Yet the book rises to an almost passionate disappearance, so handled that volition is lost in the shifting context that surrounds it. The taxi is irrefutably deserted; its driver knows nothing. Let me quote again from the novel, its last few lines:

> At that moment a crowded streetcar was passing by, filled largely with native dock workers in blue overalls. Inside it the dim lights flickered, the standees swayed. Rounding the corner and clanging its bell, it started up the hill past the Café d'Eckmuhl-Noiseux where the awning flapped in the evening breeze, past the Bar Metropole with its radio that roared, past the Café de France, shining with mirrors and brass. Noisily it pushed along, cleaving a passage through the crowd that filled the street, it scraped around another corner, and began the slow ascent of the Avenue Gallieni. Below, the harbor lights came into view and were distorted in the gently moving water. The shabbier buildings loomed, the streets were dimmer. At the edge of the Arab quarter the car, still loaded with people, made a wide U-turn and stopped; it was the end of the line.

How could any film do that? Consider the unavoidable brutishness of movie and the camera's crushing reluctance to take on doubt. (The camera is a Tunner.)

If the camera were to hold on the empty cab and then gently pan away with the glide of the crowded streetcar behind it, we would become certain Kit is on the car. No matter how casual the movement, the connection is incriminating; and there is no doing it and then denying the linkage—the movies are a poor form in which to tell lies. (Their lies are so passive and automatic they do not need to be told.) A pan asserts that Kit is one of the swaying standees. Then she is alive and possessed by some vestige of purpose. She has escaped, or moved on; she may have a notion of living in the Arab quarter, or in emptier parts beyond it. The sequel of pursuit raises its dull head—surely Tunner would go after her.

Whereas the beauty of Bowles's closure is enigmatic and open. The prose account can notice or feel the streetcar without betting on it. As often as you read the last sentences of the novel, it seems not just impossible but unnecessary to say whether Kit is on the streetcar or whether the ordinary flow of traffic is part of a city and a continuity that no longer know her. She has gone away from the story, and merged with the life outside the frame. As the novel ends, different readers can believe she is free, or nonexistent now; yet most who have traveled with the book will retain both possibilities. The slight yet fateful incident has ebbed away into its surrounds, and in the process Paul Bowles has rendered up the notion that meaning and being do not matter enough to impress the desert or the ceaseless shuffle of the crowd.

Other films have approached this sensibility—and most of them are by Antonioni. In L'Avventura, when Anna vanishes on the island, the process of detection leads into an absence that is metaphorical, spiritual and a premonition of fragile memory. At the end of L'Eclisse, a sustained yet impassive observation continues at the urban intersection where a couple fail to meet. In Blow-Up, the figure of Thomas is erased or swiftly wiped from the green of the park. And in The Passenger (cowritten with Mark Peploe), the Jack Nicholson character has a touch of Port as he surrenders to scenarios and a life other than his own. He goes away from real circumstances he cannot endure or satisfy into a fiction. Once he makes his blind date at the Hotel de la Gloria, the camera wanders into its courtyard in the late day, ruminating, luxuriating, barely hearing the bump of his murder inside.

That prolonged camera movement is one of the most intricate and emotionally subtle the movies have ever dared. It is not just a stylistic parent to Bertolucci's movement, it is a more demanding and compassionate inquiry than he has yet thought to risk. Movement in Antonioni is a sign of the fading will; but in

Bertolucci, too often, it is the flourish of decoration. And so, with far greater departures from Bowles's story, *The Passenger* comes closer to the wistfulness of *The Sheltering Sky.*

A story has stopped, or receded; and we see that life goes on, untidy, yet so mysterious it begins to urge larger questions on us. But these passages expose the fuss and vanity of tightly organized plots. Something else beckons, truer to the camera's capacity for observing without deciding. It is as lovely and abiding as the light, or the spaces that wait to be rewarmed by tomorrow's sun. If there is a future in movies, then somehow they need that air of mere duration and continuity. What else can humor the fearsome convulsiveness of plot? If only the obsessiveness of our few worthwhile directors could look out and away from their cruel conspiracies.

We need some sense of the last movement of *L'Eclisse,* the possibility of a North African town in which Tunner concedes there is no finding Kit, or the last twilight of *The Passenger* ("Hotel Exterior. Sunset. We see the building in medium long shot. The street, passing cars. An everyday life which goes on. It becomes night"). Or even the desolation of Alcatraz and the stretch of night across San Francisco Bay in *Point Blank* after Lee Marvin's Walker has declined to come out of the shadows to prolong the deadly game. . . .

And just suppose if, in *Vertigo,* instead of going into the tank after Kim Novak's fake, seductive dive, James Stewart had looked up, felt that liveliness around the bay—and gone away.

(1991)

How People Die in Movies

The seven screenwriters are decent men and women. Four of their children have been in Non-Violence Awareness programs. The parents ration the children to an hour and a half of TV a day—and they drill the baby-sitters in the rule. They are all devout in the faith that there are too many guns in America. Not to mention greater Los Angeles. They have written letters to senators urging resistance to National Rifle Association pressures. But they have a problem with this script.

"What do we do with Arthur?"

"Arthur's a loose end."

"He did love Dolores."

"And he was useful in our second-act bridge."

"Arthur *was* the second-act bridge. Now he's spare."

"We kill him?"

"We have to. We leave him around, the audience is wondering. How?"

"Arthur could get ill."

"Illness is a year, it's doctors."

"It's got to be quick. We're over two hours already."

"Suppose Roger shoots him? In a fit of hitherto repressed anger?"

"Love it. That makes Roger stronger, which is good for Angie."

"And it gets Roger put away, too."
"Ground clearing."
"We do it as a sudden epiphany. Ten-second scene."
"Bang bang, Arthur."

> *This is the way the world ends*
> *Not with a bang but a whimper.*
> > —T. S. Eliot, "The Hollow Men"

> *Gittes pulls the car door open and Evelyn falls out. Her*
> *face is covered with blood. She is dead, shot through the*
> *back of the head, coming out through her left eye.*
> > —Robert Towne, *Chinatown,*
> > the screenplay

> *The mass of men lead lives of quiet desperation.*
> > —Henry David Thoreau, *Walden*

To illustrate the empire of bang bang, let me list the deaths in *The Godfather,* the original and first part:

- Luca Brasi, one hand pinned to the bar counter with a knife, strangulation inflating his horrified dignity
- Paulie, the treacherous driver, plugged in the back of the head in a parked car, all in serene long shot, while Clemenza takes an easeful leak in the wheat field
- Sollozzo, shot in the forehead so that an odd Indian caste mark puts a dent in his pasta
- Police Chief McCloskey, shot in the throat and the forehead; these two men are left with their tipped-over table in the small Italian restaurant like lovers' clothes thrown off in haste—there is something orgasmic in this double murder; it's Michael getting laid
- Sonny, at the toll booth, with 612 bullets (you count them)
- Apollonia, eager to drive, blown up in the car, her persimmon breasts tossed to either end of the garden

- Vito Corleone, while playing in the tomato plants on a hot day with his grandson
- two Tattaglia brothers shotgunned in an elevator
- Moe Greene, having just put on his glasses, so blood can creep through a cracked lens
- a man in a revolving door
- a man and a woman astonished in bed, naked and then quickly dead
- Barzini and Barzini's man, Barzini only after he has run to the top of some steps so that he may topple down again
- Tessio: we don't see Tessio's death, only his stooped figure being taken away and Abe Vigoda's dreadful glance
- and Carlo, Connie's husband, throttled in a car, his frantic feet kicking out the windshield so that we can see he didn't even take care of his shoes.

That's seventeen, to say nothing of a horse's head, a fish (to let us know where Luca Brasi sleeps) and at least three corpses in a montage. Not to mention Kay's hopes.

Over the years, I have taken it as an axiom that the American eighteen-year-old has seen 20,000 acts of killing in movies and on TV. Most college freshmen with whom I shared this nodded like connoisseurs: few professors had taken their youth so seriously. Yet I am no longer sure how I ever knew this fact. Having totted up one movie (seventeen deaths in 175 minutes), I suspect the statistic is rather conservative. It would be as hard counting the bullets in Sonny as it might be to keep tabs on the deaths in, say, *Sergeant York, Kriemhild's Revenge, The Wild Bunch*, Alan Clarke's *Elephant, Spartacus* or *Tom & Jerry*. Let us agree that we have witnessed a lot of killings. By my age, fifty-two, with more films endured than I can remember, I wouldn't doubt 100,000. Yet in what I will call the rest of my life, I have seen just two dead bodies. From all I can gather, asking around, two is on the high side—enough to be thought a little morbid.

What a marvel that our bang-bang movies are so seldom chided for morbidity. Yet, as I recorded the deaths in *The*

Godfather, I did feel infected or aroused by the sheer exuberance and stylistic slam of the movie. I recalled that aside from *Lolita*: "You can always count on a murderer for a fancy style." In turn, that triggered the recollection of Francis Coppola admitting, long ago:

> You know, I took my kid to see a forty-five-minute assembly of some of the stuff of the old *Godfather* and I said what parts do you like better? He said, "I like when the guys get shot." Everyone is like that. Even when you're shooting the film. The second you're going to do a throat cutting or something, everyone including the crew crowds round.

He's right, of course (and he's no more bloodthirsty than most directors today). Kids—or boys—generally exult in the best balletic death scenes: it may be as close as they ever come to sissyness, preferring style over content. In the late forties and early fifties, getting out of cinemas on Streatham High Road, I galloped to the prairies of Tooting Bec Common to reenact death scenes. My friends and I vied for the spectacular bits in these remakes: it was fine to be John Wayne on the bare land that would become the Red River D ranch, but so much more liberating to be Don Diego's man who is tumbled from the saddle by Wayne's shot. Or Edmond O'Brien running through the streets of *D.O.A.*, clutching his bright stomach, loaded with irreversible poison, running for his death. Or Elisha Cook, Jr., in *Shane*, lifted off his feet and thrown back in the mud by Jack Palance's guns. Cagney in *White Heat*, seeming to go up like a rocket. There was a blooming in these deaths, a jeté, reaching for beauty. We grazed our knees and dirtied our clothes doing death falls. But we glowed in their rapture.

As time passed, I guessed some actors had the same fun and release in extravagant death scenes. Cagney and Edward G. Robinson were treasured for those cadenzas in which they occupied time and space with their delirious dance of death. "Is this the end of Rico?" Robinson asked in *Little Caesar*. Well, eventually.

Was there anything in movies so much in love with life as these whirling expirations? Slum kids could at least look forward to the brilliant strut and fret of passing.

Cagney's stricken grace leaned toward the fits and fevers of approaching rigor mortis. "Made it, Ma!" in *White Heat* was only a veteran's fond tribute to the death throes from *Public Enemy, He Was Her Man, Angels with Dirty Faces* (one of the first "showtime" deaths, proof that acting can get you over that hump) and *The Roaring Twenties*. Cagney yearned to throw himself about, to smell extinction, tousle his hair and let his eyes see oblivion. He expanded in death scenes, he grew lithe and poetical. It was only then that he could disclose his passion for movement and his love of the precarious. Death gave this would-be real-life radical his greatest sense of insurrection.

If you doubt the nihilistic élan in Cagney's demises, then look at how bitterly Bogart went to his deaths. He never liked losing control. In such predicaments, we feel the truth in Louise Brooks's observation that "Humphrey" was a socially correct young man who liked to keep his cool and his distance. Bogart tensed up when he had to die: his body often folded in on itself, like hired evening dress packed in a suitcase. If he had to "act" in death, it was his worst acting. In *The Roaring Twenties* Bogart is intimidated, whipped and mocked by Cagney, as if he were Liston being taught psychic danger by Cassius Clay. It's notable that in *High Sierra* Bogart's Roy Earle dies in extreme long shot, without benefit of triumphant staggering against the skyline. *High Sierra* was Raoul Walsh (who made *White Heat*), but *Sierra* is drugged by Bogart's depressive reticence. Bogart's glory learned a lot from *High Sierra*: he developed a smoldering, still fatalism, the chance for a few wry words before conclusions he had foreseen. But Cagney's death hound was always lit up by the surprise—the discovery!—of bullets.

We know of actors who held a nearly contractual right not to perish in fiction. To stay the hero, Wayne, Gary Cooper and, more recently, Clint Eastwood walked up and down in the shadow of death, yet kept a beacon key light on their ever more haggard faces. As one of those not swept away by *Unforgiven,* I note the greater historical and artistic plausibility if William Munny had died on his mission rather than revert to that reassuring bringer of death. The film might then conclude with a simple scene of the forsaken Munny children, dying in their cabin from cholera or loneliness. But the Munny who had lost such edge and youth did pick up quickness at the end. Then he rode home in a grim spirit, condemning all the fates and movie conventions that had made him be lethal.

The comfort in Munny's regaining deadly impact surely extends to Eastwood himself. No matter how far this moviemaker has poked and prodded old genres, no matter his candor with age and fatigue lines, he cannot do without looking good and potent. He is—and he knows it—the last classic star. Thus, allegedly, he spent time researching Secret Service agentry for *In the Line of Fire* but still indulged the cockamamie of a sixty-year-old jogging along beside the limo and the sentimentality of a service that keeps such maverick problem children on the payroll. Even then, the ludicrous fun of *In the Line of Fire* depends on John Malkovich's fastidious killer. He is a delicious tribute to the bliss of murderous daydreams. The fantasy appeal of *In the Line of Fire* is a balanced two-hander, but it is Malkovich who knows the whole thing is just a game. It is so often our killers now who are blessed with wisdom and insight. They are the only characters allowed to turn to philosophy or talk for the sake of talking.

It would not be out of order if Malkovich crooned into the phone, "Frank, don't be petulant. You know, and I know, we're just playing checkers for the audience, and they love to think about killing, and you're there just to waste me at the end so they feel OK about it. I've told you all along I'm ready to die for the picture—but, Frank, are you really ready to stop a bullet?"

And Clint is not: the thought of it seems indecent and un-American. On the other hand, Malkovich is a master of all those infinitesimal droops and melancholies that could while away a whole film with dying—"As I Lay Dying" seems to be the dream in Malkovich's remote eyes. Kirk Douglas in that ebullient youth of his seemed to crave horrid execution, agonies to prompt his throbbing cry, and movies where he could be mutilated, marred and generally pecked at by those birds of story who knew his needs. Lee Marvin has the world-weariness that chooses to be a killer-for-hire only to stay awake. Thus, in Don Siegel's *The Killers*, the actor-assassin who is gradually clearing the film of life, mortally wounded himself, can say (to Angie Dickinson), "Lady, I'm just too tired. I haven't got the time." A career and an attitude are made lucid. James Mason was another actor born to see the sense in his own extinction—think of *Odd Man Out*, *North by Northwest* and *Lolita*, or even *Heaven Can Wait*, where he is in charge of death's best hotel.

And who can mistake the self-discovery in William Holden, gazing down from the top of the pool in *Sunset Boulevard*, the hack who finally has a drop-dead story to peddle?

Death is so slick in film, it has become tongue-in-cheek. "If history has taught us anything," Michael Corleone will announce in *The Godfather, Part II*, "it says you can kill anybody." That line portends the resolute evil with which Michael orders his older brother Fredo dead—in a rowboat on desolate Lake Tahoe. It inspires confidence that any Hyman Roth can be taken out in broad daylight at an airport. And it tickles us to think that Michael may have assented to events in Dallas on November 22, 1963—as *In the Line of Fire* makes plain, killing a president is not that difficult.

But Michael's line signals a more pervasive mastery: that movie can kill whomever its weary, plot-crazed eye falls on. It can put Shelley Winters on the bottom of the lake in *The Night of the Hunter* (so that we marvel at the coup); it can consign Janet Leigh to the swamp after a scant forty minutes of *Psycho* (outraging stardom's expectations); it can make a studious tracking of so many serial killers for connoisseurs, so long as the killers are caught before the final crawl—except that after *The Silence of the Lambs* these killers may roam the earth if they are nicely spoken, have discerning tastes, and if they remember to call Clarice now and then.

There's a giggle in the end of *Silence of the Lambs* as Lecter goes a-roaming. There was a more smothered chuckle in the setup for *Sunset Boulevard*, a way in which contempt for Hollywood began to turn against the audience; there is malice and self-loathing in the camp superiority that betrays our disbelief. Long before the clamor to be on death's side, in such titles as *Die Hard, Lethal Weapon, The Terminator* and *Death Wish,* our movies had made deals with the glamour of death. The timing and polish of our well-made melodramas were like the ingenuity of Malkovich's gun in *In the Line of Fire.* They were to die for.

Deathliness is in the mise-en-scène. Think of the killings in *The Godfather:* isn't the consciousness observing them that of a Corleone? These deaths are not messy or untidy. The attitude is proud, masterful, in love with meticulous detail. Nothing in the sensibility disturbs the remorseless efficiency of vengeance, or departs from the managerial pleasure in seeing intricate plans work sweetly.

There is gallows humor in the spatial tranquillity of Paulie's death—the windswept location; Paulie's stupid patience; Clemenza's ruminative urination; the faraway bump of the shot to match the lovely long shot: it is a kill-master's dream with Paulie the spare pin taken out by a dab hand. When Sollozzo and McCloskey get it, we are nearly palpitating with the urge to give it to them—one reason why "they" can kill anyone is because we are such willing, voyeur accomplices. Finally, when the total elimination of enemies is orchestrated with the rite of baptism, we might be witnessing the adorable fit of nuclear physics.

Is there irony in the magnificence? Is Michael being condemned? Watch the sequence again, and there is no escaping our deranged complicity in the lethal arrangement. There is such macabre comfort in feeling a part of the Corleones. The psychic infancy that dreads all strangers has been protected—they have got theirs, and our supreme plan has been vindicated. Michael is patriarch and paranoid, for surely, one day, he will have to eliminate every family member and anyone who knows.

It's during the grease-quiet, digestive mechanics of films like *The Godfather* that we may recall how frequently film has appealed to fascists. Not that I mean to suggest some directors are readier for the jackboot than others. No, the dilemma is tougher for those of us who love film: something essential to the medium cleaves to uncorrected powers, the magic of plot (or organization) and the chance to stare at death without honoring pain or loss. Still, for the moment let's pull back from that comprehensive unease and offer an intriguing disclaimer—roughly, that these corpses don't smell—none of these guys was ever "alive" anyway. They're toons, for crying out loud!

There is something childlike in the easy dispatch of so many people as quick as a wipe. My four-year-old takes as much delight in hurling himself to many deaths, and in inflicting them with pointed finger and inner-mouth explosions, as I ever did. But did children have this game, or its risk, before moving pictures? Perhaps boys keep the game alive—and most things that depend on boyishness are becoming harder to sustain. Yet there are plenty of decent film critics, some of them women, who seem untroubled by the extended boyhood of, say, Sam Peckinpah and the very cinematic motto "If they move . . . kill 'em"—the line that introduces Peckinpah's credit on *The Wild Bunch*.

The deaths are easier to face when one gets in the habit of knowing movie deaths are akin to a bucket of dip cleaning out the premises. Dip, you may remember, is the green fluid that brings death or erasure to all toons in *Who Framed Roger Rabbit*. It works in the way water did on the Wicked Witch of the West in *The Wizard of Oz*—Christopher Lloyd's judge dies with the same cry of frustration, "What a world!" that Margaret Hamilton uttered in Oz.

Lloyd's judge actually dies twice. He is first flattened out by a steamroller: this is what reveals his secret tooniness, though it is a cunning conceit of the Zemeckis film to say some characters are flatter than others in movie's two-dimensional illusion. Then the judge reinflates his own balloon and comes on wicked again— with gestures from *The Texas Chainsaw Massacre*—before dip

takes him back to primordial ooze. He is too good a villain for
one death. Zemeckis is so wantonly inventive in *Roger Rabbit*
(and so inspired by other films) I could believe in the judge
bouncing back as often as the cat in *Tom & Jerry* cartoons.
Did that cat ever die? Or were his lives infinite? He was
reduced to fragments, blown to smithereens, electrocuted, pancaked—you think of a way to go, Hanna–Barbera did it—and
always there was the swift fade-out, fade-in, and puss was back
again, ready for worse. He was a character out of Buñuel. When
killing is so easy and such fun, and death so brief, it becomes a
way of life. And not just for card-carrying toons. We know how
reluctant the film business is to let its most vital killers take
retirement. At the end of *Halloween,* the demonstrably deceased
Michael vanished, so that he could return for sequels. As I tried
to puzzle out why Scorsese had made *Cape Fear,* I noticed the
clearly posed cue for Max Cady to grab back once more from the
river, just as Carrie came out of the black earth of her own grave.
The moment passed; it was presumably just a joke about such
tricks. But Cady could have escaped—so burned, so crushed
and drowned that he would be the harder to recognize next
time.

   With death so climactic or constitutional, ghostliness becomes
a subject for movies. Our watching from the dark, intensely
"with" the images yet powerless to intervene in their progress, is
a model for stories in which those left alive may keep some kind
of community with lost ones. After all, the thrust of movies is so
much more imaginary than actual. So there have been films in
which ghosts come back, or the living make a journey to the
realm of the dead. From *Nosferatu* and *A Matter of Life and Death*
to Beatty's *Heaven Can Wait* and *Ghost,* movies have played with
the undead (without having to hire other than the regular actors).
Some of those films have resorted to "ghostly" special effects,
superimposition, et cetera. Yet, truly, no tricks are required. No
one on-screen has a real life or corporeality. The films keep playing long after the actors die. These are toons reread as appealing
solids by our fond credulity.

Ghost hints at a way movies might—on the scent of Shirley MacLaine and Marianne Williamson—burrow into the self-help of projection. In several recent movies, there are wishful thinkings beyond the grave, psychic schmoozings: in *Field of Dreams*, Kevin Costner has the chance to meet his dead father again, so that the load of misunderstanding can be rolled away. That's not what I want an art form to offer. But that won't deter the development, and who knows if movie isn't less an art than just one of those fun boxes the Good Guys offer. We may not be far from a household video facility that could take all the hours of home movie of a loved one and then put that passed-away person into computer regeneration, so that those left behind have a houseguest-ghost to chat with.

Already, TV commercials (today's pioneering) have worked this magic with the look and sound of dead stars. And there are rumors of Jurassic Parks in northern California where that readiness is poised for new feature films—with Bogart and Louise Brooks together again at last—if only the legal details can be worked out. The one interest in the actual *Jurassic Park* was that such ghosts shared a frame with the very pale humans Spielberg had time for. Most of the time, the seams didn't show. But suppose next that we could resurrect and write dialogue for Elvis and Marilyn? Or you could have your own home video tête-à-tête with the star/celebrity of your choice—the star as ultimate pet.

The bullet goes in, and life goes out. Movie prefers it as an instant, switchlike adjustment, without suffering or waiting. Yet so much of death is in those two grim departments. How do we stand up for the very few deaths, and corpses, we may meet in our lives? They are unscripted, no matter the anticipation; and they are not there for slow-mo analysis. Are there moments in films when we have a better than bang-bang understanding of what cessation means for the passer-on and those left behind? I can think of film deaths that move me, or give me a sharper sense of the precariousness of life. In every case I'm going to list, somehow, life remains the subject:

- The deaths in *The Missouri Breaks* are epic and lugubrious, undignified yet very skilled, but the best is Lee Clayton's, asleep after his horse pissed during his love song, then awake to the snap of bracken or sinews, his own vain efforts to breathe or stay calm at Tom Logan's dry inquiry, "You know what woke you up? Lee, you just had your throat cut."
- In *Pat Garrett and Billy the Kid,* Slim Pickens realizes he has a death wound while James Coburn is still fighting L. Q. Jones. But the music rises for his death, and leads him down to the river (Pickens has been building a boat to "drift out of this damn territory"). His woman, Katy Jurado, follows him, and they gaze at each other by the water as he holds his startled face and his belly wound up to the evening light. And then we see that Coburn (Garrett) is watching the death and taking it in as evidence and responsibility. For he had hired Pickens away from the boatbuilding. And then there will be Garrett camped by another river, half an hour and months later in the film, as a vagrant family drifts by on a raft.
- In Renoir's *The River,* the little boy Bogey is entranced by the cobra at the end of the garden. He is warned. But he wants to charm the snake, and one afternoon he goes too close. We never see the cobra strike. There is just the boy's sprawled body. The loss comes not long after a siesta in which the several members of the household are seen sleeping, with the camera simmering on their breath. The boy dies, a new child is born. This easily sounds trite as a philosophy, but Renoir's structure, his camera and the sense of breathing transform the quietism so that it becomes as steady and flowing as the river and the flooding sitar music.
- There is the moment when Isabel dies in *Ambersons,* with the major gazing into the fire, speaking of the sun as the source of life—Richard Bennett rambling very near his own death— and then the fateful word, the major jerked out of his reverie, ready to die, and the rapacious embrace that Fanny has for George. Family in a few seconds.
- And then there is the death of Tom Joslin in *Silverlake Life,* the

documentary made by Joslin and his lover, Mark Massi, as they both faced the destiny of AIDS. In this case, it is the entire film, the ending of which never enjoys doubt. It takes a movie like this to remind us how gradually and faithfully death comes. Bodies diminish and waste; the lesions of sarcoma spread and join; courage and tact fail. Joslin sometimes rants out of fear and horror at what is happening to him. Months and years come down to ninety minutes or so of film, and we see Joslin seconds after he has died—a skull with skin, yet freed or deserted by life and the illness. We see so few authentic deaths on film, *Silverlake Life* can put you off movies.

I saw *Silverlake Life* on June 15 on PBS. Two days later I flew to England for my father's funeral. I was reading Philip Larkin on the plane because, for many Englishmen, Larkin has been like a life-sustaining illness: he had a sensibility I loathed, but a capacity with words that was piercing. And now, eight years after his death, Larkin is being revealed—in his *Selected Letters* and a biography by Andrew Motion—as a furtive, less than honest man, darker and more afraid than he could admit. I felt there was some kind of kinship between Larkin and my father. My father left my mother when I was being born. He lived with another woman for more than forty-five years. But he came home to us weekends and Christmases, and he never once said anything about the double life. This is Larkin in "Aubade" (he never sold the movie rights):

> I work all day, and get half-drunk at night.
> Waking at four to soundless dark, I stare.
> In time the curtain-edges will grow light.
> Till then I see what's really always there:
> Unresting death, a whole day nearer now,
> Making all thought impossible but how
> And where and when I shall myself die.
> Arid interrogation: yet the dread
> Of dying, and being dead,
> Flashes afresh to hold and horrify.

Before London, I went to Dublin to see my oldest friend, Kieran Hickey. We met on the steps of the National Film Theatre in London thirty-three years ago. He was the first naturally eloquent person I had ever known—smart, gruff, lyrical and caustic. He was a filmmaker, and a good one: he made documentaries and short fiction films in Ireland—*Faithful Departed, A Child's Voice, Exposure, Criminal Conversation, Attracta, The Rockingham Shoot*. I went to see him because he was set for double bypass surgery on June 28.

We had a fine weekend in Dublin, his house on the south side full of friends and all the things he collected. We watched a tape of *Bitter Victory*, letter-boxed yet incomplete, but with that scene where Richard Burton's officer remarks on his skill at killing the living and saving the dead. We watched Stephen Frears's wonderful *The Snapper*. Then I went to England for the funeral. My father was eighty-four. He had had a stroke from which he never regained consciousness. I went to the funeral home to see him in his coffin before the cremation.

It was him, yet the fierceness had gone, and with it the last hope that he and I would ever talk about our history. You see, I had never quite been able to make him tell me; but instead there were ways in which I had imitated him. He was cremated and I came back to America.

Kieran had his operation. It was a complete success. The news from friends in Dublin could not have been more positive. Two weeks after the operation he was to be moved from the hospital to a nursing home for further convalescence. But in a matter of hours he developed a pulmonary embolism and died. The day after he died I got a card from him, written from the hospital—"My improvement is marked." You have to believe me: he would have chuckled and said, "Oh, dear, yes," for he loved irony.

The limit to death in most of our films is that it shows what poor attention they pay to life.

(1993)

Ask the Anaconda

"Face it, honey," said the editor at *Movieline,* old enough to be my daughter. "This is your big chance." There was something solid and health insured behind her brisk expertness, as if to say that, after all, nothing else I had ever done amounted to much, not even the Ph.D. at Brown on staircases in the films of Max Ophüls. No, I had the feeling this might be my *last* chance. If I was ever going to convince anyone that I could do serious trash with commitment, this assignment had to work.

"We have been after her for five years," said the editor. "Not that I thought she'd last this long. Wouldn't you have picked her as a destruct?"

It was an astute remark (this editor is top-notch). And the great lady of the screen in question—She—had always had eyes that expected (or promised) trouble. That famous Oklahoma childhood picture—windswept by the roadside—had a fierceness that few of us would stop for. She is all she is on-screen because of some desperate, uncomfortable knowledge that would send most moderate, sensible women into steady family life and obdurate perseverance with insoluble problems—the life that leaves many Americans ready for the rush and dream of a silly movie, once a month. In her face we see a kind of courage or disaster that frightens decent people. It is both noble and destructive. That must be the attraction.

She was and is . . . well, as you will soon understand, I am
going to have to invent a name here, just as I'm not going to give
the exact address. A movie magazine, even *Movieline,* has certain
codes of responsibility. We cannot have the world arriving like a
pack of rabid dogs on her sprinkled lawn. Such animals deserve
a little constitutional protection. So She for now is . . . well, what
shall we say, do we need a contest? Gloria Stannard? Sukie
Whybrow? Dale Harkness? Yes, I like Dale Harkness, though in
my heart she is always She.

"Everything is set," the editor told me. "There is the address."
She pushed a typed card across her battleground desk. "You will
be there at 10:30 a.m., and you have ninety minutes. Don't let
them mess with the ninety. If she has to go to the john or take a
call, and if you can't be there, that time is added on afterwards to
make ninety. Ninety is non-negotiable."

You can imagine what I was meant to do in ninety minutes:
wait out her beauteous, healthy openness, break down the practiced armor of pleasantry, bring her to depths of candid and even
foulmouthed reflection, getting in the process the most piquant,
previously unpublished dish on her ex-husband, the new movie,
her "problems" with food, drink, narcotics, other men, intrusive
fans, money, CAA, PMK,* the IRS and the latest religion in her
spiritual cafeteria.

"With time for a little light flirt on the side," I supposed, as
ironically as I could manage.

The editor's eyebrows shot up in a Northridgy way. "Don't
fuck up," she said. "She has to be on the cover. We have astounding art already." Her hand swept across some color prints of la
Harkness, alluring and somehow threatened on a balcony looking
out over downtown at magic hour, coppery hued with her skin
glowing, her eyes like guns. "I aged getting these pictures," the
editor complained—yet they looked so natural, so entirely L.A.
"In the text I want the madness there for anyone to see, but I
don't want to give any of her people so much as an arrow slit for

---

*PMK is one of the leading public relations companies in Hollywood.

comeback. Get her talking, and after thirty minutes she'll be wild." Dale Harkness did not have a sedate reputation.

"Of course," I said, trying to be soothing. After all, why should anyone raised to the rhythm of movies regard ninety-minute roller-coaster rides on some beauty's soul as anything but traffic as usual? "Get her," said the editor in a not entirely kindly way. "Do this and you could write our next Sharon Stone cover!"

And so I found myself on the Thursday at tennish on a perfect, still June morning, prowling the byways of upper Benedict Canyon. For I had arrived at the place early, just to guard against any unforeseen difficulty. I had time to kill. I parked a little way up the road, simultaneously in the droop of a crimson rhododendron bush and the wistful lilt of Shirley Horn on my car tape player.

As I waited, 10:12 blinking into 10:13, marveling at how Shirley Horn makes "Disappear!" so startling but inevitable on *Get out of Town,* a black limo slid up the lane, pulsing as it moved through the dappled light, stopped outside the entrance I knew to be hers, waited and then, as a young black woman emerged from the entranceway, hands reached out of the limo and gave her a brown-paper carton large enough to contain an average-sized head. Then the limo made a prolonged shuffle of a U-turn in the lane, its muscular sheen caught like a beetle in the narrows, until at last it eased away. What mission made for so contorted a maneuver? Designer yogurts, a parcel of scripts from CAA or a rare orchid from some prince of corruption?

But I had my own business. I tested my tape recorder once more, and listened to my own whisper, "Here I am, waiting for Dale Harkness, on one of those perfect poised days that can seem suspicious in Los Angeles." I put the recorder in my bag, checked again on the extra tapes in their pouches, the typed sheets of questions, my two sharp pencils.

I got out of my car, locked it and sauntered down the lane to the entranceway. There were electronically operated gates and beyond them a short, very steep driveway, above which I could see the peak of the house's roof. No need to take my car in, I thought, not with that testing incline. I pressed the bell—nothing. I pressed again and after a long interval the buzz of static came on. I heard bumping in the background, with what seemed like cursing, and then intimate breathing and "Yes?" This had to be Harkness herself. Don't we know that voice?

I gave my name. There was no response, but the same voice seemed farther away, talking to someone else. "Shut up, I'm listening." Then it was back again, in my ear, "Say again."

I repeated my name.

"From the agency?"

"It was all arranged, Miss Harkness. Ten-thirty."

Nothing more was said, but the gates uttered a clicking noise and then parted arthritically. I went in, and the blind gates seemed in a hurry to shut me in. They clanged shut, trembly and anxious.

I went up that steep slope and discovered that it was a rampart. Beyond and below was the Harkness estate—a two-storey house, in the dark windows of which I could see the brilliant flowers of the garden reflected, and even my own hesitant figure. A tiered pool dropped, by way of a waterfall, to lawn and a lime-colored tennis court. The whole thing was wrapped around by the rampart on one side and by an audience of dark trees on the other. Yet already, at 10:30, this inner bowl was a sun trap.

I know I pondered on the natural composure and photographic rapture of the place and the legendary disorder of Dale Harkness's life and career. But, of course, she would be within somewhere, waiting, watching me through the smoked glass windows, ready to stride forward, her heels smacking on the Portuguese *azulejo* tiles. "Hi, you must be David. I'm Dale"—as if we were perfect in the parts, and friends at last free to talk.

"Come in, quick, I need you *now,* love cup." I had not even rung the bell when the heavy door opened and the unmistakable frenzy of Dale Harkness grabbed me, her cool hand clamped on my wrist and pulled me into the hallway of her house, where two large men were standing, one in dark glasses, the other shifting a gun from one paw to the other as if guessing its weight.

"There!" said Harkness, in panicky triumph. "My bodyguard. My new bodyguard."

"This is your bodyguard?" asked the man in dark glasses in a rather offensive way.

"Betcha!" she said, sounding like a little girl in a game of dare. She *was* Dale Harkness, yet she was more ragged and less finished than I had anticipated. But these two men had a dumb, intimidating presence that could have taken the shine off a star.

"He don't look like a bodyguard," said the man with the gun. The gun was by then generally pointing at me, indicating my flaws as cast.

So I said, "It'd be pretty dumb, wouldn't it, if idiots like you knew I was a bodyguard?" I just said it, without a thought. I'm sure my delivery was feeble, or in need of direction, but it was a whole sentence, with a rhythm, and it was absolutely evident from the way the two men stopped to look at each other that it counted as a line.

"Right!" yelled Dale Harkness, like a cheerleader dazzled to find her team can play.

"So," said the one in dark glasses, "he's your bodyguard and you still owe us ninety-three thousand dollars."

"Ninety-three thousand dollars is picayune! It's peanuts!"

"Keeps you bushy tailed," said the man with the gun.

"So fucking what! So what is Arthur thinking about? Does he know you're here, or did you two creeps come freelancing? Arthur knows I am good for the stuff, and Arthur does not talk about money."

"Lady, he is concerned—"

"He's *concerned* if he knows *you're* here. Right?"

She was in charge now, and it was pretty. The two fellows grew sheepish—I realized that they had no car outside. They had *walked* up to the house. They were amateurs. So I said, "Why don't you two schmucks walk back where you came before the day gets too warm?"

"Terrific!" said Dale Harkness, giving me a tough nod. "They have been arguing here for half an hour!"

Before I could give an opinion on that scene, there was a buzz behind me.

"Shit!" said Dale Harkness. "Deirdre, where *are* you?"

A black woman—the one I had seen outside—drifted into the hallway. "What is it, girl?" she asked.

"Where were you?"

"Making the white chocolate fudge. What you mean where was I?"

Had this very relaxed Deirdre been at hand throughout the conversation I had interrupted? She seemed so casual, sleepy even, not fazed by the two thugs, yet regarding me a little skeptically.

"Who's this?" she asked, nodding at me.

"There's someone at the door," snapped her boss. "You are supposed to handle that, you know."

"I had my hands in fudge." Deirdre was still licking her long fingers clean, one by one, reveling in the sweetness.

"He's the guard," said Dale.

Deirdre looked dubious. "Well, first, he can run these jerks off."

"Oh, he will, Deirdre. And I don't want any mouth from you."

Deirdre rolled her eyes and pushed a button that opened the gate. In an instant, a fresh-faced Japanese in FedEx blues was at the front door with an oblong box and a large envelope.

"Livestock," said the FedEx man.

"It'll be the anaconda," said Dale Harkness.

"Hey," said the man with the dark glasses, removing his shades to show the importance of what he had to say, and looking at his watch. "It's after ten-thirty."

"And you're still here," said Dale, exasperated, signing for receipt.

"What I mean is"—he struggled with the propriety of the case. "FedEx guarantees ten-thirty. You know? You get a refund." His buddy was nodding vigorously in the spirit that makes for jury solidarity.

"Listen, fuckhead," said Dale Harkness. ("I beg your pardon," she asided to the bewildered Japanese.) "Let me tell you something, you wretched puke. In this world—and I have been through this world, a movie star has wounds and regrets beyond your belief— there is *nothing* I would stake my life on more than Federal Express. They are rock solid. I have been in the South American desert on location and they have delivered—no matter what, with a smile and no tips allowed! This gentleman here has brought me a Paraguayan anaconda, which is not playtime. Look at him—he is smart and polite and he is *here*! And the anaconda is happy! You are here, and you should be in nursery school still, working on getting your glasses on and off. He is a servant in the cause of order."

"Anaconda velly tlicky," the Japanese burst out.

Dale Harkness paused. She blew a wisp of curl off her face and then winked at me.

"I know," she told the servant in the cause of order. "Anyone with a grain of decency would know. If I ever joined a religious order it would be you people."

The hood grunted and shrugged. He put his shades back on, perfect the first time. Spurred, I indicated the door with a tilt of my shoulder—enough to set off rheumatic twinges. But his buddy was needy still. He asked Deirdre, "Could we get a glass of water?" Deirdre looked at her boss, who spat out "Water!"

"Like a little Pellegrino?"

"We got Evian," said Deirdre.

"Same diff," said the guy.

"They don't touch the fudge," warned Dale Harkness.

She was scanning the FedEx deliveries. The oblong box had several airholes in its Perspex lid. A little way below these lay the amazing folds, vermilion, green and coffee colored, of the anaconda. Dale held the whole box in her arms, and she partook of some reverie with the exotic beast. I concluded it must be for her.

Then she broke out of her trance, parked the box on a side table and ripped at the envelope. Out fell a paperback book—and with it my heart (I believed I had all the remaindered copies): the university press publication of my thesis, "Staircases in the Films of Max Ophüls."

"Oh, right," she said, seeming more intimidated by the book than by the reptile. "This is the weasel from that magazine who's coming tomorrow. Where's the damn tape?"

"What tape?" asked Deirdre.

"They were going to send me one of the guy's movies."

"The guy from the magazine has made movies?"

"Of course not, you dope. What's he doing writing about them if he's made them? This *Offals. Letter from an Unknown Lover*— something like that. Why does everyone fuck up these days?"

"*Woman*," I said, but no one noticed.

"They don't care enough, darlin'," said Deirdre. She seemed practiced in these exchanges. "Not like you care."

Dale looked up at Deirdre, suspicious, as if she too heard the possibility of deadpan ridicule. Then she looked at me.

"What was your name?"

"David," I said. Then and there, thirty minutes or so inside the gate, and I could have explained everything. I could have given my whole name, fondly laid claim to the paperback she was holding and said, Well now, how did this little misunderstanding occur? This fuckup? Because here I am for a chat, Miss Harkness, a day early. What a difference a day makes. But I just said, "David."

"I can't stand that shirt, David. You don't mind me saying this, do you? I mean, if I'm going to have to look at you and have you around, and I'm paying, why should your shirt hurt me? Take Baby." She nodded at the anaconda. "Put him in the bath in the blue bathroom—so long as Raymond's out of there." She giggled. "Or even if he isn't. And then go to wardrobe, it's the room next door, and get yourself another shirt. Teal maybe, I am thinking, solid teal."

I was startled by the weight of the anaconda's box. "I tip it into the bath?"

"With an inch of water. Warm water. No soap. Then later we'll put him out in the zoo. They need to get adjusted. You have a thing about snakes?"

The two toughs, replenished, were on the point of leaving, and they chuckled at my squeamishness.

"Hey, Dale," said the gunman. "You want, we can handle Baby."

"Going, sweetheart?" she said, ignoring the offer. "Aren't you forgetting something?"

"Forgetting?"

"The stuff? You didn't come up here empty-handed. You've got a fat three-pound bag for Mama."

"We was expecting to be paid," said the man in shades.

"And you were told to make a delivery." She held out her hand until, grudgingly, Shades found a plastic bag of what I assumed was cocaine and draped it on Dale's arm.

"Miller time," said Deirdre.

Miserable and defeated, the overweight frighteners trooped out of the house while I went upstairs to deposit the boa and reform my image.

What would you have done? Would you have come clean, made your apologies and got out? Or would you have understood immediately that here was a god-given chance for the journalist to observe the underside of Harkness life—the chaos that would be tidied away in any regular interview? You must not suppose I have any unusual disposition toward courage or recklessness. Also, I did foresee Dale's explosions if the truth came out—and I knew already that she was more steely and dangerous than the armed enforcers who had settled for Evian. Maybe I had seen too much already—too much wildness, too much inadvertent absurdity, too much basic cocaine—just to be let go. She was trapped, without knowing it yet; but I was a prisoner, too, pinned by this lunatic luck of someone getting the day wrong. I might also be soaking up a classic scoop—Dale Harkness off guard!

Yet I will admit something else: I was somehow carried along on the sheer momentum of this unexpected "scene." This was not like life. It was enough to utter a few lines to keep the action moving. And the sensation was exhilarating. I did not want to disappoint Dale Harkness, or have the game end. I was excited just to be there with her and feel the fictional energy beating off her—like heat from an oven.

So the bizarre day went on. The bathroom I had been sent to was occupied. Or rather the bath in it was. Raymond proved to be an elderly gentleman of rather scholarly look who was reclining in the warm, soapy water reading *The Wall Street Journal* and humming Fred Astaire songs.

"His turn, is it?" he asked, folding up the paper and nodding charitably at the box of anaconda. He was like a benevolent grandfather accustomed to the follies of the household.

"If it's no trouble," I said.

"Not at all, old chap. Are you an anaconda man?"

"No," I told him. "I'm a bodyguard."

"Really?" He smiled sweetly. "Well, welcome. I'll be getting out."

He made to raise himself from the waters, so I began to retreat, mumbling about my need of a teal shirt.

"Next door," he said. "Have an explore in there."

The next door gave entrance not just to a closet but to a room fitted out with clothes racks and chests of accessories. A steaming Raymond came to share the hunt, in a voluminous dark blue robe, until a suitable shirt was found for me.

"Oh, yes, very nice," he said admiringly, when I put it on. "She's usually right in these things. Anything else?"

He directed me to shelves of hats, to accessories such as sword sticks, false mustaches, medals, monocles, parasols and many guns. It was a small wardrobe and props department, somewhere between the necessary support for ongoing productions and a dress-up trunk for children's play.

"Raymond," I asked, "what do you do in this house?"

"I run the numbers, as it were. Look after Dale's holdings and commitments. The in and out, red and black. I'm the Maurice Tempelsman of the organization, you might say. Though *organization* is a grand word. I'm very fond of her."

"Of course."

The gentle old man could pick a fellow admirer. "Isn't she a heroine?"

"Remarkable," I agreed, for I longed to have this old man say more than I could know about her.

He smiled at me. "It's so easy," he said, "to see the worst. The publicity side of it all. Don't they call her the Heart of Darkness?"

"I have heard that. Have you known her long?"

He laughed. "Do you know that old snapshot of her?"

"The child by the roadside in Oklahoma?"

"Actually it was north Texas. Everything is a little wrong by now. I took that picture. I was on an expedition hunting butterflies at the time, when I *saw* that face. I could never look at a butterfly again with quite the same awe."

Now, some of you will be Dale Harkness fans and authorities enough to know what golden stuff this is—never offered anywhere before! Moreover, there *I* was, magically placed in this strange household—the princess, her droll, black attendant, rogue warriors and this man old and wise enough to be her Merlin.

"By the way," I asked Raymond. "Her bodyguards?"

"Well, these days one has to take what one can get."

"I see," I said, lying to prolong the talk.

"Bodyguards aren't what they used to be. It's a calling now that attracts . . . unstable material. We've had some who were wrecks. Feeble creatures she had to hold together."

"And she could do it."

"A word of advice?" the old man wondered.

"Please."

"Guard her spirit first. Her nerves. A little grace goes a long way."

"Thank you, Raymond."

"We're all here for her," he told me.

Beginning to luxuriate in my shirt—it was more kingfisher than teal, but designer Italian—I made my way down the Harkness staircase. I haven't yet had space or opportunity to describe this marvel to you—uncommonly wide, in glowing walnut, with those old-fashioned low steps, and a fine Bessarabian rug with rods and runners in polished brass. And then the banister! There are houses still in Los Angeles where you glimpse the old glory and marvel that once there were haciendas that looked out on orange groves and empty fields of green. It was a place where the age of Zorro coexisted with automobiles and talking pictures.

"Wait a minute!"

There was an alcove at the turn of the staircase, with a mullioned window and a bench seat to rest on. Dale Harkness was there, drawn back in the shadow as far as possible and gazing out in anxious scrutiny. From there one could see the lane and the hood of a car parked beneath a red rhododendron bush. It did look ominous.

"See it?" she hissed. She had drawn me close to her. I could see a pulse jumping in her throat. Had she been at the cocaine already, or was this simple paranoia? I could smell her skin.

"Isn't parking permitted?" I wondered.

"No one parks there."

"It's quite innocent, I'm sure."

"It could be a stalker," she said softly, almost to herself, as if this was an old dream.

"A stalker?" It was not a word I was used to. I had visions of jobbing gardeners coming in to stake drooping hollyhocks.

She turned to look at me. "Don't you even think like a bodyguard?"

"I don't believe you have anything to be alarmed about. In fact, I know there is nothing."

"Oh, how do you know?"

"That is my car."

I saw her eyes darting this way and that, experimenting with comedy, double cross, outrage and perplexity.

"Why'd you park out there?"

I took a deep breath. "I was worried about the steep slope inside your gate."

As if for the first time, she studied me. "Or maybe *you're* the stalker."

"Me?"

"Yeah." She was flirting, but she wasn't sure. She was making a scene of it, and fear was a little aphrodisiac. "Even in that . . .

turquoise sort of color, or do I mean aqua, you're better as a
stalker than a bodyguard. Have you come here to get me, David?"
Did she know? Had she worked out the error in scheduling?
Was she teasing me? Was it her wicked design that this unpick-
ing of me was arranged to take place on a staircase? Was she
truly as adorable as I felt, as close to her as conspiracy or the
dread of being stalked allowed? Readers, I kissed her, to shut her
up or to shut those knowing eyes of hers. Why? It was as if the
kiss was already there, hanging there like a bobbing apple, and all
I had to do was lean forward and mouth it. She came toward me
and joined in the kiss without restraint—if only to get the taste of
stalker or protector.

"What time is it?" she murmured.

I looked at my watch. "Twelve," I said. My ninety was over—
yet not properly begun.

"We have to get Max."

"Who is Max?"

"Max is the child. The light of my life." She kissed me again—
Dale Harkness—just in a spirit of inquiry or browsing. "I have
Max in the afternoons this week. He's a spina bifida baby." The
beauty of her mouth saying *spina bifida.*

"Your child?" Who had ever heard of that detail in the Harkness history?

But all she said was "He calls me Mommy."

"How old is he?"

"Seven. The anaconda is for him." She kissed me one last time,
taking half a minute over it.

"Right," she said. "You sure you're not a stalker?"

Now again, you will tell me, I could have spoken up. I could
have stepped back, told my rising hard-on to behave and simply
explained to this . . . this creature, that there had been a misunderstanding. I could have beaten a woeful retreat with threats of
lawyers hurled after me. Or this woman might have nailed me,
shot me dead in the back at the threshold. I could see the head-
lines: "*Movieline* Writer Missing" and then, a few days later,
"Author Washed Up on San Pedro Beach." Everything tidied

away, with my few remaining possessions in the wardrobe room, choices waiting for future victims. How could I tell this woman I had been kissing her under false pretenses? So I kissed her again and went downstairs.

"You carry that bag everywhere?" she called softly after me. Indeed, I had not let go of the bag or the recorder. "What you got in there? Your operating tools? Or your lunch? Think we won't feed you?"

I stopped to look up at her—a staircase shot! so glorious!—"I need these things," I struggled to explain. It sounded childish.

"Bodyguard stuff, I bet." The light was falling on her sideways from the window that looked out on the lane. There must have been some green in the glass, or foliage nearby. She was untidy, but the light rimmed her mock belligerent manner. There she was, a little movie in the alcove, and I was the camera and the crowd. If you fall in love on a staircase, you know the fear of falling.

"Where do we get Max?" I said weakly.

"We go to his school. We'll take my car. It's got his chair in it— and I can handle the slope." She grinned at me, standing there, holding the light. "When I'm not out of my skull," she added.

Her car was a white Volvo, and she did drive us down to the school. There was some sort of festival there, with parents and nannies to watch the little performance put on by the children. Dale had dark glasses on, and she wore just the old, pale jeans and the sleeveless T-shirt she had been wearing all morning. No one seemed to recognize her, and she was not really more striking than a dozen of the other mothers or au pairs. This was one of the most select schools in Beverly Hills, with a dedicated Jeffrey Katzenberg room for quiet times.

Max sat on the ground, braced by a chair, watching all the games go on around him. He wore pebble-lens glasses. His head easily tipped from side to side, and he had imperfect control of his arms and hands. His legs were diminutive and folded up under him. But he laughed a lot of the time, especially whenever one of the children stopped to touch him. He was like a mascot to them. Dale did not present herself to Max, let alone embrace him. Rather, she managed to be behind him and in the background.

The other parents were constantly invading the dances and small games of the children. They were drawn there by their cameras and their video recorders, some as immense as the backpacks worn by spacemen. The event was not a thing in itself so much as something to be recorded on film and tape. It was grim and foolish the way the adults intruded on the performance, or blocked it, and bumped into each other all the time, striving to find a shot that had only innocent children in it and no other preying camerapeople. The recording was nearly religious—so many of the adults were on their knees, seeking the ineffable and longing for relics of the occasion. Dale was one of the few adults not part of this tasteless witness. But no one watched with more need.

I had to lift Max and carry him to the car. This made me as nervous as I had been with the anaconda. But the boy welcomed me with his vague, unsteady benevolence; he had great warmth and presence, but no observable personality. In the car, Dale sat beside him in the back, holding his hand and caressing him while I drove us . . . back. I nearly wrote *home*.

The rhythm of the day changed. Deirdre gave us all lunch—sandwiches and fudge, with a salad for Dale, who also did a little cocaine there in the kitchen without concealment. There was mail that had come. Raymond had business papers and checks for her to sign. She was on the phone to her agent, and then, in the space of thirty minutes or so, she had a conference call with Sydney Pollack and Warren Beatty and then one with Pollack and Anthony Hopkins, with finally Beatty calling back for a private checking-up. This was all for some venture I could not identify and something that everyone involved hailed as a bright and shining idea. In half an hour, it was over, buried, and the parties were telling each other to stay in touch.

For the next hour or two nothing happened without being interrupted. There were alarms when connections were lost or when some vital person was unavailable; unavailability was immediately taken as a bad omen, rather than just the fact of being in the bathroom or talking to a mother. Dale had her trainer come by for fifty minutes in the gym. Two Korean gardeners went across the lawn with intricate machines. Sprinklers arced this way and that. I watched small rainbows come and go. Exercise had to stop as scripts came by messenger, and then there were calls to water the new plants. There was planting going on inside and out.

For that part of the day, Dale and "her people," in the house and elsewhere, were in a furious pursuit of things that had to be done, or of movies that had to be made. Whole enterprises rose and fell, and I guessed that every day provided the same tumult.

How could real hopes survive in this chronic uncertainty? How could any prospect inspire enough belief to last? I saw how in the picture business most projects die aborted long before anything is shot. Death is taken for granted.

Max was put in the garden and in the part of the house where animals were kept. The anaconda was set beside him, and he chuckled over the great surgings in its cold skin and the rasping noise it made on the ground. It was my task to watch them both to be sure there was no mishap. But they survived together in some affection or helpless understanding, and sometimes the coils of the snake seemed to be supporting Max's enfeebled spine, like a throne.

But the two of them tired. Max was put down to nap in a cool room, while the anaconda sprawled and baked in the sun. Then a weary peace came to the house—it was nearly five—and just when it was needed, the first slant of shadow fell on the garden and the patio. I was sitting there with a glass of lemonade Deirdre had brought me. She joined me for a while and painted her fingernails out there in the sun.

"Does Max stay here?" I asked.

"No, she'll take him back. He goes back at nights."

How could I pursue the matter? Was Max a vital, treasured part of Dale's existence, or just glorified property?

"They can look after him better there," she said. "He gets his fits, you see." She had a very understanding way of putting it, of seeing how it would be beyond Dale.

"But she goes away—on films?"

"Oh yeah, but he remembers her. Anyway, she does everything for him. I mean, she pays for the home and his schooling. He's got his trust fund. Weren't for her, Max would be shut up somewhere."

I thought I dared ask her: "Is Max her own son?"

"Oh," she said dreamily, "I wouldn't know about that."

There were sounds behind us, of someone coming into the shaded living room. It was Dale, wearing a caftan now.

"You want to watch a movie?" she called out idly to the pair of us.

"Nice day like this?" said Deirdre. "I'm going dancing."

"Behave yourself," drawled Dale from the gloom of the room.

"That's my business, girl," said Deirdre. "You don't hear me givin' you lessons."

So, as if I might be proof of warnings unuttered, I strolled into the living room, where Dale was crouched over, putting a tape in the VCR. She sat on the sofa, and there was space beside her in the soft cushioning.

"What's this movie?" I said, though I knew the music for *Letter from an Unknown Woman* by heart. (You may not know this picture, readers, but you should—and it *is* available. Dale Harkness found a copy, and so may you. You should perhaps have it on in the background as you read this last part of the story.)

"It's something the guy who's coming to talk to me tomorrow likes. I thought I'd take a look at it."

"I'm amazed that a movie star should be so careful."

"That's nice," she said, her feet up on the coffee table—sandals dropped off—and there was a bowl of cocaine beside her from which she dipped now and then. She moved it so that it was between us. "Why wouldn't I care?"

I shrugged. "You are so busy."

"I'm so busy doing nothing."

This was true. The aura of excitement and purpose had accomplished nothing. Her day, from what I could see of it, was made equally of great tension or uncertainty and extensive emptiness. The atmosphere was entirely neurotic—frantic or bored—and there was a way in which the aroused energies needed release, in violence or melodrama. I saw how the cocaine might be a retaliation for the hounded soul.

"The interviewer will ask you about *this* film? Won't he want to talk about *your* films?"

"Those people don't want to 'talk,'" she said, matter-of-fact. "They want me to do or say something outrageous. Anything."

"Like what?"

"Like how the powerful people in the business are screwing me. Who I am fucking. How vain and selfish I am—because that fascinates them. And do I *ever* do drugs? Recreationally. Oh no, I say—it's never recreational. Or what are my secret fantasies and does Clinton really call me? They want me to say pull quotes— the bits they print in big type for the kids who don't like to read the whole thing."

"There may be readers who are really interested to know about you."

"They want to look at me and say to themselves, 'Look at that sweet slut.' They want to jerk off over me and they want to imagine me sucking their dick. And they want to think of murdering me."

"No, surely! These are fans."

"You should see letters 'fans' write."

"They are bad?"

"Horrible. Filthy. Degrading. Murderous." She looked at me suffering with every word, and she smiled. "When I look at the camera, I'm looking for those creeps."

"It doesn't disturb you?"

"I'm a disturbed person, David. I depend on it. That gets me up to eight or ten million a picture. So what is happening in this film?"

"Well—" I began. I sketched in the story that had slipped by during our talk. I noted the gorgeous style, the decor, the light, the camera movements, the staircase. I remarked on the astonishing air of youth in Joan Fontaine. Dale hadn't heard of Joan Fontaine. But she liked the picture. She was weeping when it was over, and we were fellow passengers in its grave journey.

"Could I do that?" she said.

"You mean die, like the woman?"

"Update it! I want that story."

"I expect it would be possible. Does the film help you with the interview?"

"Helps me understand the guy."

"Really?"

"He must be sensitive, gentle, romantic, sort of stuffed . . ."

"I daresay."

"I get horny after a good movie," she said, rolling into the cushions, into me, and tipping over the cocaine.

"Why don't you try some?" she asked, laughing to see the spill.

"Your interviewer may never show up."

She was taken aback. "Why not?"

"How long does he get to understand you?"

"Ninety minutes," she remembered.

"Wouldn't hardly take that long," I surmised.

And it didn't. Yet she was ready to say there was more to be had in the way of knowledge. And I would have followed, for I had given myself up by then. But we heard the fearsome crying of a child unlike any I had ever heard, as if imperfection in the bones might affect the sound of weeping and its grasp on despair.

She got up and went away with a speed only possible in a well-trained body.

I was alone, and I knew that now, at last, with darkness falling, I had to go. Raymond was in the hallway, waiting for me or for something. He had the brown paper parcel I had seen handed over so much earlier on that long, hot summer's day.

"Going?" he whispered. "Would you make a delivery?"

He opened the lid to the box and I saw piles of dollar bills packed and tied in that fine twine bankers use. "A hundred thousand dollars," he told me. He gave me a name and address for the box.

"An interesting day?" he asked.

"You trust this to me?"

I searched his kindly face. Where would I begin with all I wanted to know?

"Why does she have a bodyguard?" was all I could think to say.

"It reassures her."

"Of what?"

"Of having a body."

My car was covered in red blossom, transformed by the day and like a figure in an initiation. I drove to the address—in the Melrose area—and there I found a man sitting quietly alone in an upstairs room, the doors and windows open on the hot, airless evening, watching the Dodgers game. He nodded when I came in and asked me to put the box on a shelf in the closet. There were golf clubs in the closet.

"That fucking Strawberry" was all he said.

I found my editor that evening, and I said there was no reason to go into details but there had been a mistake. I should have been there on the next day, on Friday. I had to withdraw.

"It was definitely Thursday," she said, her horror rising.

I don't know what happened next; I could hardly ask. The editor was conclusively finished with me. But several months later *Movieline* ran its "Dale Harkness" interview—it was an excellent, professional job, with arresting pull quotes. I could see the actress lovely and alive to be interviewed (by someone else, of course), nervy, flighty, but giving glimpses of perilous inside stuff—the real story, as they like to think of it. And the art *was* astounding. No, I won't say which issue or who Dale Harkness is. You'd rather guess, wouldn't you?

And I have to wonder whether there was a misunderstanding, or whether for a moment or two—if not the full ninety—something like the chance of knowledge rose up in my life. Did Dale Harkness know what I was? Did I come close to recognizing her? Or was I just part of a different kind of movie, a new genre among interviews? Ask the anaconda.

(1994)

Beyond Hara-Kiri

DECEMBER 7, 1988

Today, my good friend and master, Akio Morita, head of the Sony Corporation, came into my office. He silenced my inquiry with a raised hand. And then seven times he paced the maple floor, seven steps in each direction. Forty-nine steps I counted. Then he stopped at the window and turned to me. There was a fine smile on his face. The lenses of his eyeglasses caught the late-afternoon light. His silver hair shone like icy waves.

"Would it not be pleasant," he said, "to have a motion picture studio?"

This is what I have dreaded.

JANUARY 2, 1989

Many minds have been directed toward financial analysis of the existing American studios. This is distressing work for the minds.

"Morita-san," I said. "It would seem that such wretched unfortunates as these studios are warnings to the rest of us to leave well enough alone. You recollect the tale of the leper and—"

"Not so," he said. He moved his arms in that overly dramatic way. I could tell he had been watching ancient James Cagney pictures. "This disorder shows only the decadence of the foreign rascal. He must be saved. Captured first. Captured to be saved."

"Sometimes," I said as I bowed, "the rescuer is never again his old self."

I order films for Morita from the archive—the enlightening works of Ozu, Naruse and Mizoguchi, the flowers of Japanese cinema, stories of the family, of history, of necessary sadness and resignation. Instead he insists I see *Working Girl*.

"But Morita-san," I say later, "we know truly that woman in American business is but a shadow."

"Sure," he agreed, "but women dream, and women's dreams are business."

"To lie to oneself," I repeat the old proverb, "is to make a road for others."

"Get a load of that Melanie," he says.

FEBRUARY 19, 1989

With Morita-san to lunch with Keiji Shima, chairman of public broadcasting. This is opportunity, I hope, to dissuade Akio. He describes to Shima the plan to buy an American movie studio.

"Which one?" asked Shima.

"Who knows?" says Akio. "Maybe it doesn't matter."

"Why do this, Morita-san?"

"For software," he answered. "We have hardware. But we need product. Japanese software not right—too sad, too truthful—like films *he* sends me." Akio smiled, not unkindly, at me. "We want happy software. America!"

For a very long time, Shima said nothing. Then he sighed, stood up and announced, "Great danger here."

"Why so?"

"To own American business, you must *have* American illness—suffer from it. Only people who can save or destroy America are

Americans. They are possessive people. Stick to hardware. In time, new hardware will always dictate software—the medium is the message. Americans dread the excellence of our hardware. They *need* to hate us."

"Hardware has no soul," said Morita-san. "No magic."

"These are Western illusions," said Shima.

APRIL 20, 1989

With Morita-san, I fly to New York. Special screening on the plane of rough-cut *Black Rain*. Same old slam-bang stuff, but Akio chuckles at picture's sardonic view of American suckers still ignorant of tough Japanese attitudes to business.

In Manhattan, at neutral hotel, we have secret meeting with the most illustrious Ovitz-san of CAA. He is impressive. Very still—no surplus movements. Most pleasing. He does not speak first. He is not nervous or vain. He waits for Morita-san, who waits to be waited on. Morita-san very happy with this. Excellent atmosphere of order and harmony. Ovitz-san does not laugh at movie studio scheme, but marvels at its farsightedness.

"Every studio," he said, "would be better positioned at the thought Sony might support it."

"Synergy," explained Morita-san. "Hardware and software."

"I like 'synergy' very much," said Ovitz-san. "It is not just the question but the answer. But can Sony be comfortable?"

"Comfortable?" asked Morita-san.

"Can it digest a studio and have sweet breath still?"

"Chew twenty-three times?" said Morita-san. And the two of them laughed silently together, like musicians of the mind.

"For you," asked Morita-san, "there is no conflict of interest?"

Ovitz-san reflected: "The interests are too interesting. Would you be comfortable if I offered humble advice?"

"When perhaps?" asked Morita-san. I knew he was reckoning on another meeting, in May perhaps, in Hawaii, with good golf.

"How would four-thirty be?" asked Ovitz-san.

At this second meeting, with aides, charts and slide show, he talked of MCA, Paramount and Columbia TriStar. His dense wisdom conveyed the present state of those three with great assurance and merciful optimism. It was most apparent, he said, that Sony could find comfort with MCA or Paramount.

"And Columbia?" asked Morita-san.

"The most speculative" was the reply. "The least rational."

"But maybe cheapest?" asked Morita-san. "Bargain?"

Ovitz-san did breathing exercises. "Would Sony want to be the least expensive?"

Later, after the CAA party had left, Morita-san reflected. "Ovitz-san fine man. Yet he makes me perplexed."

I waited.

"He is very Japanese," decided Morita-san. "But can man who sees so much still have 'vision'?"

"Perhaps," I said, "he has discovered there is no need to own studios."

AUGUST 10, 1989

Meeting with Norio Ohga, Sony president. He does not support the great idea: he explains Sony needs funds for next stage of hardware development—high-definition TV. But Morita-san is now determined on Columbia. When he doodles he draws lady with torch.

But who could run our studio? Ovitz-san says he is not worthy, and more useful as friend. We need proven moviemakers.

"Spielberg?" suggests Ohga-san.

"Steven would not cross over," says Ovitz. "You need the hot executive, the lucky man. Or men. The equation is so complex. It will very likely be someone who would startle you. There is no such concept as 'the right man.' Whoever you choose becomes right. It is a kind of fate." These Western mystics!

AUGUST 18, 1989

Talks with Coca-Cola on terms to buy Columbia. Much cola consumed. Many books of financial data are provided. No time to know if answers and numbers have meaning or are birds put in the branches of the tree to sing for us.

We hear stories that Matsushita also getting the same books of numbers and may be interested in its own studio purchase. Ovitz-san murmurs about the new air of competition.

I admit to Ovitz-san, "I myself have bug up ass. Looks like we might be paying a billion too much. Talking billion."

There is a pause. Ovitz-san then says, "All this shall pass. A billion here or there is history's footnote. We must grow into the future, and in the future you are getting a sweet deal."

Can we wait?

SEPTEMBER 25, 1989

Day of grief. The die is cast. Sony will buy Columbia and TriStar from Coca-Cola for $3.4 billion. This is twenty-three times Columbia cash flow—one for every chew. I show these mad numbers to Akio, and he gives me his sunny, inscrutable smile. "I told you, Columbia is not small potatoes. No reason to pay low—it adds insult to Americans. In ten years synergy will make numbers seem like fairy story. I would have paid more."

SEPTEMBER 26, 1989

It is more. We find that Columbia has just discovered debts of $1.2 billion, which we now own. Lucky bastards.

SEPTEMBER 29, 1989

And more. There have been pressures in the United States to bring
in Peter Guber and Jon Peters to run the new Sony Pictures. They
are *Batman* and *Rain Man*. Morita-san calls Ovitz-san, who will say
only that "Goobers" (our joke!) are "authentically American."
"They are respected?" asks Morita-san.
"You have to understand," says Ovitz-san, "that no one here
exactly has what you mean by *respect*. But Peter and Jon are high
profile. They are players."
"They know show business?"
There is silence. Ovitz-san can seem very far away, like someone in a farther galaxy, ahead of us in time. "They are the show.
They are stars. With them you get an attitude."
Morita-san put down the phone and gazed very long at flower
arrangement. "Who's on first?" he whispered to the fragrant
air.

OCTOBER 1, 1989

Sony Pictures will buy the Guber–Peters Company—another
$200 million: this is like tipping money. Each man will also be
paid $2.75 million a year, rising to $2.90 million over five years.
Then there is a vast budget pool—"Everyone has to have a nice
pool of his own," they say. The numbers are very high, but
Morita-san says a signal of intent must go out.

OCTOBER 3, 1989

The signal comes back. Warner Bros. claim a contractual arrangement with Guber–Peters. Why were we not told about this? They
forgot? The Goobers are not normally so silent.
"You see," said Morita-san, "how much the Guber and Peters
are *really* worth?" He is in triumph, but his hand is shaking.

Already I see that he is irked by the endless explanations from American lawyers. As they talk, the air in the room vanishes.

OCTOBER 15, 1989

The press commentary in America is disturbing. Only former President Reagan is on our side: he says at last there will be a return to "decent" pictures. (Don't worry, Guber says: people don't take him seriously.) Other leading figures in Hollywood regret that so ancient an institution as Columbia (founded in fact by Harry Cohn in 1920, only a blink ago) should pass into "foreign" control. What do they think "foreign" is? United States is all foreigners, except for Indians—and they don't run any studios (despite Guber's Indian hairstyle).

OCTOBER 21, 1989

More bad talk. Americans should know that British, Germans, Dutch, et cetera own more of United States than Japanese. But Japanese faces stick out in crowd—I wonder why—nor are there yet Japanese Jews. This American patriotism very strange. Always comes up in arguments; never seen in daily life. But Americans talk about themselves as if they were characters, not real people. There is always a script going on, and they are always in rewrite. We learn to beware most of any American who describes his own sincerity. They are doomed.

NOVEMBER 15, 1989

Warners withdraw their suit, on these terms: they get all the Burbank studio (very nice for them—Ovitz-san says we would not be comfortable in Valley air); so we have to make do with old Metro lot in Culver City, which is like slum town now. Plus we have to buy out the Warners contract with Goobers. With all these extras, Sony has paid at least $5.5 billion for Columbia TriStar—no matter that in 1982 Coca-Cola bought it for $750 million. Remember millions? Morita-san has, for days now, had the austere look of meditation, or like a man who declines to notice dead rat in his nasal passages. This cannot help his health. To save face sometimes is to destroy the head.

DECEMBER 1, 1989

Alan Levine is hired to be president of Columbia Pictures Entertainment. Levine is the lawyer of Guber–Peters Company. I thought we bought that company. So don't we own Levine already?

DECEMBER 18, 1989

Jeff Sagansky leaves TriStar. Peters says it's the same old musical chairs time.

JANUARY 9, 1990

Dawn Steel resigns from Columbia. Why is everyone leaving?

FEBRUARY 27, 1990

So others may come. Mike Medavoy takes the old Sagansky job.

MARCH 20, 1990

Frank Price is new chairman of Columbia. Peters says everyone is concentrating now on new office decoration. Floristry business in town reported up by 572 percent. But garish arrangements to our eyes.

APRIL 18, 1990

We hear reports of enormous expenditure from new regime. Not that we get much reaction. Many of our calls are not taken. We hear that "it's impossible to talk to the Japanese." Peters-san is said to be earnest user of company airplanes—to fly girlfriend here and there. He works at home and wears casual clothes—Morita-san bewildered ("Is Peters-san sick?"). And Peters is spending maybe another $100 million to refurbish the studio—always bills for flowers, office furniture (much of it Japanese!). Also, ugly stories of excessive personal behavior. Peters-san had been advised that Japanese feel distaste for shows of personal glory. Whereupon, Peters said, "Hey, you don't understand. I'm fucking Lew Wasserman now!"

"What is that?" asks horrified Morita-san. "Such perversion?"

APRIL 21, 1990

After research I can report that in above remark *fucking* is not verb but adjective. Wasserman-san (fine man, great gentleman, example in our business, formidable hair and spectacles) above reproach. *Fucking* here is full of esteem—can be used to describe anything. Example of double meaning: "This fucking script is not fucking Robert Towne."

AUGUST 11, 1990

Morita-san makes discreet personal visit to Los Angeles to better appreciate the culture. He is alarmed at opulence of the new studio and at brazen signs of milking the Japanese. Very condescending attitudes. He tells me that Peters-san, who was formerly a hairdresser, is rare mixture of artist and gangster who shouts to himself all the time, using lines from screenplays. Morita-san very unhappy to find that such a movie character walks about in real life and disposes of Sony money. Sony money not funny money. No one now can tell us exactly what purchase has cost. "Wait for the pictures," they say. Morita-san dines with Oliver Stone to explore ideas—returns home before dessert with migraine condition. "At least I didn't throw up," he says.

DECEMBER 31, 1990

For this last year, Columbia TriStar had 14 percent share of American box office. Very poor. A pickup deal from Carolco, *Total Recall,* makes money, but only a small share goes to Columbia. Anyway, it is hardly the kind of picture former President Reagan meant. There are many losers, too: *Texasville* (cost $20 million, box office $1 million). "Wait till next year," says Guber-san. "Fucking next year," says Morita. He does not look well, and he says that in Hollywood if one does not look well there follows lack of respect.

MAY 8, 1991

Rejoicing! Peters-san resigns. But his new company has deal with Sony, still. In one year and a half, he has muddled more heads than any hairdresser manages in a lifetime. Impossible to estimate final amount of money directed to Peters's friends, associates, et cetera—they are all "friends." Hollywood is just a board game played with real money, and a place where everyone gossips all the time on the phone. No secrets, no discretion, no reserve. It is now said that the Goobers have inflated the cost of all professional services in movies. Ray Stark—always a force at

Columbia—is reported as saying, "The Japanese have done nothing yet. But the nothing is a zero added on to every check."

AUGUST 20, 1991

Again, Morita-san visits Los Angeles. He is taken to the set of *Hook*, the picture Steven Spielberg is making for TriStar. He tells us he is amazed by the production design and the whole world made for the movie, but still he cannot understand a story based on the desires of children, with adults wanting to return to childhood. I suggest that "the lost boys" could be our code name for the Guber people. In Japan, to cultivate childhood would be deemed regressive and unhealthy. At the same time, Morita watches Warren Beatty's *Bugsy* in production. "More childhood," he reports. "The twelve-year-old's wish to be treated like a gangster. I see it before—*Bugsy Malone*." And the real Bugsy had to be eliminated because he preferred romance of Las Vegas to business. A lesson for us all?

OCTOBER 3, 1991

Mark Canton is new chairman of Columbia, replacing Frank Price. No one ever stays—no responsibility.

DECEMBER 31, 1991

Better news; Columbia TriStar have 20 percent of the box office for the year. Motion picture division shows a 60 percent increase in revenue. However, Sony Corporation reports its biggest ever loss at $110 million. Many failures in the year: *The Taking of Beverly Hills; Hudson Hawk* (estimated cost $60 million, revenue $8 million). *Boyz N the Hood* is very profitable, but no one at Sony can understand it. Again, for Carolco, Columbia does nicely thank you, distributing *Terminator 2*. Morita-san asks, "When do we do our own Arnold picture?" *City Slickers* is another hit, and pretty cool flick. *The Prince of Tides* opens well on Christmas Day. There is nothing I can believe in that picture, except that Miss Streisand believes in it and it is *her* picture— make her feel good. It is worrying after this movie to learn that many Columbia executives are also in analysis. Part of search for health. Such bullshit.

FEBRUARY 18, 1992

Hook does well; correction; it does "well." It will gross over $100 million. But turns out it cost at least $80 million—before promotion costs. New worlds not cheap; lost boys have expensive tastes. Picture cannot break even. *Bugsy* gets best picture nomination (*Prince of Tides,* too), but again *Bugsy* makes nowhere near enough revenue to cover all costs. Warren Beatty bitter that we have neglected his picture in favor of *Hook*.

FEBRUARY 28, 1992

Guber-san has been saying for months now things would get better. He saw departure of Frank Price in that light (but it turns out Price got $15 million handshake). Guber has defended every venture and becomes morose if questioned—no place for constructive criticism in the American system; volcanic praise is the norm. Everyone always looking on what they call the "bright side"—Morita-san has called this the "blight side." Where is fear? I wonder. Fear, dread and doubt, those strong feelings? Now *Radio Flyer* opens, cost $30 million (I am told this could be "conservative"—only the lies are conservative; revenue, $4 million).

APRIL 1, 1992

We learn that *Radio Flyer* actually cost $41 million.

DECEMBER 31, 1992

We have been making some modest adjustments in personnel arrangements. This leads to ugly press stories of firings. Nineteen ninety-two has been a year of many uncomfortable hours in the dark: not just *Radio Flyer,* but *Hero, Year of the Comet* and *Mr. Saturday Night* (this last something that Canton-san had been promising as a terrific picture). But then there is mysterious *A Few Good Men,* in which great star and mighty marine commander deliberately breaks down on witness stand so that "blight side" may be maintained. Audiences do not notice: they like the picture. We have a hit. I have amusing talk with Ovitz-san on this.

"Ovitz-san," I ask. "*A Few Good Men?*"

"Now there is a nice product," he says.

"But very foolish."

"You know that. I know that. But what do we know? We know nothing—no one in Hollywood knows anything. The point is, and I think this is instructive, can we live with ourselves—can we be at ease—can we perform—knowing nothing and facing tomorrow without needing to visit the bathroom every ten minutes? You take my point? Steadfast in ignorance: think about it. The two things that will kill you, my friend, are knowledge and decisions."

Where is honor? Where is worth? This is not just disaster; it is darkness. The American way, I see now, is to be mad politely and entertainingly and to have your millions guaranteed in the back end. Big bonus; soothing payoff. Everyone has his deal here. Somehow, Sony must acquire the fortitude to be proud of things like *A League of Their Own, Basic Instinct* and *Bram Stoker's Dracula* (we have hits!). I see wisdom of something written very neatly on the walls in Columbia executive washroom—this I had puzzled over for eighteen months: "I will come to work every day. I will take the shit and deny reality. I will take the money. I will kiss the ass. But nowhere in my contract does it say I have to see the pictures. I like them already. I am *very* high on them."

JUNE 20, 1993

Old Japanese proverb I coined yesterday: pick the fruit day by day, and when your arms are full of sweetness you will fall into the latrine. Our hits vanish like mist in the sun. *Last Action Hero* has opened: our Arnold. We once recited at the boardroom table, "We want it, but only if the price is right," and then added, "Or if Arnold is in it." Now the great Arnold (very amusing man in meetings) has put us in it. And he is still smiling; artists must not let themselves be dragged down. It seems that the picture cost $82.5 million to produce and another $52.0 million to promote. And by the end of summer we may have income of $20.0 million.

AUGUST 10, 1993

But first, summer, the summer of Heidi-Ho, Heidi Fleiss. First it is said that her sometime lover and "business adviser," Ivan Nagy, had an office at the studio. Rumors follow that Michael Nathanson, our president of production, and even Mark Canton may have been clients. No truth to this, but Nathanson jumps gun: issues denial before accusation. Canton speaks: "I am hardly being biblical when I say that the people who are spreading the poison are going to have to drink from the same well." Must they all talk like dumb movies?

Nathanson promoted—replaced by Lisa Henson, child of Muppets. He will concentrate on "administrative matters." Stare at ceiling? No disgrace anymore—this is the way pioneered by Nixon. Hara-kiri now is done with rubber swords on prime time.

SEPTEMBER 15, 1993

I begin to see the light. We have more hits—*Sleepless in Seattle* (telephone ad), *Cliffhanger, Groundhog Day* (at last I like one of our movies) and *In the Line of Fire* (which shows how to kill a president in great detail). Of course, we are in crisis because of *Last Action Hero*, and so we are having to make more eliminations.

There is a story in Los Angeles that Canton-san fell asleep while being shown *The Age of Innocence* by Martin Scorsese. Not so, says Canton; only thinking and listening to Joanne Woodward. He telephones Morita-san and describes plot of film at immense length to prove he was awake. Morita-san drops off during call.

Columbia has had to put many developing projects on hold. Barbet Schroeder, it is said, goes in to see Canton-san with Bushido sword and threatens to disembowel himself if he doesn't get green light. Canton-san says, "We always give director first cut."

NOVEMBER 17, 1993

Guber-san is given a new five-year contract with Sony Pictures Entertainment. Sometimes it is enough to write down the worst news with one's finest penmanship. And it is said that Medavoy-san is likely to leave.

DECEMBER 2, 1993

Morita-san has cerebral hemorrhage. No recent Japanese of his stature has been so drawn to America—or so humbled by it. It is the great power of America—its virus—that it spreads hope, the search for happiness and moral untidiness in the world. And movies are a great symptom of the illness.

DECEMBER 21, 1993

Guber-san speaks at New York event. He warns against putting faith in hardware and technology: "We can expand our businesses to the farthest points of the earth, re-create movies in a dozen new formats and technologies, blaze new pathways into home entertainment, but there is no substitute for the shared emotion of going to the movies, the twentieth-century version of the tribal campfire."

DECEMBER 23, 1993

Alone in screening room, I see *Geronimo*—at last an Indian picture. Who is interested in this? Who can persuade themselves that anyone is interested? The lonely campfire.

MAY 1, 1994

Quietly—as if with garbage cans on our feet—we are attempting to sell some of our studio. No interest. Why should there be? *I'll Do Anything* opens after much recutting and elimination of songs. They didn't do enough.

SEPTEMBER 10, 1994

I see rough cut of *Mary Shelley's Frankenstein*. Beyond horror—horrendous. Will this Shelley woman sue?

SEPTEMBER 29, 1994

Guber-san resigns, with the air of a man much afflicted, much wounded, much relieved. He says he needs more time to explore his own creativity: "It's the natural evolution to somebody who has done the high-wire act, to want to own the circus. Now I'd like to touch the cloth and hear the music, to touch the TV, the movie. If I was going to be in the fire, I wanted to feel the result more directly, more personally."

DECEMBER 31, 1994

Research suggests Sony may have spent over $10 billion on the studio venture. Steven Spielberg, David Geffen and Jeffrey Katzenberg are forming a new studio. Sony is approached about presenting definitive exhibit to celebrate one hundred years of movies for 1995. Two thousand prints of *Last Action Hero*?

Morita-san is comfortable.

My retirement. I shall go at last to watch the water and the sun in my favorite city of Kobe.

(1995)

Follow the Money

The first time you see *The Last Seduction,* you curl up with the sheer fun. The second time, it has become a ghost town of mannered femme fatalism and story stupidities. But still a wind blows through the forsaken place, a mournful stirring to match the sickly and nearly decayed eyes of Linda Fiorentino. You begin to realize that, despite the deadpan lines and stark attitudes she uses for nakedness on first encounter, she was dying.

She didn't have an idea in the world what to do with life, and so the precious bag of money—the object of her bleak exercise— is like a slow-acting painkiller, a tombstone waiting to stand above her, the one dick that cannot be offed. Indeed, when you see her at the end of the movie, in a black stretch limo, with a full-length dress slit up to her thigh, she isn't going anywhere. She isn't living it up. She's just the figure of death floating around town, like Maria Casares in Cocteau's *Orphée.* She couldn't handle the money.

Who can? I have been noticing the frequency of what I take to be the most reverent, erotic and fatal image on the American screen now. You see it everywhere, not just in movies but in so many television commercials. It is there, over and over, like the answer and the dream, the destination and the question. When it appears, the characters on-screen tend to sigh, and smile, and expand, as if in assent or confirmation. There is a whispered or felt yes, as if to say, This is it, this is us, and the mystery of the play. And audiences respond in a similar way. They know the setup in advance. They know that the briefcase that is being opened up for the camera is a mouth, a naked lady and the waiting grave filled, row upon row, with neat stacks of Andrew Jackson, Ulysses S. Grant and Benjamin Franklin. Getting rich can teach you history, and the severe color scheme—off-white, sage green, black and gray—is like a mouth of caries, the revelation of disease in the realm of magnificent, cosmetic dentistry.

Why do we smile and sigh if the meaning is so grim? Is there some sort of tacit death wish at work? You have to follow the money, remember, to come upon the most terrible meanings. That is offered in *All the President's Men* not just as a guide to inquiry but as early warning that maybe money has eclipsed evil and all other aspects of human nature.

Among the many smart touches in *The Last Seduction* there is the opening in which Clay (Bill Pullman) rendezvouses with two kids under the Brooklyn Bridge. He has a chic briefcase packed tight with pharmaceuticals while they have a shabbier, rather beaten up metal case filled with $700,000 in used but "clean" presidentials. For a moment, Clay thinks the kids mean to double-cross him: they put a gun to his head. But only so that they can tip the cash on the ground—you know these kids have no respect for money—and make off with both cases. Obviously, in this era of the magical close-up, you can't have too many cases.

This leaves Pullman with the challenge of getting home with the $700,000. He stuffs his shirt with the packs of money so that he looks no odder than an actor going to audition for *Junior.* So he returns to his Bridget (Fiorentino) and disgorges. She does a little kiss-and-lick with the money, never noticing any taint on it, though when Clay offers himself for some of the same her disdainful nose wrinkles and we appreciate the stale odor of fear-funk he carries. So he heads for the shower, while Bridget equips herself with a canvas bag for the money and slips off into her own sardonic looking-glass world.

Bridget is so smart-ass at talking idiots into the floor, but so dumb in the big picture. Her grand getaway goes no farther than Beston, upstate but very down-market, where this sultry, rich bitch on the lam is reduced to the level of a nice suburban home, a decent boyfriend and a job! Anyone who talks like this Bridget ought to go much farther west and be throwing the money away on tactical nuclear weapons, clothes beyond John Dahl's budget, a pair of leopards and a Francis Bacon triptych. Or at least a Salmon P. Chase to keep in her underpants—Chase, by the way, is the $10,000 bill (and he was secretary of the treasury under Lincoln). A woman on the run ought to relish a Chase.

But this girl is a sad escapee. What does she do but take up a cute mirror name, Wendy Kroy, that shows her homesickness for New York. She isn't liberated; she hasn't broken out; she hasn't fooled that dread illness behind her eyes. Like everyone else in Beston, she stagnates. She calls a lawyer, pursues a divorce and begins to bargain with her $700,000. The soaring, innovative genius that Fiorentino could bring to the role is betrayed by Dahl's hapless storying, and by the film's anal reticence with money. Bridget ought to buy, gamble, promote or take over promising parts of Nevada or the banking system. But the entre-preneurial spirit only flirts with the idea of insurance rip-offs, a fancy concoction of James M. Cain and telephone computers. So she hides the loaded canvas bag in the attic. She doesn't even take one evening to roll naked in a sea of Franklins while listening to Mozart and Vivaldi, using a crisp McKinley (the $500 bill) as a dildo. Her flair is so *noir* and verbal: she could be the grand-daughter of Dorothy Malone from *The Big Sleep*.

So often in our movies, the world and its wonders are encoded in such big bundles—the great orgasmic passing of Go, the ulti-mate Gucci bag packed airtight with Madisons (the $5,000 bill, celebrated in the book of *The Long Goodbye*). But the world that is yours, and ours, is so bare and unimaginative. There is a rhap-sodic passage in De Palma's *Scarface* on money itself, the dirty, wrinkled pages of its endless book, like bedclothes after nights of fucking. Tony Montana has made it; he has a realty corporation for digesting the money. He has eliminated enemies, he has woken the scrawny Elvira and claimed her in a dead rival's satin sheets. The money starts to build. Forests of it, the notes riffling through counting machines. Thugs arrive at the Miami banks with sackloads of the shit. The WASP bankers rear back, offended by such flagrant plenty. They do not dare show Tony's raw glee at having it. There is even that lovely moment, when he marries Elvira, and hurries her down to the lake in the garden to show her his gift, a tiger, on the island. What else is money for—unless it's feeding slaves to the tiger?

Montana has no other idea for the money, except to convert the off-white stuff into the bright white of cocaine. The boxloads of untidy cash become idyllic mesas of coke on his own desk. And so the simplistic notion is reiterated that money equals death and destruction. The pharmaceuticals that Clay renders into $700,000 in *The Last Seduction* are not going to be of long-term benefit to the kids of New York. And thus, the sentiment goes, Bridget/Wendy has gone off with the proceeds of death and exploitation. That is one reason why she is made inert or dispirited by the money. It is a drug for her, a muffle on her undoubted wit and inventiveness. And it is in having money, Elvira and a Miami mansion that Montana confronts his limits. So few movie characters like Tony think big. They tip face-forward into the cocaine or into money's gloomy moralizing. They don't think to buy the Dolphins, the governor and twenty-three savings and loans—let alone a stake in the new, post-Castro Cuba. They so seldom make the elegant moves into charity dinners, corporate life and "respectability." Or movies.

Tony's exultation, the moment in which he looks up at the blimp with its message, "the world is yours," and is one with it, is so brief. On the up-slope before it, he has been cocky, brave, funny, horny; afterward, he is a slob, an addict and a fool. Success and money, here, are so much more safely dreamed of than possessed. That self-righteous subtext—that rich people are cursed—reminds me of the astonishing determination of Walker (Lee Marvin) in *Point Blank,* to get the $93,000 that is his due. However one reads that beautifully enigmatic film—whether it is death's dream or life's struggle—Walker is an implacable but unthinking force of honor (or automatic debit), intent on his rightful if illicit money. Pursuit takes him up the ladder of the Mob (in movies, the makers of monetary order)—not that he notices or cares—so that his zeal serves as a purging instrument for the Mob CEO, Fairfax (Keenan Wynn).

But a moment comes, at night at the abandoned Fort Point (within sight of the island Alcatraz, where it all began), when Walker is to be paid off. He is there with Brewster, another Mob executive. But Brewster stands in the illumined courtyard, while Walker watches from the dark of an upper gallery. The helicopter comes in; it leaves a parcel and withdraws. As Brewster calls out to come and get it, a shot is fired. Brewster dies beside the parcel. A moment later, Fairfax appears. He calls out to the darkness and to Walker, "Our deal's done." We see Walker back off into the blackness. Then the gunman appears. Was Walker, too, about to be shot? Does he flinch from showing himself? Or is the dreamer receding as he reaches the climax of his revenge, knowing that a parcel of money is too dangerous, too ridiculous or too sacred to be touched? We see a sliver of Walker's face, which then slips into the dark, like a blade going back into its sheath.

"Walker, this is the last time," Fairfax shouts out, and then, "How do you like that?" to the gunman.

"I like it," says the assassin, making a move to reclaim the parcel.

"Leave it," orders Fairfax.

Is it real money, regarded with contempt now, or as a paid debt? Or was the parcel only full of blank paper bills?* We never know, but the $93,000 has become just the tag in a game or a myth. It will remain at Fort Point, uncollected, like a W. C. Fields bank account. No wonder so many tourists go there now, discreetly searching for the parcel. In their dreams the $93,000 is identity and answer: the sum equals I am.

So Walker dies, or retreats perhaps, educated in the precarious state of being on a ladder. Maybe he just creeps away and goes

---

*Do they use *real* money in movies—or blanks, as with ammunition?

back into "America," with the obliging and fond Chris (Angie Dickinson); perhaps it is his ambition now to be unremarkable, earning the average wage. Or maybe he recollected the wisdom of so many American films, that money will ruin you and cast a blight on your life. Money, the movies do say, is something the wise man learns to laugh at—unless he's a gross player.

Of course, the movies lie a lot, no matter how earnestly some of us address their spiritual virtues. So it's uncommon in movies for cash, dough, the moola, itself, to be made fun of. On the contrary, rich men are made to do the rueful act, à la Charles Foster Kane, and murmur the sad homily of how they might have been very great men if they hadn't been born so rich. At such solemn moments, we might note the rugged, blunt amiability of such as Rupert Murdoch, who seems unabashedly cheerful and moderately happy despite every superstition in the culture that wealth and ownership make a psychic wound. No, if you want to find misery and madness in our world, it is quicker to test the collapsed lives that sleep in doorways.

Occasionally a movie does catch the sheer glee of money, cash, greenbacks, the wad. The nicest thing about *The Brink's Job* is how, even in Boston, it is assumed the world is peopled by idiots—from the cops and Edgar Hoover and the Brinks employees all the way to the seven deadbeat dreamers who find the candy store is wide open. Was Warren Oates ever better than as Specs, the hard man who boasts of artillery, D Day and being tortured by the Japanese, but who begs just a gesture at pressure so that he can cave in? Peter Falk and Allen Goorwitz (as he was at the time) are brothers-in-law who seem to be in each other's clothes by mistake—Falk's pants have room for a getaway truck.

After these seven dwarves actually pull off the job, there is a moment when they gambol and frolic in the money and the bills drift in the air like feathers in *Zéro de Conduite*. (It also harks back to an earlier scene in which Goorwitz is swept away on a cascade of candy balls.) Apparently, when their weary counting of all the bills is done, it comes to more than a million and a half. This is so far beyond their dream as to be daft. Falk gets his wife a fur coat.

Oates and Kevin O'Connor rob a clothes store—just to show they haven't gone soft—and wear the garish new togs with price tags still attached. But the image and brief bliss of these grubby blue-collar rogues with serious money is endearing and lyrical. There's hardly anything in American film that so catches the decent, conservative obstreperousness of the criminal classes, or the fatuousness of money.

Of course, the end titles to *The Brink's Job* do admit that these scruffy ruffians served just fourteen years in prison and then led "comfortable" lives. Why not? Less than $50,000 of the million and a half was ever recovered. So I'd like to think that the boys were able to move to Newton and have vacations in Las Vegas. Then again, maybe the $1.45 million was laundered to make movies like *The Brink's Job*.

Walon Green wrote *The Brink's Job* (from Noel Behn's book), and his ragamuffins do remind one of the taller, harder guys whose bunch is shot to pieces in San Rafael for the sake of so many bags of steel washers. (You have to rub your eyes to believe that Warren Oates is in both gangs, he's so much more richly conceived in *The Brink's Job*.) Green wrote *The Wild Bunch*, too, but with Sam Peckinpah cocking a gun over his shoulder, and so the air of Mark Twain that graces the Boston film goes Hemingway-esque with the Pike Bishop gang. They are idiots, too, but they have honor, like men always checking their armor fly to make sure it isn't unzipped.

So the absurdity or tragedy of risking life and losing comrades (as well as murdering bystanders) is supposedly redeemed by the discovery of fatalistic pose. For myself, that facile irony only underlines the human truth of a Walker stubborn enough to go the extra miles for ninety-three cents. Most of us are pretty humorless about money we've earned that never comes. Even *The Wild Bunch* was made in the era of "pay or play." In other words, ironic mirth over monies gone with the wind is as common in the Hollywood Hills as snowdrifts. As in so many things Peckinpah, "honor" is the threshold to romance and white lies, as well as the excuse for a stupidity that no one would tolerate in life.

But surely Peckinpah was remembering that famous conclusion to *The Treasure of the Sierra Madre*—the work of a chronic gambler—in which the much struggled over gold joins a dust storm to the accompaniment of Walter Huston's sardonic laughter. John Huston enjoyed that airy humor and its suggestion that the efforts of men are all vanity; he made several films with the same godforsaken nonchalance. So at the conclusion of *Treasure,* the treasury is all good works: Walter Huston proposes to live contentedly like a man who would be king among the sweet Mexicans, while Tim Holt goes home to be a better person. As for Dobbs, he is dead—because he took the money too seriously. But that bogus stance is a fruitful model for American movies, in which "treasure" is a wicked temptation that may divert pilgrims from the trek toward a simpler, less ambitious life. So in amassing a vast fortune, Chaplin discovered the common man he had striven so hard to surpass.

I never much believe in that Hustonian laughter, or admire it: it seems a sort of arrogance, an assertion of gambler's class, and not so far from the streak of cruelty Huston and Peckinpah shared. Compare it with the somber emptiness left by fatigue and dismay in the face of Sterling Hayden at the end of *The Killing.* This is Kubrick's most concentrated plan movie; yet it also has the oddest bunch of believable people he ever mustered—think of Jay C. Flippen, Elisha Cook, Jr., and Marie Windsor, Timothy Carey and Maurice Oboukhoff.

Everything builds and rebuilds toward the instant when the bulging sack of money comes flying out of the back window of the racetrack administration block. The bad cop Ted de Corsia puts it in his trunk and drives it to the motel where Hayden will collect it. Money on-screen has few more desperate or poetic scenes than Hayden driving down a back road to transfer the bills to a suitcase large enough for a corpse. There's such abundance, yet we grieve and fuss over stray notes that spill free. The naggy meticulousness of Kubrick's approach has made tellers of us all—that's why we feel for the Hayden character, and see him age at the airport check-in counter where he learns his case won't qualify as carry-on luggage. Hayden always had abandoned eyes, and he seems to know he's ruined before the suitcase goes on the luggage cart—top corner position—and then topples off as the driver swerves to avoid the damn dog. One bump on the tarmac and it's open. There's a blizzard of money in the slipstream of an airplane engine. It's one of the most harrowing death scenes in pictures if you're counting the demise of dreams. The great bag of money—it is $2 million—is turned to fragments in a few seconds.

Supposedly it could be retrieved: there might have been a great screwball comedy about people at the airport, weeks and years later, hunting down the errant bills. But the classic desirability of the big bundle is less in the paper chase than in that solid block of bills, impacted hope, that also resembles a coffin or a headstone. That kind of dream is to be possessed, held close, lived in even—but not spent. It embodies manhood, virginity and identity, its ownership is for movie characters the implant and insurance that permits them to live as if money doesn't matter.

That has always been the chief subtextual way of getting money on the screen. It wasn't flashed around, but it was there in rooms larger and houses grander than characters might afford in real life. The money was there in so few movie people having to work, or worry over work. It was the newness of their automobiles, the freshness of their teeth, the laundering of their wardrobe and the semireligious gift of backlighting. It was in the constitutional good looks and the way everyone spoke at least $300-a-week dialogue. In that sense, the Hollywood movie has always been an advertisement for the nation's supposed bounty and the conscientious pursuit of happiness. For decades, most movies offered a world, a look and a luster which—if revealed onstage as the curtain rose—would have been greeted with the heartfelt applause of shared ideals and destinies. Movies were properties for us to desire, places we wanted to be. "Put the light where the money is," they used to say.

We may be too cynical, or guilty, for that splendor now. It is the humanist orthodoxy to be antimaterialistic: we are all exhilarated by the concerto of domestic explosions at the end of *Zabriskie Point* (especially if, when we go home, our place is intact still). The wealth and extravagance of picture making—the display of money—now frequently provokes explosion and disruption: the collision of vehicles; the eruption of buildings; the columns of fire and smoke; the spectacular zapping of so many humanoids. Creatures and cities are invented and generated to be blown apart. There is a surging schizophrenia in the boasting of assets before blowing them to smithereens.

Such spasms of ownership, of money, are now more characteristic of our movies than anything that might come under the heading of auteurism. The voice or style of artists is nearly lost in the medium's deep, digestive debate over having things and demolishing them—whether money, material or dreams. But the noble venture of auteurism always preferred to look away from money or business history. Too much of the best writing on film, and the best film journals, studiously neglected the money. And so our verdict on the career of every alleged artist has been lopsided.

By now, the public has moved on ahead of auteurism. Many newspapers run weekly box-office charts. America is regaled by the discovery (as of May 1995) that *Forrest Gump* is still in the red (at last the feather of mystery and wonder brushes that film). We face the blunt fact that Mike Ovitz is only going to quit CAA for MCA if somehow a designer case containing $200 million will be handed over. (After all, an agent only ever made 10 percent; he has catching up to do.) And in *Striptease*, Demi Moore will break all records for women by getting $12 million for doing a little lap dancing. Who says they don't write rolls (and heaves) for women? We know such guys are doing it for the dough. We have mixed feelings about the discovery, but we are old enough for mixed feelings. And no one is ever going to *get* American film without grasping the treacherous mix of beauty and the numbers.

I have a proposal that might add mustard to our movies. In watching sports on television, we take the stats for granted. As

Barry Bonds comes up to the plate, the image acquires his average, home runs and runs batted in. So why not in movies a similar line that would include salary and points for this film plus career profitability? I got the notion watching *Indecent Proposal,* which seemed, for a few minutes at least, one of the most intriguing American films of recent years.

After all, this movie actually talks about the recession of the early nineties, and it has the young married realtor Demi saying, "I'm scared—we don't have any money. What are we going to do?" Woody Harrelson's answer is indicative of how movies think. They go to Las Vegas with the $5,000 his father has loaned them. St. Vegas's dance is the automatic response to cracking poverty (after all, poverty is a matter of luck, isn't it?). At first Woody is hot: he turns his stake into $25,040 at the craps table.

This leads to a sex scene with Demi in cool white underwear on a bed strewn with money. It's not exactly Trina in *Greed,* but for Adrian Lyne, style always reminds us of ads. And the scene knows that money is aphrodisiac, that the contrast of flawless Demi in white with grubby money is a turn-on. The intimation of ordinary prostitution is there well before Robert Redford's prim offer. Redford isn't right for the part. He has grown old trying to be sensitive: he has the glazed look of the Sundance catalog. The part needed more coldness, and zero charm—if only Barry Diller could be coaxed onto the screen.

But there is a knockout scene to come: Woody and Demi (so many stars now have kids' names) are in bed again and they start to talk about the offer, maneuvering for the money without wanting the responsibility of the decision. The scene could be longer, wilder, funnier: still, it's a rarity on our screen—two people talking turkey about money. After that, the picture's shot. The ad allure sets in, love looms and Demi's self-hyping hard stare and her loose-change voice are wasted. This could have been a scathing movie about someone learning how exciting money can be. And Demi Moore has the ravishing, empty eyes that it requires. It needed Buñuel perhaps, or Bresson (who did make *L'Argent*)—or Louis Rukeyser.

Another failure in *Indecent Proposal* is that the $1 million Redford pays for Moore (Oliver Platt's shitty lawyer knows he could have got $2 million—and the negotiation should have been extended) is delivered as just a credit note at the Vegas casino. We never get Demi and one million bills in the same shot—like beauty and the beast. What a *Vanity Fair* cover it could have been, with the naked lady made of money. As ever, the serene solidity of money has a surreal potential that begs to be pushed.

Yet I wonder if even that image didn't reach its climax forty years ago. For the greatest of all the fateful opened cases is the leather-strapped steel box that glows and growls in *Kiss Me Deadly.* In the Mickey Spillane novel that Robert Aldrich and A. I. Bezzerides departed from, the case contained a few million dollars from a drug deal. It is part of the audacity of Aldrich's movie that the box contains . . . well, God knows what it is exactly. Let's call it the ultimate deterrent among possessions, a force that scalds the inquisitive touch and is ready to burn like nitrate film.

Tarantino quotes the idea in *Pulp Fiction,* of course, and Buñuel has his magical box in *Belle de Jour.* But no one has ever matched Aldrich's savage fairy-tale ending and the box that no one can resist, or survive. It is the only explosion in movies that accounts for the desolate landscape at the end of *Greed.*

(1995)

The Technical Sense of Money

1. Day. Interior. The enormous living room of a fine house in the Hollywood Hills. KAREN SPECTOR is about 35, sensationally beautiful, smart, nervy, a great star, but with an edge of anxiety, as if she has foreseen her future closing in on her. RICHARD, 34, is a screenwriter, and he is carrying a script. He wears sneakers, chinos and an old tweed jacket, whereas Karen wears an Armani dress.

RICHARD: So, I could leave the script with you. I need to go get my glasses repaired. You could read it while I'm gone.

KAREN: Your poor glasses! What happened? You worked so hard?

RICHARD: My kid threw them on the floor.

KAREN: I have a child, too. He's . . . somewhere.

RICHARD (polite): Right. So . . . there would be time for you to read the script. Then, when I get back we could talk.

KAREN (with authority): No, I don't want to read it. Not yet.

RICHARD: Not yet?

KAREN: I know it's going to be too important. I want to save that experience. And if I read the script too soon it gets locked.

RICHARD (perplexed): Locked?

KAREN: Sure. I read it, I fall in love with it—I'm less open to changes.

RICHARD: Changes? Already? You haven't read it yet.

KAREN: Growth, Richard. Isn't it true, when you're writing— you have to stay open?

RICHARD: Well—

KAREN: It's a living thing. You don't know where it's going to go. Isn't it all an adventure for you, Richard?

RICHARD: I guess. But I have to *pick* the words, too. Make the decisions.

KAREN: Of course you do! God knows, you do. But isn't there always . . . oh, I don't have the words—the flux? The sheer fucking flux, Richard.

RICHARD: The flux?

KAREN: It could be this; it could be that. It's like you meet someone and you don't quite know how it's going to work out. The uncertainty, Richard. Don't you love that?

RICHARD: But I saw you—not Demi. My agent said Demi.

KAREN: I know you did, Richard, and I thank you. And Demi is terrific. But . . . ?

RICHARD (grins): Yeah, she's not what I saw.

KAREN: You saw sophisticated, didn't you?

RICHARD: I guess that's it.

KAREN: You see, I haven't read it, but I know.

RICHARD: So what do we do?

KAREN: You tell me the story—nutshell it—and I give the script to Monica, my assistant. I trust her implicitly.

RICHARD (dubious): Pitch it to you?

KAREN: Uh-huh.

RICHARD: Gee, I always hate that.

KAREN: You're shy. I'll help. You need a drink?

RICHARD: No, no, thank you (takes the plunge). It's called *I Married an Iron Man*.

KAREN (a little cry as if pierced): Oh! I like it.

RICHARD: There are these iron man athletic events. Triathlons. The competitors have to swim several miles, cycle several more and then there's a mini-marathon, a foot-race. The three in a row.

KAREN: I don't believe it.

RICHARD: And they stage these things in very spectacular places—Hawaii, Mexico. Anyway, our heroine is a top iron man triathlete.

KAREN: Women do it! Oh God, I am creaming! That's *me*? *I* do all that? Richard, you are amazing. I *love* activities.

RICHARD: Obviously, it's a terrific physical test. A lot of the time the actress is going to be in skintight Spandex giving her all.

KAREN: The actress! Don't tease me, Richard. Did you know I am only nine percent body fat?

RICHARD: Really? So there's this guy, he's an investment banker. And he's looking for Miss Right. And he meets Alice—

KAREN: Alice! Richard, Alice is hardly it.

RICHARD: Well, sure, the names can be changed.

KAREN: You see, you see. It *is* open.

RICHARD: Well, the banker meets our heroine, and he's crazy about her.

KAREN: And her he . . . or whatever?

RICHARD: Yeah. But she's always training. She's obsessed with her event.

KAREN: I love it.

RICHARD: So he has to try iron man himself, just to be with her, to keep up with her. You see?

KAREN: But he's not as good as she is?

RICHARD: Nowhere near. But she loves him. And he nearly kills himself trying to be worthy of her. And they never have enough time together.

KAREN: They fuck?

RICHARD: Well, sort of, but they are interrupted—and he's too tired from the training.

KAREN: Oh, the lamb.

RICHARD: Anyway, it will end—

KAREN: Don't tell. I just want to absorb the idea. *Iron Man*— that's all you need to say, with just a full-figure me in one of those suits—lovely, in love and sweating.

RICHARD: *I Married an Iron Man.*

KAREN: Go mend your spectacles, Richard. You're going to need them.

2. Later that day. Poolside at KAREN's home. She is on the cellular phone, talking to HAROLD, at her agency. Karen is a telephone virtuoso, like Navratilova at the net. We hear only her end of this call.

KAREN: Harold, where is Mike? . . . This is the second time this week. . . . He is? In Canada. How weird. . . . No, so long as he knows, I'm comfortable. It's just that I get unsettled if I don't feel Mike is "there." You know what I mean? . . . OK, well Richard has given me a first look at the script, and Monica— What? You have seen it, too? . . . Oh, I see, Geoff thought you should see it, too. Yeah, I know Geoff is

Richard's agent. . . . So, what do you think? . . . You like
it . . . Monica is wild for it. She said it was like *Bringing Up
Baby* with aerobics. . . . How do I feel? I am inclined to do
it if the deal is sweet enough. . . . Richard is adorable. He's
very shy, very young—like *my* age. . . . Yeah, Monica said
the dialogue would set new standards. Witty was the word
she used. . . . The people are too smart? . . . Harold, if I
may say so, I think I have always had the thing of making
intelligence basic and sensual; remember what Kael said
about *My Pulse*, sweetheart? . . . Yeah, I bet it's engraved on
your soul. . . . Well, sure, we could dumb it down a bit. . . .
Richard wants to direct. The fox! That he did not say. . . .
He has done nothing before, right? . . . Everyone needs
help, Harold. Even Mike needs help—that's why he has
you—Oh, I have to take this call. Get back to you. (She
goes to call waiting) Yeah? Ken! . . . I know, I know, what is
Michael doing? . . . Right, my gardener said he had heard
that yesterday at his judo class. Why would he do that?
Don't tell me—the money. . . . He would want a quarter of
a billion? Right . . . right . . . Ken, I love your perspective.
. . . Well, the script is good. I think maybe it's great. . . . We
should, I agree. . . . The Ivy at one, gotcha.

3. Next day. At the Ivy restaurant. KAREN is lunching with
KEN, her lawyer. He is 40, very slim, very suave.

KEN: I just feel that things at the agency are . . . uncertain. And
this is a big decision for you. I don't want to see you
exploited again.

KAREN: Again?

KEN: *Riddle Diddle* is a hundred and thirty domestic. Foreign, I
have always said, will be colossal. And you made seven.

KAREN: Personally, seven was manure on my roses.

KEN: *Then,* seven was terrific. And I'm not knocking Mike— though we have always said actresses were not his thing. Demi is twelve in *Striptease.*

KAREN: Which will be a day-old hot dog.

KEN: But it gives Demi a plateau. It gives you a hill. And your points on *Riddle Diddle* are net.

KAREN: They'll come in in time.

KEN: So will the Cubs. Karen, I hate to see you futurize like that. And I hate to tell you points net is playing chess in the gulag.

KAREN: So?

KEN: I see you as a gross player here. Points off the first dollar. Karen, what are you, thirty-seven?

KAREN: Six. Which you know.

KEN: Kid, I can tease you. This picture, you're going to have to be in shape—fascist shape, right? You want dessert?

KAREN: Fuck off.

KEN: What I'm saying—and talk to your doctors—that regime at your age and you could get a butch look. The dew dries.

KAREN: No way!

KEN: I haven't read the script—

KAREN: Nor me.

KEN: —but don't you have to be athletic a lot of the time?

KAREN: All of the time.

KEN: My point.

KAREN: Ken, the point of the picture is that every woman in the audience wants to look like a lean machine *and* me at the same time. We can double in the long shots. I'm not doing all the uphill cycling shit.

KEN: Can you swim?

KAREN: I can float.

KEN: Who's the guy going to be?

KAREN (speculative): One of the Toms?

KEN (reflecting): I like it. That gets you in double figures. For dignity they have to give you that. And Mike is out of reach?

KAREN: That's why I have you.

KEN: With you and a Tom, both gross, this is a fucking expensive picture. What's the script like?

KAREN: Monica says it's the best romantic comedy since *Sleepless*. But it's physical.

KEN: Yeah?

KAREN: Sure, there's the athletics, and the guys get it on. There is a lovemaking scene on Kauai at sunset on a cliff. She strips off her Spandex suit. She's wet with sweat. He licks the salt. Monica read me the scene.

KEN: I bet she did. So can Richard direct this big a picture? Has he *written* this big a picture?

KAREN: If we let him direct, we can ball-break him on his money, right?

KEN: Oh, sure. You know, I am thinking beyond this.

KAREN: Yeah?

KEN: I see Nike, Schwinn—who makes swimsuits? I see merchandising. It's like Michael Jordan.

4. Day. Exterior. Crosscutting from one highway to another. KEN and GEOFF, Richard's agent, on car phones.

KEN: Geoff?

GEOFF: Ken? Does she like it?

KEN: I think we all think it's promising.

GEOFF: It's made for her. Richard—this is just between you and I—he has always been crazy about her. He *saw* her in this, all on his own. I couldn't stop him.

KEN: You mean, this is spec?

GEOFF: This is spec. Richard wanted to keep some power on it.

KEN: Power?

GEOFF: He wants to direct.

KEN: Pretty big stuff for a first-timer.

GEOFF: He understands it, Ken. You can't buy that.

KEN: I wouldn't try.

GEOFF: So Karen likes it?

KEN: I don't believe she's finished it.

GEOFF: Uh-huh. Demi liked it.

KEN: She's read it?

GEOFF: No, no, Ken. She got coverage is all.

5. Later that day. In the agency office, KAREN is with HAROLD.

HAROLD: So, is this something we want to do?

KAREN: It could be. What does Mike say?

HAROLD: I speak for Mike.

KAREN: So what do you say?

HAROLD: Richard isn't of a mind just to sell the script? Sell and get out. How do you like Richard?

KAREN: He wants me.

HAROLD: You mean, like, he *wants* you, or he *wants* you?

KAREN: I mean, I can handle Richard. What I want to know is can the agency package me?

HAROLD: Mike and I have been talking about that.

KAREN: Like Tom or Tom?

HAROLD: Which would you fancy?

KAREN: Well, Tom is cuter, but Tom has comedy.

HAROLD (chuckles): You're a kick! By the way, Warren asked me to tell you of his interest.

KAREN: Warren! He's read it?

HAROLD: I wouldn't want to go that far. But he is looking, for a new kind of alignment for himself on-screen.

KAREN: He's the banker?

HAROLD: I could believe Warren as a banker.

KAREN: Listen, Harold, this goes no further.

HAROLD: Sealed.

KAREN: Back in 'eighty, 'eighty-one, I told Warren then I didn't intend him to have a heart attack on my account. This guy has to do triathlon stuff, you know. I'm not having Warren on my conscience, not now he has the little ones.

HAROLD: I only said I would mention it. And Warren now would be a little more economical than the Toms.

KAREN: Harold, you are speaking for Mike in this? Mike is suggesting Warren?

HAROLD: No, Mike is undecided. Warren called me. What about Daniel Day-Lewis?

KAREN: Shouldn't the guy be American?

HAROLD: I guess.

KAREN: This is very mainstream, very commercial, Harold. Ken told me he felt the agency was being a little passive about it.

HAROLD: Ken is on this?

KAREN: I talk to Ken.

HAROLD: You pay him, you pay us.

KAREN: Ken says I should be a gross player.

HAROLD: Ouch! I always worry about an actress going gross.

KAREN: What has Hanks taken out of *Gump* so far?

HAROLD: Thirty, I believe. But he took a chance.

KAREN: What is the chance on gross if I had ten per—

HAROLD: Or seven and a half?

KAREN: This picture has to do a hundred, right? Comedy, happy ending, sex, the body stuff, the competition. It does a hundred mill, at ten I've got five million. I take at least two up-front. We are not yet talking foreign. What is the risk? Whereas—

HAROLD: Whereas, we might get you fourteen mill up front. No worry, no waiting. No accounting.

KAREN: Fourteen?

HAROLD: That's what Mike wondered.

KAREN: You could get it?

HAROLD: We would ask it. Look, Karen, this picture is you. "Karen Spector is Iron Man." Can you see the poster?

KAREN: I saw it. Straightaway I saw it.

HAROLD: But then I think we have to consider a lesser figure with you. Some nice guy who can do comedy.

KAREN: You're not going to tell me Matthew Modine?

HAROLD: Honey! I don't know who I would mention. Alec Baldwin maybe I would mention.

KAREN: A banker? Alec would rob a bank.

HAROLD: Maybe we find a nice five, a four or a five, and maybe we can do the whole thing for thirty-five. . . . I'm assuming it's enough for Richard to dry your sweat and everything for change?

KAREN: A mill.

HAROLD: He should be smiling.

KAREN: He will.

6. Next day. On the wilder section of Mulholland Drive.
RICHARD is walking, looking for someone. He sees KAREN on a knoll, with a racing bike, posed for him, in a Spandex suit that is black, lime green and flame red. The effect is somewhere between knockout and disturbing.

KAREN: Hi!

RICHARD (truly startled): Well, how about you!

KAREN: Is this the look?

RICHARD: I should say so. Did you bike all the way up here?

KAREN: You want me to be honest?

RICHARD: Good question. It might be safer if you lied.

KAREN: Oh, I love your dialogue. Actually, I drove. Monica is parked in the Nissan round the bend.

RICHARD: So you just staged your little scene?

KAREN: Little! Getting into these clothes is not so little. I wanted to impress you.

RICHARD: You have.

KAREN: Come see the view from over here.

They start to walk down the southern slope. On a DISSOLVE we come to the two of them in the grass, the city below in a smoky mauve sunset. KAREN is sufficiently out of her suit and RICHARD sufficiently in her to get an R.

KAREN: Oh, my God, Richard, you are so agile. You must work out.

RICHARD: Just my fingers working on the keys.

KAREN (deeply appreciative): I could have guessed that. So, you love the view, or what?

RICHARD: You showing me the city to tempt me?

KAREN: I'm showing you more than that.

RICHARD: So?

KAREN: So what?

RICHARD: There's an offer?

KAREN: You're very young.

RICHARD: I think we're the same age.

KAREN: That's what I mean.

RICHARD: But at that age, Karen, movie star, you're close to old.

KAREN: Is that nice?

RICHARD: How much?

KAREN: How much what? Are you getting hard again?

RICHARD: To write and direct.

KAREN: Seven hundred and fifty thousand. Oh!

RICHARD: Sorry, did I hit a tender spot?

KAREN: Again, please.

RICHARD: Two mill.

KAREN: That is outrageous! A mill two.

RICHARD (looking at the desolate place): You know, Karen, up here—know what I could do?

KAREN: What?

RICHARD: I could do a mill five.

KAREN: Done.

RICHARD: If the per diem's sweet.

KAREN: Sweet as sweat.

7. Day. On different highways, HAROLD and GEOFF on their car phones again.

GEOFF: So Richard has a deal personally with Karen.

HAROLD: Uh-huh.

GEOFF: Does Mike know that?

HAROLD: Mike hasn't mentioned it.

GEOFF: I did the paper with Ken.

HAROLD: It's pay-or-play?

GEOFF: Not exactly. There are contingencies.

HAROLD: Karen owns it. Dare I ask how much?

GEOFF: I have to hold that for the moment, Harold.

HAROLD: Has money changed hands?

GEOFF: In the technical sense of money, no.

HAROLD: Well, this is very nice for everyone.

GEOFF: So we are thinking, Harold, which Tom?

HAROLD: Berenger or Hulce?

8. Next day. A psychotherapist's office just off Wilshire.
LEON, 50, fat, absorbent, is listening to KAREN.

KAREN: So, Leon, what I need from you now is deep work on my motivation.

LEON (his voice is oddly flat—monotonous or drugged): I know we can clear that up. What's the bind?

KAREN: It's philosophical.

LEON: Of course it is.

KAREN: I mean, first of all, the numbers are blue sky, you understand?

LEON: They're hypothetical.

KAREN: Right. But I can ask hypotheticals?

LEON: Hypotheticals unlock the soul.

KAREN: OK. Well, there is this picture, written by such a sweet kid, Richard. And I don't want to tell the story, but this is a sensational opportunity. For *moi*.

LEON: Uh-huh. Academy Award?

KAREN: Could be. Could be radical image remake. Could be truckloads of money.

LEON: The issue is the money?

KAREN: You are a genius, Leon. There is the prospect of being a gross player.

LEON (deadpan): Wow.

KAREN: I could go for, say, two mill up front and ten on the gross.

LEON: Ten?

KAREN: Say it's eight.

LEON: Say it's seven and a half.

KAREN: Or they are discussing fourteen million done and done.

LEON: What a drama.

KAREN: I am seething.

LEON: It's a good script?

KAREN: I believe so.

LEON: You've read it? Read it all?

KAREN: Whoever knows with scripts?

LEON: Isn't that the truth. I thought *My Pulse* stank.

KAREN: It did.

LEON: Your biggest hit.

KAREN: Which is why I don't put so much stock in reading a
     script.

LEON: You are fucking Richard?

KAREN: Technically.

LEON: So? The motivation?

KAREN: Right. Am I instant gratification, the prestige, the clout,
     the now, the check as long as King Kong's dick, or am I
     going to go the long haul, back my judgment, have some
     sort of *Gump* and clean up till the end of the century? I
     mean, am I now, or am I then?

LEON: And are you broke?

KAREN: Come again?

LEON: Karen, you owe me for six months and eight on little
     Max.

KAREN: Let me tell you one thing, once and for all.

LEON: Please.

KAREN: You are a healer for the ages.

LEON: Sweetheart.

KAREN: No, it's true. And you have words for me I have to hear.
     But too much money talk unhinges me. You will be paid,
     you know that.

LEON: I know, I know.

KAREN: If you like, just as a gesture, I will have the Schnabel brought down tomorrow. Yours. As a deposit.

LEON: I hate the Schnabel.

KAREN: So what do you want?

LEON: I might take Max.

KAREN: Leon, you are depraved.

LEON: It's listening to people like you all the time. I get inspired.

KAREN: So what should I do?

LEON: I could tell you I needed time to think about this. I won't do that. I see this. I see you on *Entertainment Tonight,* with to-die-for hair, saying you can't confirm the fourteen million, with a shit-eating grin, and I think you are a well woman for a week or so. Get it while you can. You really swim and run in this picture?

KAREN: How did you know that?

LEON: Tom told me.

9. Later. The gym in KAREN's house. She is working on the NordicTrack, with MONICA watching—30, plump, plain but with sly eyes.

MONICA: You have realized: you'll have to cut your hair.

KAREN: What do you mean?

MONICA: I've been looking at footage of these triathlons. All the girls have short hair. Swimming, running, they want less resistance. There was one who had shaved her head.

KAREN: Cut real short?

MONICA: Cropped. Like boys. Sorta cute.

KAREN: People expect my hair.

MONICA: For this money you make a sacrifice.

10. Next day. KEN's office downtown. He is with KAREN.

KEN: So here is where we are. I have talked to Harold and he is talking to Mike. Our package is you, the script and what's-his-name, and we have a producer's position. I am confident with that we can get eight and a half on the gross. You with me?

KAREN: Of course I'm with you. Have you heard about the hair?

KEN: What hair?

KAREN: These women cut their hair. They have to be streamlined.

KEN: Uh-huh. Well, we have three places, we have Warners, Paramount and DreamWorks, I would say "frenzied"—

KAREN: Yeah?

KEN: Jeffrey has called three times today already.

KAREN: Steven left me a message. It was neat. He said, "If E.T. could ride a bike, why not you, Karen?" Isn't that nice?

KEN: Steven is a very human being. Anyway, DreamWorks and Paramount have already conceded that you are gross—so long as the guy is right. Now, are you listening?

KAREN: Listening!

KEN: I have one word for you—Seinfeld.

KAREN: Oh!

KEN: Just my reaction. A very fresh take. Right age, attractive, automatically funny.

KAREN: Yeah, you know, I wonder, would I be funny with a comedian?

KEN: Karen, face it, the guy gets the laughs in this script. He makes a fool of himself.

KAREN: There has to be sharing, though, Ken.

KEN: We can get it in the polish. I agree, by the way, that your character needs just a little punching up, laugh-wise. Harold has talked to Robert and Elaine. Four or five big laugh lines, I think, will do it.

KAREN: Is Seinfeld interested?

KEN: His people are fascinated.

KAREN: What money would he be?

KEN: Well, they're talking parity, of course, what do you expect?

KAREN: Parity is for beans! He has never done a movie.

KEN: It's only a position. But would you be comfortable with him?

KAREN: I love his show. But then more than ever I think I need my hair.

KEN: I believe the hair can be finessed.

KAREN: What about the up-front?

KEN: I am hearing two mill.

KAREN: Shit, Ken, on two mill with you and Harold, with the withholding, I don't clear much more than half a mill on signature.

KEN: At this time of your life, this is the enlightened way to go.

KAREN: My monthly on the house is twenty-five thousand, and then there is Max's father. And I am behind. And I am going to have to pay for the hair problem.

KEN: There are merchandising deals I can close in two weeks.

KAREN: Which is not much front end, right?

KEN: Not a lot, right. We can float you a loan.

KAREN: I have too many of those.

KEN: What are you saying, Karen?

KAREN: You think Luigi or Gunther for the hair?

11. Later. KEN in his office, calling the agency.

KEN: Harold, this is Ken.

MIKE: This is Mike.

KEN: Mike! How are we? Can we talk?

MIKE: I have no comment, Ken. You know that.

KEN: So Karen's thing.

MIKE: Naturally.

KEN: She is uneasy.

MIKE: She does her best work then.

KEN: Mike, confidentially, what is your view on it, gross or not
for her?

MIKE: Ken, it's a sophisticated piece. It's an elegant picture.
Now, I know we've got offsetting factors—we've got a lot of
skin, we've got the race, Hawaii, all of which I think I like.
And we're going to clean out the fitness and carotene crowd
first weekend. But then I say there are a lot of out-of-shape
people in America—I read this a lot—and I wonder if they
are intimidated.

KEN: Sophisticated and intimidated?

MIKE: Am I hearing *Love Affair* again, I ask. And I would be
happier if someone like, say, Sydney was doing this.

KEN: Is Sydney available?

MIKE: I think he might be.

KEN: He is a proven on comedy.

MIKE: With Sydney you get a lot. How are you with Richard?

KEN: The deal is constructed in a pretty intricate way.

MIKE: You could dump him?

KEN: For change we could. Though Karen likes him.

MIKE: She adores Sydney.

KEN: She reveres Sydney.

MIKE: Might make her more calm.

KEN: The hair is worrying her.

MIKE: Some guys like the clean pussy.

KEN: I don't get you.

MIKE: The pubic. Triathletes shave it all off.

KEN: No kidding! I don't think we need to go for that level of realism.

MIKE: So she might like it up-front?

KEN: Now is always appealing with Karen.

MIKE: What has been talked about?

KEN: Fourteen.

MIKE: So twelve is in there?

KEN: Who knows?

MIKE: And Branagh, I believe, would kill for it. So he is helping us.

KEN: Branagh?

MIKE: Didn't Harold tell you?

KEN: I missed it. He could direct.

MIKE: After *Frankenstein*, not even traffic.

12. Next day. KAREN's house. The dressing room. She is seated at the mirror, with GUNTHER working on her hair. He is about seventy, tall, frail and gaunt.

GUNTHER: See, if I cut it on the line of the chin—like Louise Brooks.

KAREN: Uh-huh.

GUNTHER: When you're swimming, it's like a helmet. That nice, yes? And when you run, we lacquer it very heavy so it just bounces. With your tits.

KAREN: Right. It has to have life. It doesn't look older?

GUNTHER: Not if your neck is fine.

KAREN: Below the brain I am steel.

The phone rings. KAREN picks it up.

KAREN: Yeah, Ken. . . . Right. . . . Oh, really. . . . Mike said that?
He is an angel. . . . Uh-huh. . . . Sydney is a possibility? . . .
Well, God, Ken, I don't know what to say. I mean, this is
Richard's child, and truly I believe that Richard has a
phenomenal talent. . . . No, I do not just mean that. (Aside)
Thanks, Gunther, I'll call you.

GUNTHER leaves.

KAREN: Gunther has been here. I think we have a look. . . . So
Sydney would direct? . . . Hold on a minute, Ken.

She goes to call waiting.

KAREN: Richard, how are you? What? . . . I heard no such
thing. . . . Well, of course I value Mike's input. Who
doesn't? . . . Look, Richard, I hear your anger, but I have
someone on hold. I'll get back to you. . . . Of course, I will.
'Kay, Bye.

She goes back to her first call.

KAREN: That was sulky Richard. . . . I know. . . . Of course he
will. . . . So DreamWorks would do it with Sydney? . . .
What will they go to? . . . No, Ken, I think I at least want to
know the up-front. . . . Of course I understand the gross
ramifications. But if I never know what they would have
paid I will feel cheated. . . . I've got another call. . . . Yeah, if
it's Richard again, I'll tell him to call you and stop harassing
me.

She goes to call waiting.

KAREN: Hallo? Who is this? . . . Camille! Good God, girl, how
are you? . . . You're doing what? A piece on what's wrong
with Hollywood . . . for Tina! That is such a great idea. . . .

Me? . . . Well, you know as well as I do, the business is
being ruined by the money, by the suits at the top who get
an idea and then package a picture around it. . . . It's a
dumb idea, it costs too much, and it bores the public. . . . I
wish you *would* quote me. . . . Exactly, they are not hands-
on. They don't know pictures. . . . What am I doing?
Camille, I am working with a truly inspired writer. . . . No,
I can't say a word yet, but if it works it could be the picture
that secures my old age, if you'll pardon the expression. . . .
No, be vicious, whip 'em, level 'em. This town needs it.
And you, sweetheart, I miss you.

KAREN puts the phone down. MONICA comes in.

MONICA: Busy, busy?

KAREN: I am having to think about so much I think I am going
to die.

MONICA: Your eyes look great.

KAREN: Thanks.

MONICA: Like Karen Spector eyes.

KAREN: I hope so. You know, I am very tense.

MONICA: I can tell.

KAREN: You wouldn't want to give me just a little head, would
you?

13. A few days later. LEON's consulting room. He is there
with KAREN.

LEON: So, you're famous.

KAREN: I guess.

LEON: Twelve and a half million for one picture.

KAREN: It's eleven actually, or ten-eight, I think. The rest went to the original writer.

LEON: Bye, bye, Richard.

KAREN: Know what he did? He sent me a note: "Well, thanks a lot." I have it memorized. "Actually I despise the movies. I only wrote this script because I have a friend dying of AIDS and I want him to have as nice a time as possible."

LEON: Bitch.

KAREN: And he added, "Camille sends her love," which I think is a threat. She's doing some magazine piece on Hollywood as hell.

LEON: Oh, come on, they're always doing that. Public loves it. So who is the guy in your picture? They know that yet?

KAREN: Don't tell a soul. Val Kilmer.

LEON: Oh, I like him. So why are you blue?

KAREN: I'm just tired. You cannot know the intensity of the deal period.

LEON: Tell me.

KAREN: You have to be very bold, very exposed, and you have to lie a lot. Adrenaline! I'm wiped out.

LEON: But the movie—

KAREN: Please! I have to go to the gym every day. My diet you would not believe. I'm still not sure about the hair. And this movie will be a grind! All that open air—the open air is not really me.

LEON: Anticlimax.

KAREN: I'm listless, Leon. I feel I've shot my wad.

LEON: There's the money.

KAREN: I guess. Know what Ken is doing?

LEON: Tell me.

KAREN: He is having the studio deliver a briefcase packed with hundred-dollar bills.

LEON: Like in the movies!

KAREN: Yeah, I guess there's that to look forward to.

LEON: And the trades said it was one of the great scripts of the nineties.

KAREN: I'll let you know, Leon.

(1995)

Happiness

This July 4, we had an invitation to a party in Bolinas. Nothing happened.

We drove out with an old friend, catching up with her news, realizing anew how much we liked her. The weather got better after about eleven, and it was hot already for the parade in Bolinas. An untidy conga line of agricultural vehicles, dancers and drummers stopped at a junction and drew in members of the crowd. I danced for a minute or two with our son, Nicholas, on my shoulders in what I was raised to call the flying angel position. People said it looked like fun, but the thing about a flying angel is that the horse can't see the angel's face. Nothing happened.

We walked back to Warren and Amy's farm for barbecue. Amy had laid on everything with the simplicity that makes guests think of perfection. No one has reason to wonder how difficult it is for her—that is her grace. There were hamburgers and salads on tables in the open, and then round the corner of a hedge fruit, homemade pies and a good Ridge zinfandel. Desultory yet quite vicious croquet was played. Small children who had never met before fell into savage, exultant conspiracies. We lost a ball in a hedge. There was talk, a little sleeping, and anyone could walk off into the fields where Warren grows scholarly lettuces and rare rosemaries.

Nothing happened; yet it took all afternoon in a gentle swell of holiday and ease. Is happiness the absence of story?

Of course, I cannot be sure nothing happened. This serenity could be a matter of my not having noticed. Sooner or later, noticing means something to worry over. Suppose my picnic was someone else's *Partie de campagne,* that Renoir sketch in which a tablecloth on the grass, a swing and a chance view from a window lead to meeting, to lovemaking and the engorged close-up of Sylvia Bataille, so satisfied, so pensive already, and then, later, in different weather, a sadder re-encounter on the same riverbank when Henri tells Henriette, *"Tu sais, j'y ai mes meilleurs souvenirs."* For me that day in Bolinas the sun stayed out—I got burned, I found out later—but that doesn't mean there wasn't some rueful overcast for someone else, some surge of hope or regret, and even private tears gazing down on the rows of lettuce. I hope not. I wouldn't want the memory marred. But will I remember as well without some "event," some incident that led to this and that? Moreover, I'm forgetting everything—last week I couldn't summon up a date for *Run of the Arrow.* Scholarship falls with synapses' seeds.

Yet if I went to the movies, I'd be as demanding as everyone else: have something happen, I'd urge. Driving home from Bolinas, Lucy and I talked over the story possibilities: suppose so-and-so became interested in him. . . . She said she thought there was a Hardyesque structure in view, with ramifications down the ages. I could see it, but feared it might bring an end to sweet Bolinas days if imagining went too far.

There's the puzzle: to be so desperate for story in the dark, and to be some kind of storyteller by profession or malady; but to go in fear of "story" settling in under the sun—as if "story" were the worst rain. To pursue happiness—or to walk away from the pursuit? It sounds like the ending of *Point Blank* again.

This wondering has set in over the last year with the occasion to review several old movies for no professional reason. ("You'll find one," Lucy promised.) This has been Nicholas's third year, and he has acquired the habit of watching the VCR. Lucy and I are nervous about this: we dread having a TV kid—we want someone unlike ourselves. We would prefer him to "do something," which means playing with blocks, toys or kitchen equipment, putting on our clothes, throwing things out of the window—or doing nothing, I suppose, except having grand afternoons wash over him. He is unimpressed by such lofty ease. He likes to watch movies, and he has a bunch of favorite tapes.

They all frighten him, for one reason or another: the judge in black in *Roger Rabbit;* the dinosaurs in *King Kong,* and the "natives"; the fighting in the Flynn *Robin Hood;* the wolf in *Into the Woods*—that full-bodied creature *is* breathtaking; George Sanders's Shere Khan in *The Jungle Book.* Beyond these bogeys, he is alarmed but beguiled by the great imponderable of whether the characters in movies will come out of the screen to get him, or whether he could get in there with them. That suspense holds him more than the stories, many of which he cannot grasp. (And I think he loves watching just because he hasn't gone stale on the stories.) But he knows he enjoys being afraid, and he asks himself all the time if he is enjoying it enough, whether it is fun or happiness.

So we try to watch with him, to talk over the mystery. Which means that I have seen *Meet Me in St. Louis* and *The Black Stallion* some thirty times in the last year.

Though it came from MGM in 1944, *Meet Me in St. Louis* deserves a place in this daft genre I am hoping for, of movies in which nothing happens. Of course, there are "things," events, routines, numbers and action. And the musical has always been the genre with the best shot at physical exhilaration unencumbered by consequence. In so many musicals, we sit wearily as the story line maneuvers as ponderously as a rhinoceros backing into a chair to cue the "number." In any desert-island selection of all-time happy movie scenes I would want Astaire and Eleanor Powell doing "Begin the Beguine" in *Broadway Melody of 1940,* or more particularly the tap finale, with both of them in white on a shining dark floor—how is it that so common and forgettable a movie has one of the greatest sequences ever done? (Is there a clue here in how movies can be watched? The way a rainbow appears on a dull day?) I'd want Astaire and Cyd Charisse, too, doing "All of You," in *Silk Stockings,* but only if the island has CinemaScope.

Meet Me in St. Louis is a musical; yet it has no big numbers. I like it because it seems done in the spirit of home theatricals. That's what makes the cakewalk so enchanting. The teenage kids are having a party, and the infants have crept out of bed to sit on the stairs and watch. They are discovered, and Tootie (Margaret O'Brien), the youngest, must be indulged before being sent back to bed. With one of her older sisters, Esther (Judy Garland), she does a party piece, "Under the Bamboo Tree." The number is brief, gently orchestrated and geared to the phenomenal but six-year-old capacities of Margaret O'Brien.

Nothing happens. Tootie does not glimpse the meaning of life or determine to be *Funny Girl;* a poltergeist fails to materialize; no Uncle Charlie comes to visit from the East with his cigars and his burden. O'Brien and Garland just sashay here and there, with a delicate air of untidy rehearsal. Minnelli covers them with a kind of camera grace that we may never see again—it was the genius he shared with such as Cukor, Ophüls, Ozu, Hawks and Lang, so different and so unified in their accommodation of human figures and surrounding space. I treasure how little else is happening, because it is in that absence that one feels the bonds of family and the precious banality of the occasion. One sees the two actresses watching and watching out for each other, trying to be sisters. With so much affection and respect, and with the little show to put on, what else could happen? Plain lives are so full.

Meet Me in St. Louis is not simply a musical. It is a yearbook, done in four quarters, or separate episodes, that needs no more than the order of seasons and the scarcely felt approach of the moment when the family, the Smiths, will leave St. Louis. For the father (Leon Ames) is to be posted and promoted to New York City. The year passes: the summer crises of hot evenings and what time dinner should be served; the child's huge antici-pation of Halloween and the peril in confronting Mr. Bruckoff; Christmas, its dance and the mistaken plot to embarrass the

visiting girl—storms in teacups, flurries in snow globes. Then
comes the second moment between Esther and Tootie (it is the
privacy they deserve), when Garland sings "Have Yourself a
Merry Little Christmas." Tootie never notices how Esther's eyes
widen when John Truett appears at his window across the way.
The threat to her St. Louis Christmas is too great. The song
soothes her, and arouses her. She runs down to the garden, a
place of blue, moonlit snow with the amber splash from the
window's light, and smashes the patient snowmen.

Then something happens—the decision that nothing will
happen. Alonzo Smith overhears his child's anguish (parents will
listen). He feels the anxiety the moving means to all the family. So
he decides they will remain in St. Louis, that "greatest" town—
"Right here in St. Louis!"—even if it is all built in Culver City. The
film's yearning for home and family overcomes any sense of
change, movement and adventure. This was 1944, when many
people wanted to be home and together for Christmas. So the
film affirms the virtues of ordinariness, of abiding and of letting
passing time slip by and over us. Until it creeps up, like a shroud.

I had not appreciated, until I watched it over and over with a
child, how grown-up a film *Meet Me in St. Louis* is, how loaded
with doubt and mystery. Lucy and I have found ourselves puz-
zling over the ending, with its Smiths all in St. Louis for the
World's Fair, assuring themselves how fortunate they are and
how central St. Louis is. (Lucy's mother was actually born in St.
Louis, the real place—and could have been Tootie's daughter.)
But another truth is evident: the Smiths have forsaken the
American chase. Esther and John Truett have a brief talk, and it
shows us their first disagreement. She looks at him quickly, to
check, and there is worry in Garland's avid gaze. Can the marriage last? Should it, for this modern, emotional woman?

That urge I have to extend the stories of films is in some part
a longing for them to join with life and be worthy of it. To be as
good and plain as life. Esther is set to marry her John Truett at the
end of *Meet Me in St. Louis,* and one may see it as the sleep of
sweethearts . . . or the imprisonment of happiness. Esther is too

much Judy Garland to be settled—don't her eyes bulge with the hope of experience? The people in these movies are actors and actresses, one of the least secure callings we know. They stare past all satisfaction, looking for something to happen. But there is a trace of that look in Lucy's mother. She left St. Louis, found happiness and its opposites, and—I suspect—reckons that nothing much has ever really happened. She has great young eyes still; unsatisfied.

The pathology of acting and the suppressed context of happy endings may be a more potent interaction than whatever it is that occurs inside nuclear warheads. I have little doubt as to which explosion has most affected Americans.

For decades, our movies have had protection from the happy ending, and grown up crooked because of it. That conclusion is not just a resolution in which most of the people we like in a story feel pleased. It has invoked the chronic repetition of advertising: go away from this theater with energy, so that you will come back again; go out into the world determined to try harder and dream more longingly, for the wishing in stories will carry you—will carry all of us (for discrimination is not fair or American)—all the way home.

There is a limit, however. Once happiness is reached, the story, the projection, the providing darkness must all cease. Happiness cannot be risked or inhabited. In *Meet Me in St. Louis,* we are supposed to believe that Alonzo Smith has made the heart's decision; that Esther Truett will never waver. But the Alonzo we see is weak, changeable, weighed on by family, a man so uneasy he must pretend to be strong and irritable. Go forward fifteen years from the end of *Meet Me in St. Louis,* from the Louisiana Purchase Exposition to the end of the Great War, and what might we see? Was John Truett killed at the front, or on the way there in an accident? Did he stay in the Midwest making munitions? Did Alonzo start to drink? Did he cheat at the bank? Was there even some flicker of an Uncle Charlie in him, some rage at how his caution had retreated from challenge? And Esther? Did she leave John to go after Tootie, who had run away from home? Is Tootie wild, always in search of Halloween? Does Esther go after her, less pursuing happiness than trying to prevent disaster?

Such lurid proposals expose my cast of mind. Yet I think they speak to some force built up in us—a need for revenge on the happy ending. (It is the shabbiest political promise, for life goes on, falling short of bliss.) It is so much more likely that Alonzo, Esther and Tootie did little except put on weight and conservative attitudes. They had fine days when nothing happened, yet the day's image of peace stayed with them, to be recollected in tranquillity and fatal illness. They also knew months of unobtrusive failure, habit and quiet desperation, waiting for Christmas or the mail. They became the people who go to movies, not those who hold the light on the screen. But from time to time, they realized, they had been happy. And there are Smiths still in St. Louis who have observed their children, the distinctions of flavor in a good catsup, open-air opera in Forest Park, and Stan Musial.

That level of experience does not make it to the movies. There is an obvious explanation: such quiet days are not diverting enough; people go to movies to escape uneventfulness and anonymity. One can hear production executives laughing away a sequel as unmusical as *Waiting in St. Louis*. Yet the 1944 film—a hit—is, truly, a study in endurance. With great guile, that film replaced story with domesticity. There are other American arts where a relative lack of melodrama charms us: I am thinking of the paintings of Edward Hopper and the novels of Willa Cather. In Hopper's *New York Movie* and in Cather's *The Professor's House*, for instance, unremarkable existence persists in the proximity of some larger dramatic event. In both, happiness and existence work in tidal ambivalence. I go back to such mysteries more and more as the best American films seem increasingly emphatic, rigged, hysterical, fanciful and unhelpful.

The ruthless orthodoxy of shitface happy endings, preceded by amazing mayhem, has made the texture of movies both camp and frenzied. Thus the life in films threatens our real existence, as fantasy and plotting strip away responsibility. (Put it like this: two people—Richard Nixon and Travis Bickle—got away with things in the mid-seventies in ways that should not have passed.)

I don't know whether this alienation has been growing. Maybe *The Birth of a Nation* and *Citizen Kane* have as little footing in real life, and as much reliance on deranged egotism, as *Bonnie and Clyde* or *Taxi Driver*. We spend so much time in the dark watching people do and say things that are rarer than snow in Death Valley. In even the cities of this "dangerous" country (arguably also the most protected on earth), how many viewers have examined a dead human being, much less seen one killed? And how many hundred thousand pretend deaths have we hung on, from Cagney's antic strut to Kane's dropping the ball, all the way to the slowed orgasm of Warren Beatty and Faye Dunaway in *Bonnie and Clyde*? And don't we know that today in the places where films get the green light, more and more projects depend on whether the characters can die or convey death in novel ways? The movies are a killing shop.

Like any parents, Lucy and I worry over this with Nicholas. The films "fit for children" contain so much blithe violence, and such a steady accumulation of momentous, fearful incident. In moviegoing, there has always existed the apprehension that anything could happen. The razor attends the eyeball. No wonder we grow nervous, or jittery. No wonder dictators aspired to this dark—for they depend on dread and excitement.

In the middle and late fifties, my mother believed I was seeing too many films, or being too affected by them. She asked about the films I was seeing; she reckoned that they were adding to the youthful angst that came from nuclear testing in the atmosphere and the various manias of an innocent age. So I would recount the narratives of James Dean, *Men in War, Run of the Arrow, Sweet Smell of Success, Vertigo, Touch of Evil, Fear Strikes Out*, to say nothing of *The Seventh Seal, Les Diaboliques, Peeping Tom* or *Hiroshima, Mon Amour*.

The kid I was shrugged off her advice. Not to look at the worst was unresolute, ungrown-up, I declared. (And nothing in James Dean indicated priggishness in adolescents.) But this courage was so youthful. Older people have to concede how much listless ordinariness there is in life. And like most movie buffs, I never encountered, or admitted, the commonplace. Mood music kept it away.

This dilemma took on a fresh shape in the summer of 1984, when I was one of five people on the selection committee for the New York Film Festival: Richard Roud, Richard Corliss, Jim Hoberman and Molly Haskell were the others. We assembled in the first two weeks of August to watch all the films and tapes we could. But Molly was in and out. Her husband, Andrew Sarris, was desperately ill. (No one then guessed that Roud, the most vivacious of us, would die first.) Molly would sometimes arrive from the hospital in mid-screening. The rest of us cringed to notice how doggedly death, disaster, ghastly violence, fatal illness and funeral greeted her from the screen. We longed to have some sunny comedy, some picnic movie, waiting for her. The particular films we suffered need not be named, but I have no reason to think 1984 was an unusual year. Has your recent filmgoing been less heavy with exaggerated menace and gloom?

I've had enough of it. In examining *Meet Me in St. Louis* that closely, I've seen an everyday subtlety our picture business refuses. Lest this sound only self-righteous, or like abandoning the faith in a film magazine, I should add that I have pursued happiness in the past with a movielike force that brings me shame now. I came to this country leaving wife and children. I had my reasons, and the situation had a complexity too great to be described here—which is also a way of saying I doubt I could ever make it coherent. But I sought an escape then from unhappiness and ordinariness. And even if I had my Renoirish reasons, that did not help the hurt reasons of others. So many movie philosophies are a boon to selfishness.

The situation was real, but I think I acted like someone in a movie. Even now, my better or patient friends may observe spasms of behavior or the ugly mouthing of "lines" that belong in movies. This can seem like drunkenness, though it is rarely that. Rather, it is an influence that I am trying to discard, and there is no point in blaming the influence. I'll keep the blame—that much greed is legitimate. Nothing helps more in this attempt than another wife and child, and lasting ties with the older children. And few things threaten the remission more than good movies. Thankfully, that threat is smaller, year by year.

Nicholas's passion for movies alarms me. And he has seen a dozen or so, many times, at an age when I had seen nothing. But he watches in the living room, in daylight, where we are interrupted by meals, visitors, the phone and his need to use the potty. I feel grateful that he does not know the frenzy or ecstasy I miss most now in going to the movies: the huge palaces, the dense crowd, the dark and the screen as big as the Hindenburg. The small screen may be the proper place for movies now—a kind of methadone.

We watch *The Black Stallion* a great deal, and I have come to admire Carroll Ballard's eye for marvels in the mundane. He sees hesitations, times of day in the light, off-guard angles. That adds to the film's fragmentary feeling. The story bumps along from one mood to the next. Shots do not match, but they are sustained by the swing of the editing. Ballard's wandering eye needs a very secure story line to have a chance of staying in work. *The Black Stallion* has a given destination, its cockamamie, wondrous race.

Nicholas loves the race, and he has not yet seen that Alec and the Black must always win. He rides his rocking horse and uses a bear hat and ski goggles for the hood that Alec the Mystery Rider throws off in midrace.

Sometimes Nicholas wants to go straight to the race—he has hints of a producer. But I like to cue the picture in well ahead for a scene that grows richer. Alec (Kelly Reno) is at home with his mother (Teri Garr). She is lounging around reading, her feet up on the table—it takes daring to make a mother so lazy and natural, so close to a slut. Alec puzzles her by volunteering for housework. Then he tells her the Mystery Horse in the papers is their Black, and he, Alec, means to ride the horse in a big race. By arrangement, Henry (Mickey Rooney) comes by, to beg the mother's consent. She is furious, afraid, anguished. Of course, we know she has to agree: this is a film, and there were producers. Still, Teri Garr is given a long scene of pause, looking out of the window, in which the grief of widowhood and the fear of losing Alec make her pretty face pinched and bleak. It may be the best thing she has ever done, and nothing happens, or nothing much more than that instant in Chris Marker's *La Jetée* when the still comes to life and poised melodrama is surpassed by mere breathing alertness and the witness of time passing. There is still nothing more beautiful or significant in movie than watching a face think and time elapse. That is the greatest motion in pictures, a small promise of mortality.

Teri Garr looks away out of the window. It reminds me of all those windows in Renoir—from *La Chienne* to *French Cancan*—the windows that gently enact change, time and a larger context in which reasons grow smaller. I wish more films had that urge to look away from plot, to pan past the stars, to see further lives and their gestures toward story. The reason I prefer to watch sports on TV is that context of all the players, plus the crowd and the placid field. There is action in sport—fierce, acute, even desperate for the instant. But it never matters. It is nothing but play. TV sport is so intensely visual—yet nothing happens. Nor does anyone really bother to make it pictorial, beautiful or picturesque. Seeing the movement of time is enough.

The "film" that has done this best for me lately is my taping of the Broadway production of Stephen Sondheim's *Into the Woods*. That show has two parts, the first a seeking after happiness and wish fulfillment, the second a study of what comes after happy endings, with a few stunned survivors emerging from magic like creatures coming out of earth's early slime.

How can one argue that there are worthwhile films in America now beside the achievement of Sondheim? He mixes the anthology of fairy stories as easily as he does the medieval and the modern, the air of set piece and impromptu aside, the sensibilities of adult and child, and the moods of ever after and aftermath. To watch *Into the Woods*—which is a show, a chapbook of stories—is to see how archaic and statuesque our high-tech films have become.

The show is as beautiful and as troubling as the close to Mizoguchi's *Ugetsu Monogatari,* when the potter comes home from his terrible pursuit of happiness. It is night, and in a circling camera movement we find the tableau of wife and child, intact and as bright as light. He marvels in his good fortune and sleeps in peace. But when he wakes there is only desolation. It was a dream, a mercy and a torment for a man consumed by dreams. As the ghost of the Baker's Wife sings at the end of *Into the Woods*:

> *Sometimes people leave you*
> *Halfway through the wood.*
> *Do not let it grieve you,*
> *No one leaves for good.*
> *You are not alone.*
> *No one is alone.*

Sometimes happiness is knowing why you are crying. Until *Into the Woods* I never quite understood why I weep whenever Esther sings "Have Yourself a Merry Little Christmas" in *Meet Me in St. Louis* and comes to the line "Someday soon we all will be together." They are together. Has she seen so far ahead to separation and then the hope of reunion? Has she guessed that one day remembrance will be their unity? Or does she mean death?

(1992)

The Blue in the Air

Not long ago, there was a time when I was traveling more than usual. As those research trips arose, I realized that I was in the habit of carrying *Democracy* with me; I mean a paperback copy of Joan Didion's novel *Democracy*. It was a slender volume, smaller than my hand, and I could slip it in the outer flap of my book bag at the last moment, along with Tylenol and air tickets. Or put it in a coat pocket.

This would not have happened if I hadn't liked the book. It had always intrigued and pleased me. Yet I believe I had chosen it so as to know it better. There had seemed from the first time I read the book something elusive, or recessive, in it. Something to travel after. It asked for practice or duration, application and patience. That was a matter not just of several readings but of living with the book, waiting for one's mind to open to it, rather as, with a person, one adapts and grows into an accommodating shape.

So *Democracy* resembled a passport, something built into the idea and business of travel. I might not always read it on trips, though I usually had need of a page here or there, even a page at random, waiting for customs; I knew the book well enough to enter into it at any point. Sometimes, on flights from California to London, say, I could read the whole book. For while *Democracy* spans years and continents, it is not long or dense. So much has been left out. That was part of its seductiveness. Sometimes the book is like a vapor trail left on the bare sky as opposed to the huge, striving labor of flight with the 301 crammed lives on a 747. Didion did not deny the messiness in life; she can catch it as quickly as a pang of headache. But she prefers the silver dart of fate, the journey measured from afar.

Not that the novel was a defense against travel, a way of taking my mind off the hubris of walking on air. I enjoy flying: I like the civil atmosphere and the preparatory excitement of airports. It seems to me that people behave well at airports—they are obedient, attentive, poised. Anticipation brings us closer to grace, though the grace comes in diverse forms—reunion or departure. After all, we are packed at the airport, all ready. There is a subdued sense of crisis, or suspended peril, in flying that makes people generous to one another. And *Democracy* hints at grandeur in souls, even an offhand ecstasy, without quite addressing those things.

I love the ease, the height, the views, the faint flush of grayness that is dawn in Europe as one crosses Iceland. I like the exactness that can pick a line that guides the aircraft down the proper runway at Heathrow or to alight on some speck of Pacific island. Joan Didion loves flying, too; or, at least, she lets the language of *Democracy* love it. The book has raptures on long flights, oceans traversed at night and the surprising kiss of intimate, tropic air on landing. There is a lot of flying in the book, and the flying is like a preparation for the love that links the hero and the heroine. Flying is their thing; the largeness of the Pacific is the map on which their courses are charted.

My intent is not to review *Democracy*. I am actually recommending it rather as one might advise the use of Dramamine, Air India or mineral water on long flights. For I found something constitutionally valuable in *Democracy* during travel. It supported the times of waiting and encouraged the romance of hope. *Democracy* involves a murder, a case of madness and a number of mundanely narrow people—to say nothing of the decline of the

American empire. But its lovers are airy and winged. They trust
the destiny of eventual meetings and inadvertent rendezvous:

> She did not really expect to see him but she never got off a
> plane in certain parts of the world without wondering
> where he was, how he was, what he might be doing.
>   And once in a while he was there.

Of course, this book—my used and battered *Democracy*—
was acquiring sentimental or even superstitious association. The
book looked thumbed over; and it was never a sturdy object.
Sometimes, before going away, I could not find the book, and
panic and search ensued—as if it might be unsafe to fly without
it. It had become a talisman, a gesture to good luck. I added to
this load over the years by using a letter from my son as a book-
mark. This letter was written on blue airmail paper, and it
assisted the mood of the story of *Democracy*. Indeed, it seemed to
me that the book itself, with the airmail fringe showing beyond
the pages, might have made a suitable illustration for its own
jacket.
  Several years passed, and the book was soaking into me. It
enriched me: there were occasions when I would see or hear
something in life and be reminded of *Democracy*, its imprecise
but sure meaning for America, and the laconic but tender way of
talking that Joan Didion had found for her hero and heroine—
Jack Lovett and Inez Christian Victor. I admired those lovers,
and I suppose I wanted them to be together, or happy. Yet they
were most eloquent when separated, when continents apart
perhaps, or in the same room blocked by the presence of others.
I'm not sure if Didion's way of writing about them, and how
they talked, would work as well if they were simply alone
together.
  Let me quote a passage that illustrates Didion's way with this
love story. She is, on the one hand, very dry, cool and oblique; she
limits herself to a certain level of external observation. Moreover,
in a story that touches on Washington and the style of official

secrecy and cover-up, there is a faint edge of jargon or obfusca-
tion in the writing, an echo of discreet, not to say evasive, reports.
But then suddenly there comes an explosion of clarity and feeling
that seems all the bolder after the drone of muffled civility. It is
like an urgent cry rising above the murmur of talk and engine on
an airliner.

Jack Lovett has met Inez Christian. She is seventeen, and he is
more or less twice her age, as well as married. They meet again—
all of this on Oahu—when he finds her in a stalled car with a
drunken boyfriend (Robert Strudler) sick to his stomach. Jack
drives them home:

> Her feet were bare and she spoke even more precisely, as if
> to counter any suggestion that she might herself be drunk,
> and it was not until later, sitting in the front seat of Jack
> Lovett's car on the drive into town, Robert Strudler asleep in
> the back with his arms around the prize plush dogs, that
> Inez Christian gave any indication that she remembered
> him.
>
> "I don't care about your wife," she said. She sat very
> straight and kept her eyes on the highway as she spoke. "So
> it's up to you. More or less."

There is no deeper romantic conversation between them, just
the bare indication of meetings where we are to assume love has
been made. That or the passing of other secrets. Inez's statement
is abrupt; it may dislodge some readers. It is nearly studied in its
unexpectedness, like a movie line, with Inez refusing to look at
him, and Lovett's gaze, lovelorn, swinging toward her. But even if
one wonders whether Didion could bring herself to write the
love scene or the lovers' talk (she is drawn to unease and things
drifting apart), the moment aches with desire and love. The
quickness helps us believe in their liveliness.

Jack and Inez never come together without impediment. I
won't spoil the story for you, if you haven't read it. But in not
working out completely, the scheme of events only intensifies

their rapport and leaves Jack and Inez seeming like the last fine people alive. That, I think, is the natural light that settles, however briefly, on real lovers.

Anyway, I wanted you to have a flavor of the book to help you understand how it became like a prayer book in my travels. Well, a large journey came my way. My father had died in England, and there was the funeral to be attended. At the same time, my oldest and closest friend, Kieran, who lived in Dublin, was about to undergo heart bypass surgery. I would go to Dublin to spend the weekend with him—the last before he went into the hospital— and then go on to England for the funeral. *Democracy* went with me.

The weekend in Dublin was a delight. I recommended *Democracy* to Kieran, and talked about its rich terseness, the span of years, and Didion's feeling for tropical air and light. The book was on the table beside my bed. I believe I read a page or two one night over the weekend. Then I woke in the middle of the night and reached out for my glasses, which were on the table, too. Later, I remembered the sound of a slap that must have been *Democracy* falling on the floor.

In any event, I packed and went on to London and the funeral. Kieran and I embraced, and I wished him luck; I told him I knew it would go well. And I left the book on the floor in the gloom. In London, I spoke to Kieran on the phone, and he said he'd found the book. He would send it on to me in America. Perhaps he was reading it first. We buried my father. I went back to America. Kieran's operation had gone well. He was reckoned to be making a full recovery, and then in an hour an embolism killed him.

I never got *Democracy* back. Somehow it was lost. Was it left on Kieran's table in the hospital room? Did a curious nurse go off with it? Or was the book just absorbed in Kieran's large library? I didn't pursue it; I was happy to have it be his. Then for a year or so I was without a *Democracy*. I felt reluctant to replace it. If I ever thought of doing so I found that my paperback edition was now out of print. The book had become a classic: it had gone from Pocket Books to a larger Vintage format. But a few weeks ago, in a used bookstore, I found a copy of the old small paperback. It could have been mine, though my son's letter was absent. So I bought it, and I am getting back into the habit of keeping it with me.

The novel is better than ever, or I seem to be a more understanding reader. On a flight from San Francisco to Los Angeles, I read one passage as many times as the flight allowed. It's the first meeting of Jack and Inez, so long ago, on her seventeenth birthday. Carla was Jack Lovett's wife. I feel I was there at the party, and I realize that my second wife is my junior by nearly enough the gap between Inez and Jack. Gaps are everything.

"Why are you wearing sunglasses," Jack Lovett said.

Inez Christian, startled, touched her glasses as if to remove them and then, looking at Jack Lovett, brushed her hair back instead, loosening the pin that held the gardenia.

Inez Christian smiled.

The gardenia fell to the wet grass.

"I used to know all the generals at Schofield," Cissy Christian said. "Great fun out there. Then."

"I'm sure." Jack Lovett did not take his eyes from Inez.

"Great polo players, some of them," Cissy Christian said. "I don't suppose you get much chance to play."

"I don't play," Jack Lovett said.

Inez Christian closed her eyes.

Carla Lovett drained her paper cup and crushed it in her hand.

"Inez is seventeen," Dwight Christian repeated.

"I think I want a real drink," Carla Lovett said.

There's another bomb dropped—poor Carla Lovett is not much more than a crater in *Democracy* where the explosion of noticing has occurred. And yet it's so discreet a bomb—has Cissy or Dwight even heard it? In a way, I suppose, this is what is called cinematic writing (and Didion has done scripts and meditated on the dreadful lure of movies). You can see the close-ups of Jack and Inez; the cutting that lets them touch in their minds;

the witless, unaware others; and Carla's claw of a hand crushing the paper cup. Yet it would be crass on-screen, too obvious, too tied together. There wouldn't be room to breathe for the sexual stealth.

The prose account helps us see while keeping the occasion open to all the ways of missing the explosion. It's writing that has absorbed the movies and then gone on to all the farther fields. The prose lets us feel the different figures in the group and the different degrees of awareness. It lives in the gaps that film is compelled to splice together. In Didion's one-sentence paragraphs, white space becomes a part of her writing—there is a visibility in writing, a balance of black and white.

The page, the pages. A book, even a beaten-up paperback, can be such a treasury. There's even a book within *Democracy*. Later on, when Inez is briefly "with" Jack, he has to go away, to Saigon, for its fall—the ignominy of Vietnam is the book's great warning to all our hopes for democracy. So the lovers are apart again. Inez is in Hong Kong in an apartment Jack has used from time to time. There are traces of another woman there, someone not unimportant to Jack once, though "it doesn't matter," he tells Inez, "it's fine." Someone who has left

a paperback copy of *Homage to Catalonia* in the drawer of the bed table. In Inez's experience all reporters had paperback copies of *Homage to Catalonia* and kept them in the same place where they kept the matches and the candle and the notebook, for when the hotel was bombed.

That unnamed woman is another aspect of Carla Lovett: figures not *here* now, yet not unimportant and all in the same slow dance of apartness. "Anyway we were together," Inez tells the narrator of *Democracy,* Joan Didion herself (there but not quite there, a ghost in her own book). "We were together all our lives. If you count thinking about it."

And who can discount that thinking? Jack and Inez are so seldom with each other in a settled or secure way—but they hardly need it. There are affinities that exist more fruitfully in the imagination and that can rise above the grim proximity of people who are together sixty years and who ignore each other.

Democracy, for me, has come to embody the perpetuity and the power of gaps. I have left people in my life—or tried—one woman for another, as well as three children. Not that the leaving can ever be complete, or wants to be. There are wounds and loves that live on absence; the thinking keeps them open. The lost, those given up and the dead are stirring, magical figures; no wonder real companions sometimes envy them. From that, it is a modest step of sympathy or imagining to be aware of absolute strangers, people we will never meet—that woman hanging from a tree in Bosnia (she at least had her picture in the papers), or let us say a tall, thin man who is walking slowly up a hill in Lisbon (he did not exist until now, and is still only a fiction, no matter how many real men in Lisbon might fit the part).

Apartness is the beginning of a community to which democracy aspires. There are so many with whom we have been distantly together, waiting for the coincidence of meetings. And there is no finer subject in the end than the resonant gaps that separate us, the space filled in by what Inez regards as the reason for being here and there—"Colors, moisture, heat, enough blue in the air."

(1996)